I0092072

Anonymous

The Socialist's Friend

containing a collection of meditations and prayers compiled and translated from

approved sources, for the use of members and leaders of confraternities

Anonymous

The Socialist's Friend
containing a collection of meditations and prayers compiled and translated from approved
sources, for the use of members and leaders of confraternities

ISBN/EAN: 9783337285005

Printed in Europe, USA, Canada, Australia, Japan

Cover: Foto ©Andreas Hilbeck / pixelio.de

More available books at **www.hansebooks.com**

THE

SODALIST'S FRIEND:

CONTAINING

A COLLECTION

OF

MEDITATIONS AND PRAYERS

Compiled and Translated from Approved Sources,

FOR THE USE OF MEMBERS AND LEADERS OF CONFRATERNITIES.

SS. C. J. M.

DEDICATED TO THE "CHILDREN OF MARY."

PUBLISHED WITH THE
APPROBATION OF THE RT REV. BISHOP OF PHILADELPHIA.

Philadelphia:

PETER F. CUNNINGHAM, CATHOLIC BOOKSELLER,
216 South Third Street.

1861.

Entered according to Act of Congress, in the year 1860, by

PETER F. CUNNINGHAM,

In the Clerk's Office of the District Court of the United States, in and for
the Eastern District of Pennsylvania.

INTRODUCTION.

THIS volume has no pretension to supersede other Manuals of Devotion, but merely to serve a friendly purpose to the faithful Sodalist.

Many young persons acquire the habit of practising meditation and performing Novenas, preparatory to Festivals, during a temporary residence in some Catholic institution of learning, but on retiring thence, feel the want of numerous helps which were rendered to them in their social meetings, and especially in their customary exercises of mental Prayer. To remove this impediment to leading a regular and pious life in the world, these familiar means of adhering to their good resolutions have been compiled.

Credit has been given to the authors from whom the Meditations have been selected, and the Indulgences that are named as belonging to any Prayer or Exercise of Piety have been taken from the Raccolta. The Considerations for the Six Sundays of Saint Aloysius, were copied with a little modification from the Pious Guide.

It is humbly commended to the "Children of Mary," with the prayerful hope that it may maintain and increase their solid piety.

MANHATTANVILLE.
Feast of St. Louis de Gonzague, 1859.

TABLE OF MOVABLE FEASTS.

Year.	Domin. Letter.	Gold. No.	The Epact.	Septuagesima Sunday.	Ash Wednesday.	Easter Sunday.	Ascension Day.	Whitsunday.	Corpus Christi.	Sun. after Pent.	First Sunday of Advent.
1860	AG	18	7	Feb. 5	Feb. 22	April 8	May 17	May 27	June 7	26	Dec. 2
1861	F	19	18	Jan. 27	Feb. 13	March 31	May 9	May 19	May 30	27	Dec. 1
1862	E	1	*	Jan. 16	March 5	April 20	May 29	June 8	June 19	24	Nov. 30
1863	D	2	11	Feb. 1	Feb. 18	April 5	May 14	May 24	June 4	26	Nov. 29
1864	CB	3	22	Jan. 24	Feb. 10	March 27	May 5	May 15	May 26	27	Nov. 27
1865	A	4	3	Feb. 12	March 1	April 16	May 25	June 4	June 15	25	Dec. 3
1866	G	5	14	Jan. 28	Feb. 14	April 1	May 10	May 20	May 31	27	Dec. 2
1867	F	6	25	Feb. 17	March 6	April 21	May 30	June 9	June 20	24	Dec. 1
1868	ED	7	6	Feb. 9	Feb. 26	April 12	May 21	May 31	June 11	25	Nov. 29
1869	C	8	17	Jan. 24	Feb. 10	March 28	May 6	May 16	May 27	25	Nov. 28
1870	B	9	28	Feb. 13	March 2	April 17	May 26	June 5	June 16	24	Nov. 27
1871	A	10	9	Feb. 5	Feb. 22	April 9	May 18	May 28	June 8	26	Dec. 3
1872	GF	11	20	Jan. 28	Feb. 14	March 31	May 9	May 19	May 30	27	Dec. 1
1873	E	12	1	Feb. 9	Feb. 26	April 13	May 22	June 1	June 12	25	Nov. 30
1874	D	13	12	Feb. 1	Feb. 18	April 5	May 14	May 24	June 4	26	Nov. 29
1875	C	14	23	Jan. 24	Feb. 10	March 28	May 6	May 16	May 27	27	Nov. 28
1876	BA	15	4	Feb. 13	March 1	April 16	May 25	June 4	June 15	25	Dec. 3
1877	G	16	15	Jan. 28	Feb. 14	April 1	May 10	May 20	May 31	27	Dec. 2
1878	F	17	26	Feb. 17	March 6	April 21	May 30	June 9	June 20	24	Dec. 1
1879	E	18	7	Feb. 9	Feb. 26	April 13	May 22	June 1	June 12	25	Nov. 30
1880	DC	19	18	Jan. 25	Feb. 11	March 28	May 6	May 16	May 27	27	Nov. 28
1881	B	1	*	Feb. 13	March 2	April 17	May 26	June 5	June 16	24	Nov. 27
1882	A	2	11	Feb. 5	Feb. 22	April 9	May 18	May 28	June 8	26	Dec. 3
1883	G	3	22	Jan. 21	Feb. 7	March 25	May 3	May 13	May 24	28	Dec. 2
1884	FE	4	3	Feb. 10	Feb. 27	April 13	May 22	June 1	June 12	25	Nov. 30

MORNING PRAYERS.

✠In the name of the Father, and of the Son, and of the Holy Ghost. Amen.

Blessed be the most holy and undivided Trinity, now and forevermore. Amen.

Most holy and undivided Trinity, one God in three persons, I adore Thee with profound humility, and offer Thee, with my whole heart the homage due to Thy Divine Majesty. O my God, I return Thee thanks for the innumerable favors and benefits which I have received, especially for my preservation during the past night. I consecrate this day to Thee, and desire to employ it wholly in Thy service, I offer Thee all my thoughts, words, actions and sufferings. Bless them O Lord, that they may all be animated by Thy love, and may tend to Thy greater honor and glory.

Adorable Jesus, Divine model of that perfection to which we should all aspire, I am resolved to become like Thee, mild, humble, chaste, zealous, patient, charitable and resigned, I will, in particular, exert all my efforts not to fall this day into the faults I so frequently commit, and which I most earnestly desire to correct.

O My God, thou knowest my weakness and that I can do nothing without the assistance of Thy grace; do not deny it to me, O My God! but proportion it to my wants, give me sufficient strength to avoid evil, to practice all the good Thou dost expect of me, and to suffer all the afflictions Thou mayest be pleased to send me.

Pater noster, qui es in cœlis, sanctificetur nomen tuum: adveniat regnum tuum: fiat voluntas tua, sicut in cœlo et in terra: panem nostrum quotidianum da nobis hodie; et dimitte nobis debita nostra, sicut et nos dimittimus debitoribus nostris: et ne nos inducas in tentationem; sed libera nos a malo. Amen.

Ave, Maria, gratia plena; Dominus tecum: benedicta tu in mulieribus, et benedictus fructus ventris tui, Jesus.

Sancta Maria, mater Dei, ora pro nobis peccatoribus, nunc et in hora mortis nostrae. Amen.

Credo in Deum, Patrem omnipotentem, Creatorem cœli et terræ; et in Jesum Christum, Filium ejus unicum, Dominum nostrum; qui conceptus est de Spiritu sancto, natus ex Maria Virgine: passus sub Pontio Pilato, crucifixus, mortuus, et sepultus: descendit ad inferos: tertia die resurrexit a mortuis, ascendit ad cœlos; sedet ad dexteram Dei Patris omnipotentis. indeventurus est judicare vivos et mortuos.

Credo in Spiritum sanctum, sanctam Ecclesiam catholicam, Sanctorum communionem, remissionem peccatorum, carnis resurrectionem, vitam æternam. Amen.

Confiteor Deo omnipotenti, beatæ Mariæ semper virgini, beato Michaeli Archangelo, beato Joanni Baptistæ, sanctis Apostolis Petro et Paulo, omnibus Sanctis (et tibi, Pater,) quia pec-

Our Father, Who art in Heaven, hallowed be Thy name: Thy kingdom come; Thy will be done on earth, as it is in Heaven: Give us this day our daily bread; and forgive us our trespasses as we forgive those who trespass against us: and lead us not into temptation; but deliver us from evil. Amen.

Hail Mary, full of grace, the Lord is with thee; blessed art thou among women, and blessed is the fruit of thy womb, Jesus.

Holy Mary, Mother of God, pray for us sinners, now and at the hour of our death. Amen.

I believe in God, the Father Almighty, Creator of Heaven and earth; and in Jesus Christ, His only Son, our Lord: Who was conceived by the Holy Ghost, born of the Virgin Mary; suffered under Pontius Pilate, was crucified, dead, and buried; He descended into hell: the third day He arose again from the dead; He ascended into heaven, and sitteth at the right hand of God, the Father Almighty; from thence He shall come to judge the living and the dead. I believe in the Holy Ghost, the Holy Catholic Church, the communion of saints, the forgiveness of sins, the resurrection of the body, and life everlasting. Amen.

I confess to Almighty God, to blessed Mary ever Virgin, to blessed Michael the Archangel, to blessed John the Baptist, to the Holy Apostles, Peter and Paul, and to all the saints, that I

cavi nimis cogitatione, verbo et opere: mea culpa, mea culpa, mea maxima culpa. Ideo precor beatam Mariam semper virginem, beatum Michaelem. Archangelum, beatum Joannem Baptistam, sanctos Apostolos Petrum et Paulum, omnes Sanctos (et te, Pater,) orare pro me ad Dominum Deum nostrum.

Misereatur nostri omnipotens Deus, et dimissis peccatis nostris, perducat nos ad vitam æternam. Amen.

Indulgentiam, absolutionem et remissionem peccatorum nostrorum, tribuat nobis omnipotens et misericors Dominus. Amen.

have sinned in thought, word and deed, *through my fault, through my fault, through my most grievous fault.* Therefore, I beseech the blessed Mary ever Virgin, blessed Michael the Archangel, blessed John the Baptist, the Holy Apostles Peter and Paul, and all the saints, to pray to the Lord our God for me.

May the Almighty and merciful Lord have mercy on us, forgive us our sins, and bring us to everlasting life. Amen.

May the Almighty and most merciful Lord, grant us pardon, absolution and remission of all our sins. Amen.

Holy Virgin, Mother of my God, who art also my Mother and Patroness, I place myself under thy protection, and throw myself with confidence under the wings of thy mercy. Be thou, O Mother of tenderness, my refuge in trouble, my consolation in trial, and my advocate with thy Divine Son, this day, every day of my life, and particularly at the hour of my death.

Angel from Heaven, my faithful and charitable guide, obtain for me the grace to be docile to thy inspirations, and always to direct my steps in such a manner as never wilfully to stray from the commands of God.

Great Saint, whose name I have the honor to bear, protect and pray for me, that like thee, I may serve God faithfully on earth, and glorify Him eternally in Heaven.

Act of Faith.

O my God! I firmly believe all the sacred truths which thy Holy Catholic Church believes and teaches, because Thou hast revealed them, Who canst neither deceive nor be deceived.

Act of Hope.

O my God! relying on Thy infinite goodness and promises, I hope to obtain the pardon of my sins, the assistance of Thy grace, and life everlasting, through the merits of Jesus Christ, and by the intercession of His Blessed Mother and all the Saints.

Act of Love.

O my God! I love Thee above all things, with my whole heart and soul, purely because of Thine infinite perfections; and I love my neighbor as myself for the love of Thee; I forgive all who have injured me, and ask pardon of all whom I have injured.

Act of Contrition.

O my God! I am most heartily sorry for all my sins; I detest them above all things from the bottom of my heart, because they displease Thee, my God! who alone art worthy of my love, on account of Thy amiable and adorable perfections; and I firmly purpose with the assistance of Thy holy grace, never more to offend Thee, and to do all that I can to atone for my sins.

Lord Jesus, be pleased to shield with the protection of Thy Divine heart, the Cardinal protector of the Society of the Sacred Heart of Jesus.

Grant, O my God, that during *Meditation*, all my thoughts, and all the intentions of my heart and soul, may tend entirely to thy greater honor and glory.

Come, O Holy Ghost! replenish the hearts of thy faithful, and kindle in them the fire of Thy love;

send forth Thy Spirit, and they shall be created, and Thou shalt renew the face of the earth.

O God! Who by the light of the Holy Ghost, didst instruct the hearts of the faithful, grant us by the same Holy Spirit, a love and relish for what is right and just, and the constant enjoyment of His comforts, through Jesus Christ our Lord. Amen.

Hail Mary, etc.

—◦✸◦◦✸◦—

Questions on the Meditation:
USEFUL FOR SELF-EXAMINATION ONCE DURING THE WEEK.

Did I read the Meditation with care, and endeavor to fix the Preludes and Points in my memory?

Did I recall the subject to mind before going to sleep?

Did I reject every idle thought, and dwell upon the Meditation, when awaking during the night, and while dressing in the morning?

Before the Meditation, did I recall God's holy presence?

Did I take a posture favorable to meditation?

Did I give to it the full time prescribed by my rule?

Have I exercised my mind and heart diligently in reflections and affections?

Have I been faithful to the additions, viz: forming colloquies, foreseeing the occasions of self conquest, and taking practical resolutions?

NIGHT PRAYERS.

✠ In the name of the Father, etc.

I adore Thee, O my God, with the dispositions with which the presence of thy Sovereign greatness inspires me. I believe in Thee, because Thou art infinitely good; I love thee with my whole heart, because Thou art supremely amiable; and I love my neighbor as myself for the love of Thee.

What thanks, O my God, should I not return Thee for the many favors Thou hast been pleased to bestow on me. Thou hast thought of me from all eternity; Thou didst draw me out of nothing; and Thou dost continue daily to load me with innumerable blessings. Alas! my God, what can I return to Thee for such bounty. Unite with me, ye blessed Spirits, in praising the God of mercies, who never ceases to confer favors, even on the most ungrateful and unworthy of all his creatures.

Come, Holy Spirit, Eternal source of light, dispel the darkness that conceals from me the malice and deformity of my sins. Grant, O my God! that I may detest them if possible as much as Thou dost, and that I may dread nothing so much as to commit any in future. What would I not give, O my God! had I never offended Thee? but since I have been so unhappy as to displease Thee, I am resolved to testify my grief by leading a more regular life. I renounce all my sins, and the occasions of them, especially those into which I have had the weakness so frequently to relapse; and if Thou wilt give me Thy grace as I most fervently hope and implore, I will strive to fulfil all my obligations, and nothing shall be capable of witholding me when called upon to serve Thee.

Our Father, etc.

Hail Mary, etc.

I believe in God, the Father Almighty, etc.

I confess to Almighty God, etc.

Bless, O Lord, the repose I am about to take, in order to repair my strength, and thus become better enabled to serve Thee. Holy Virgin, Mother of God, and after Him my only hope, my good angel, my holy patron, intercede for me; protect me during this coming night, through my whole life and particularly at the hour of my death.

Pour down Thy blessings, O Lord, upon my parents, benefactors, friends and enemies. Protect all those placed over me in authority, whether spiritual or temporal. Succor the poor, all who are in prison, the sick, the agonizing, and the traveller. Convert the hearts of heretics, and enlighten the minds of infidels.

O God of bounty and mercy, take pity on the souls of the faithful suffering in Purgatory; deliver them from their torments; and grant eternal life and rest to those for whom I am bound to pray.

Litany of the Blessed Virgin.

Kyrie eleison.	Lord have mercy.
Christe eleison.	Christ have mercy.
Kyrie eleison.	Lord have mercy.
Christe audi nos.	Christ hear us.
Christe exaudi nos.	Christ graciously hear us.
Pater de cœlis Deus, miserere nobis.	God the Father of Heaven, have mercy on us.
Fili Redemptor mundi Deus miserere nobis.	God the Son, Redeemer of the world, have mercy on us.
Spiritus Sancte Deus, miserere nobis.	God the Holy Ghost, have mercy on us.
Sancta Trinitas, unus Deus, miserere nobis.	Holy Trinity, one God, have mercy on us.

Sancta Maria,	Holy Mary,	
Sancta Dei Genitrix,	Holy Mother of God,	
Sancta Virgo virginum,	Holy Virgin of virgins,	
Mater Christi,	Mother of Christ,	
Mater divinæ gratiæ,	Mother of divine grace,	
Mater purissima,	Mother most pure,	
Mater castissima,	Mother most chaste,	
Mater inviolata,	Mother undefiled,	
Mater intemerata,	Mother inviolate,	
Mater amabilis,	Mother most amiable,	
Mater admirabilis,	Mother most admirable,	
Mater Creatoris,	Mother of our Creator,	
Mater Salvatoris,	Mother of our Redeemer,	
Virgo prudentissima,	Virgin most prudent,	
Virgo veneranda,	Virgin most venerable,	
Virgo prædicanda.	Virgin most renowned,	
Virgo potens,	Virgin most powerful,	
Virgo clemens,	Virgin most merciful,	
Virgo fidelis,	Virgin most faithful,	
Speculum justitiæ,	Mirror of justice,	
Sedes sapientiæ,	Seat of wisdom,	
Causa nostræ lætitiæ,	Cause of our joy.	
Vas spirituale,	Spiritual vessel,	
Vas honorabile,	Vessel of honor,	
Vas insigne devotionis,	Vessel of singular devotion,	
Rosa mystica,	Mystical rose,	
Turris Davidica,	Tower of David,	
Turris eburnea,	Tower of ivory,	
Domus aurea,	House of gold,	
Fœderis arca,	Ark of the covenant,	
Janua cœli,	Gate of heaven,	
Stella matutina,	Morning star,	
Salus infirmorum,	Health of the weak,	

Ora pro nobis. (center column)

Pray for us. (right column)

Refugium peccatorum,
Consolatrix afflictorum,
Auxilium Christianorum,
Regina Angelorum,
Regina Patriarcharum,
Regina Prophetarum,
Regina Apostolorum,
Regina Martyrum,
Regina Confessorum,
Regina Virginum,
Regina Sanctorum omnium,
Regina sine labe originali concepta,

Ora pro nobis.

Agnus Dei, qui tollis peccata mundi, parce nobis, Domine,

Agnus Dei, qui tollis peccata mundi, exaudi nos, Domine,

Agnus Dei, qui tolis peccata mundi, miserere nobis,

Christe audi nos.
Christe exaudi nos.

V. Ora pro nobis, sancta Dei Genitrix.

R. Ut digni efficiamur promissionibus Christi.

OREMUS.

Gratiam tuam, quæsumus, Domine, mentibus nostris

Refuge of sinners,
Comforter of the afflicted,
Help of Christians,
Queen of Angels,
Queen of Patriarchs,
Queen of Prophets,
Queen of Apostles,
Queen of Martyrs,
Queen of Confessors,
Queen of Virgins,
Queen of all Saints,
Queen conceived without stain of original sin,

Pray for us.

Lamb of God, Who takest away the sins of the world, spare us, O Lord,

Lamb of God, Who takest away the sins of the world, graciously hear us, O Lord,

Lamb of God, Who takest away the sins of the world, have mercy on us.

Christ hear us.
Christ graciously hear us.

V. Pray for us, O holy Mother of God.

R. That we may be made worthy of the promises of Christ.

LET US PRAY.

Pour forth, we beseech Thee, O Lord, Thy grace

infunde: ut qui, Angelo nuntiante, Christi Filii tui incarnationem cognovimus, per passionem ejus et Crucem ad Resurrectionis gloriam perducamur. Per eundem Christum Dominum nostrum. Amen.

into our hearts; that we, to whom the incarnation of christ, thy Son, was made, known by the message of an angel, may, by His passion and cross, be brought to the glory of His resurrection. Through the same Christ our Lord. Amen.

Lord Jesus, who, through Thy tender love for the Church, thy spouse, hast been pleased to open to her the riches and sweetness of Thy Divine Heart, grant us that our hearts may be enriched with the treasures therein contained, and replenished with its overflowing delights.

O Lord of infinite clemency, who for the salvation of sinners, and help of the afflicted, hast given to the blessed Virgin Mary a heart like to that of her Divine Son, and hast made it a source of meekness and mercy, grant, we beseech Thee, that those who honor this Immaculate Heart, may through its merits and her intercession become according to the Heart of Jesus.

Lord Jesus, be pleased to shield with the protection of thy Divine Heart, our Holy Father the Pope.

Glorious Saint Michael, Prince of the Celestial Hosts, and protector of the Universal Church, defend us, we beseech thee, from all enemies visible and invisible, in particular from fire.

O my God, I believe in thee, I hope in thee, and I love thee with my whole heart.

Memorare.

Remember, O most pious Virgin Mary, that no one ever had recourse to thy protection, implored thy help, or sought thy mediation, without obtaining relief. Relying on thy goodness and mercy, I cast myself at thy feet, and do most humbly supplicate thee, O mother of the Eternal word, to adopt me as thy child, and take upon thyself the care of my salvation.

O let it not be said, my dearest Mother, that I have perished at thy sacred feet, where no one ever found but mercy, grace and salvation.

Angelus Domini.
TO BE SAID MORNING, NOON, AND NIGHT.

Angelus Domini nuntiavit Mariæ; et concepit de Spiritu Sancto.

The angel of the Lord declared unto Mary; and she conceived of the Holy Ghost.

Ave Maria, gratia plena; Dominus tecum; benedicta tu in mulieribus et benedictus fructus ventris tui Jesus.

Hail Mary, full of grace, the Lord is with thee; blessed art thou among women, and blessed is the fruit of thy womb, Jesus.

Sancta Maria, Mater Dei ora pro nobis peccatoribus, nunc et in hora mortis nostræ. Amen.

Holy Mary, Mother of God, pray for us sinners now and at the hour of our death. Amen.

Ecce ancilla Domini;
Fiat mihi Secundum verbum tuum. Ave Maria, etc.

Behold the handmaid of the Lord; be it done unto me according to thy word. Hail Mary, etc.

Et Verbum caro factum est, et habitavit in nobis.

And the Word was made flesh; and dwelt among us.

Ave Maria, etc.

℣. Ora pro nobis, sancta Dei Genitrix.

℞. Ut digni efficiamur promissionibus Christi.

Hail Mary, etc.

Pray for us, O holy Mother of God.

That we may be made worthy of the promises of Christ.

OREMUS.

Gratiam tuam quæsumus Domine, mentibus nostris infunde, ut qui angelo nuntiante, Christi Filii tui incarnationem cognovimus, per passionem ejus et crucem, ad resurrectionis gloriam perducamur. Per eumdem Christum Dominum nostrum. Amen.

LET US PRAY.

Pour forth we beseech thee, O Lord, thy grace into our hearts, that we to whom the incarnation of Christ thy Son was made known by the message of an angel, may by his passion and cross, be brought to the glory of his resurrection. Through Christ our Lord. Amen.

Regina Coeli.

TO BE SAID DURING THE PASCHAL TIME.

Regina cœli lætare; Alleluia.

Quia quem meruisti portare; Alleluia.

Resurrexit sicut dixit; Alleluia.

Ora pro nobis Deum; Alleluia.

℣. Gaude et lætare Virgo Maria; Alleluia.

℞. Quia surrexit Dominus vere; Alleluia.

Joy to thee, O Queen of Heaven; Alleluia.

He whom thou wast meet to bear; Alleluia.

As he promised, hath arisen; Alleluia.

Pray for us to him; Alleluia.

Rejoice and be glad, O Virgin Mary; Alleluia.

For the Lord hath risen indeed; Alleluia.

Deus qui per resurrectionem Filii tui Domini nostri Jesu Christi, mundum lætificare dignatus es; præsta, quæsumus, ut per ejus Genitricem Virginem Mariam perpetuæ capiamus gaudia vitæ.— Per eumdem Christum, etc.

O God, who didst vouchsafe to give joy to the world, through the resurrection of thy Son, our Lord Jesus Christ, grant we beseech thee, that through his Mother, the Virgin Mary, we may obtain the joys of everlasting life. Through the same Christ, etc.

~⊙⊚⊛⊚⊙~

Acts before Communion.

1. O Jesus, King of Glory, I dare present myself in the Banquet Hall, though covered with tatters and reduced to profound misery; I should never have had the boldness to appear before thee in this state, hadst thou not deputed towards me one of thy servants, to invite me to take a seat at thy table; consider my great poverty. By an effect of thy mercy, thou canst deliver me in the Communion I am about to make.

2. What will become of me, O Jesus! when thou wilt require of me a rigorous account of all my thoughts, words and works? I now make to thee the humble confession of all the outrages I have offered to thy divine Majesty; pardon me, O God of clemency, pardon me. I present myself before thy throne of mercy, and humbly entreat thee not to condemn me when thou wilt come to judgment.

3. O Jesus, thy adorable body was torn in pieces by the scourging at the pillar, and thy precious Blood

flowed in torrents for love of me; why can I not now, and at the hour of death apply to my soul the merits of that precious Blood, which the Psalmist justly entitles the remedy that calls from death to life. My evil propensities seduce me, the deceitful world allures me, and Satan constantly spreads out his snares; come to my aid or I shall be lost. I flee to the Holy Eucharist; take compassion on me, defend me, and suffer me to walk in thy company: whither thou goest I will go.

4. O God, infinitely holy, I offer thee my Communion to obtain the grace of being loved by thy adorable Heart, in order to learn how to imitate thy virtues better, and to be able to lead an interior life. I desire also to make reparation for my own irreverences, and those that others offer thee in the Sacrament of the Eucharist; I offer it for the exaltation of the Church, for the conversion of sinners, and for the deliverance of souls from Purgatory: I offer it in a special manner for (N.) and I desire to have the intentions requisite for gaining the Indulgences it may procure me.

O Jesus! my love and my life enter into my poor heart; it desires thee, O hasten, it languishes to receive thee; accept it, it gives itself unreservedly to thee; fix its inconstancy, sustain its frailty; let my heart and thine form but one same heart. I entreat all these graces by thy tears, by thy sufferings, and by thy precious Blood. Bless me, and enable me henceforth to accomplish thy adorable will in all things.

Method of hearing Mass on days of Communion.

I present myself before Thy altar, O my God, to assist at the Divine sacrifice. In mercy prepare my heart for the gentle and salutary effects of thy grace; govern my mind and my senses, and by thy precious blood efface all the sins of which thou dost perceive me guilty; I detest them for love of thee, and humbly implore their pardon. Grant, O sweet Jesus, that uniting my intentions with thine, I may devote myself entirely to thy glory as thou hast sacrificed thyself for my salvation. Amen.

THE PRIEST AT THE FOOT OF THE ALTAR.

Lord, I come to supplicate thee for the life and nourishment of my immortal soul. I will feel no anxiety or sadness at the view of thy tabernacle, because thy Divine heart invites me, and Mary whom thou hast given me for mother presents me. Enlighten my faith, purify my heart, sustain my weakness, and send me from the height of thy

throne, that sublime wisdom which gives grace to
to thy children to know the dignity of the Sacraments, the holiness of thy law, and the majesty of
thy presence. O my soul, advance with confidence
towards the holy mountain; you are about to receive
a God who fears your eternal loss, and who wishes
your salvation. Publish abroad his praises, admire
the prodigious effects of his charity, say to the Lord:
God of goodness, thou desirest to nourish me with
the bread of Angels, grant me the fervor of the
Blessed who reign with thee in heaven.

CONFITEOR.

"Father, I have sinned against Heaven and before
thee, and I am not worthy to be called thy child."
I sinned through my own fault; I cannot repeat
this acknowledgment too frequently in order to do
homage to truth, and to humble my pride. I have
abused thy graces a thousand times! Immaculate
Virgin, the sanctuary of God made man, Angel of
the desert that prepared the way before him; faithful Disciples, who listened to him with docility, and
who received in faith at the Last Supper, and Blessed
souls who possess him in Heaven, join me in imploring grace, and your prayer will be heard. His
mercy will itself speak, and will disarm the Divine
justice; and may I thus be prepared for admission
to the table of my God.

AT THE INTROIT.

The Lord has opened the gates of Heaven; he
has caused manna to descend as food; he gives us
the bread of Angels. Thy bounty, O my God, has
prepared it for the humble heart. Be thou forever
blest, O God of Israel, who can alone accomplish
such prodigies in my favor.

God the Father, God the Son, and God the Holy Ghost, three persons in one God, be merciful to me a sinner.

AT THE GLORIA IN EXCELSIS.

Glory to God, whose justice is avenged by the perpetual sacrifice of so noble a victim! Peace and consolation to men of good will on earth, and who witness a God daily effacing himself to save them and feed them with his own substance. I praise thee, O Lord, I bless thee, I adore thee, I am lost in wonder at the view of the prodigies of Thy love; shall I allow them to become useless to me through the criminal dispositions of my heart? I will no longer reject the peace thou dost offer me! I will endeavor to acquire that good will of which it is the source! Appease, O my God, the strife which so often rises in my heart, and causes the flesh to combat against the spirit.

AT THE COLLECTS.

O Lord Jesus, who hast deigned by a new act of beneficence, to open to Thy Church the ineffable treasures of thy heart; grant that we may render love for love to that adorable heart, and by worthy homages atone for the injuries it suffers, and has suffered in the Sacrament of thy love.

AT THE EPISTLE.

Wisdom has built herself an abode, she has cut seven pillars, she has immolated her victims, she has mingled wine, disposed her table, and sent her servants to invite on the bulwarks and from the city walls, saying: Whosoever is simple, let him come to me. And she says to such as lack wisdom: Come, partake of the bread that is offered to you, and drink the wine that I have mingled for you, come forth from childhood and walk in the ways of innocence.

The bread of Angels becomes the bread of the children of Adam. O unheard of prodigy! the Lord is the food of the weak, the bondman and the needy. One God in three persons, whom we adore with our whole hearts, deign to visit us; introduce us into the banquet hall. All our desires tend to the happiness of being seated at thy holy table.

"Jesus said to the multitude of the Jews: I am the living bread which came down from heaven. If any man eat of this bread, he shall live forever; and the bread that I will give is my flesh for the life of the world. The Jews therefore strove among themselves, saying: How can this man give us his flesh to eat? Then Jesus said to them: Amen, amen, I say unto you: Except you eat the flesh of the Son of man, and drink his blood, you shall not have life in you. He that eateth my flesh, and drinketh my blood, hath everlasting life; and I will raise him up at the last day."—JOHN vi, 51–55.

I believe, Lord, that thou art here, really present to give thyself to me, and that thou dost renew, in the sacrifice of the Eucharist, the same mysteries of which I read in the Gospel. Thou showest thyself to me on this Altar as it were enveloped in swaddling clothes, and known only to the celestial spirits and to the humble of heart. I see thee forgotten and deserted by christians, as thou wert by the Jews at

Nazareth. Thou dost immolate thyself on this new Calvary for the salvation of each one of us. Thou remainest buried in the tabernacle as in a tomb. Thou dost bestow thy body on the faithful, thy body glorious, and forever victorious over the empire of death. I envy not the happiness of those who saw thee during the course of thy mortal life, for with the eye of Faith I discern here the Messiah, whom the Patriarchs and the Prophets so ardently desired to behold.

AT THE OFFERTORY.

O infinitely merciful God, I offer thee my heart, deign to change it, to bless it, to sanctify it; renew in it thy image that has been so frequently disfigured by sin; change its vicious inclinations into a happy propensity to virtue; destroy sin in me with as much promptitude as thou wilt destroy these substances, of which naught will remain but the sensible appearances; let me become by the assistance of thy grace, worthy of possessing thee on earth, and of reigning with thee eternally in heaven.

AT THE WASHING OF THE PRIEST'S FINGERS.

Efface, O Lord, the slightest stain that sin has produced in my heart. Suffer not my soul to perish with the guilty; though I am not innocent, deliver me from my iniquities through the merits of the Sacred Heart of Jesus.

AT THE PREFACE.

O my soul, let us soar to heaven and give thanks to the Lord our God. It is indeed just, O holy Father, it is most reasonable to glorify thee, to thank thee at all times and on all occasions, as our God and Benefactor. It is by Jesus Christ that the Angels and the Powers of Heaven, with Cherubim and Seraphim, celebrate with delight thy glory, and chant thy immortal praises. May I, great God, unite my voice and my sentiments to their transports and heavenly songs, and cry out with them: Holy, Holy, Holy, is the Lord, the God of Hosts; heaven and earth are full of thy glory. Blessed be he that cometh in the name of the Lord, and who is about to descend on this Altar, and then into my heart.

AT THE CANON.

God of mercy, hear our petitions, bless thy Church of which I am a member by the grace of Baptism, and which bestows on me its treasures, by giving me the adorable person of her divine Spouse; bless our holy Father the Pope, with all Bishops and Priests, and grant to all those whom thou hast called to the holy ministry of the altar, the spirit of zeal and piety; maintain them in the purity of the faith, and render me constantly docile to their salutary instructions. Protect our country in peace, and enlighten all who govern it in their eternal as well as their temporal obligations. Mercifully regard all who are present at this holy sacrifice. Comfort and strengthen the weak, the poor, and such as are in trouble; awaken and pardon sinners, enlighten those who are in error, convert the impenitent. I pray for all, O Lord, because thou art the universal Father, thou art sacrificed for all, and it is thy pleasure that we have all one heart and mind.

My soul, behold your King, who comes to you full of meekness and tenderness; he veils the splendor of his divine majesty, so as to allow you a more free access to him. Admirable condescension, it is a prodigy that God alone can effect.

O Jesus, true bread of the strong, celestial manna, which bestows upon man a blessed immortality, I adore thee, be thou the life and nourishment of my soul. A tender confidence in thee, leads me to implore from thy divine Heart that degree of love with which it ought to be inflamed for thee.

AT THE ELEVATION OF THE CHALICE.

O precious blood of my Redeemer, shed for my salvation, thou art all my hope: wash me from the least stains, and apply to me thy infinite merits: sanctify my soul, preserve it unspotted, and be to me a pledge of eternal happiness.

CONTINUATION OF THE CANON.

The Heavens are open, the Holy of holies has come down to earth, this altar has become the throne on which the majesty of the Most High resides; Angels surround it, and with the liveliest sentiments of love and respect, make atonement for the contempt, forgetfulness and indifference of men.

And thou, O my Lord, whilst these sublime intelligences are prostrate before thee, thou askest my poor guilty heart, and more, thou wishest it wholly. Grant then, O Jesus, that it may be thine, and without division. Let my desires, O blessed Lord, correspond to thy tenderness, and let me receive by love what love alone can give me. I love thee, but increase this sentiment in my too cold heart, so that I may say as truthfully as did thy Apostle: "What shall ever separate me from the love of Jesus Christ?"

AFTER COMMUNION.

"I have found him whom my soul loveth, he is mine, and I will never leave him. What can I desire in Heaven, and what can I henceforth love on Earth, except thee, the God of my heart? What shall I render to the Lord for all his mercies?

O soul of Jesus, sanctify me.

Heart of Jesus, inflame me.

Body of Jesus, save me.

Blood of Jesus, inebriate me.

Water from the side of Jesus, cleanse me.

Passion of Jesus, strengthen me.

O good Jesus hear me, never suffer me to be separated from thee—hide me within thy wounds.

Defend me from the malice of the enemy. Call me at the hour of death, and command me to dwell with thee, that with thy saints, I may praise thee forever and ever. Amen.

AT THE PRIEST'S BLESSING.

O Lord, bless me by the hand of thy minister, with thy most abundant benedictions—let these place the seal on all the graces that thou hast just granted me.

AT THE LAST GOSPEL.

At that time, Jesus said to the multitudes of the Jews: My flesh is meat indeed, and my blood is drink indeed; he that eateth my flesh, and drinketh my blood, abideth in me, and I in him. As the living Father hath sent me, and I live by the Father, so he that eateth me, the same also shall live by me. This is the bread that came down from heaven. Not as your fathers did eat manna and are dead. He that eateth this bread shall live forever.—JOHN vi, 56–59.

Acts after Communion.

ACT OF FAITH.

O unspeakable happiness! it is true that my Saviour has deigned to visit me—yes, he has come, so that I may be entirely his and he entirely mine. O infinite bounty and infinite mercy! God unites himself, soul, body, blood and divinity, with my poor erring soul. O my soul, awaken all thy sentiments of Faith, consider the holy Angels surround thee, adoring their God; adore him with them, banish every other thought, collect all thy affections, offer them to God, with strong faith and ardent love.

ACT OF ADMIRATION.

Come, all who adore the Lord! come and admire with me his prodigious mercy, power and wisdom. But thou, O my Lord, where dost thou find thyself? Alas! in a heart far more unworthy of thy presence than was the stable in Bethlehem, in a heart full of imperfections, self-love and miseries. O God, in imagination I embrace thy sacred feet, assist me, O blessed Spirits, and thou O, Mother of God, in celebrating the mercies and prodigies of grace that God has deigned to operate in a heart so little worthy.

ACT OF THANKSGIVING.

My Lord, and my God, I thank thee with my whole heart for the ineffable favor that thou hast just granted to me, I would gladly offer thee worthy thanks; but alas! what thanks can a miserable wretch like me offer. All that I can do is to repeat continually—God is mine, the Highest and Holiest reposes in my soul—which is the vilest and the most miserable of abodes.

My God, I give myself wholly to thee, I desire to be all thine, I offer thee my understanding to be occupied with thy greatness; my memory that it may incessantly recal thy benefits; I offer thee my will, that it may be henceforward conformed to thine, I consecrate to thee my heart with all its sentiments and affections; I offer thee my body and my senses, that they may be so many victims devoted to thy service. Deign, O infinite Majesty, to accept the sacrifice that I make to thee of all that I am and have. Come, O consuming Fire, and destroy whatever may displease Thee in my grateful, and henceforth faithful heart, dispose of me, O Lord, according to thy holy will, I resign myself without reserve to thy amiable and over-ruling Providence.

Holy Virgin, deign to present this offering of my being to the ever blessed Trinity, and obtain for me the grace of being faithful to my promise, to the very last sigh of my life.

ACT OF PETITION.

O adorable Saviour, since thou hast come to grant me a share of thy graces, and thou dost will me to ask for them, I will pour forth my heart before thy tabernacles; I desire neither earthly goods, nor worldly honors, nor riches, neither the vain joys of this fleeting world. What I desire, what I conjure thee to grant me, is a sincere sorrow for the sins I have committed; a clear and strong light, which will manifest unto me what road I should pursue; an inviolable fidelity in thy service; in fine, thy love and the grace of final perseverance. Change my heart and give me a new one, one in accordance with thine, submissive to thy orders, inflamed with holy

love.   I do not merit this grace, but I petition for it
by thy merits, by those of thy holy Mother, by the
love thou hadst to thy Eternal Father, and by that
which thou dost entertain for me.

Ask special graces for yourself, and for the persons in whom
you are interested. Do not forget sinners; ask for their conversion. Pray also for souls in Purgatory, and for all who may
need your prayers.

A Method of hearing Mass for the Dead.

THE PRIEST AT THE FOOT OF THE ALTAR.

Out of the depths I have cried to thee, O Lord: Lord, hear my voice.

Let thy ears attend to the voice of my supplications.

If thou, O Lord, wilt mark iniquities, Lord who shall stand.

For with thee there is merciful forgiveness, and by reason of thy law, I have waited for thee, O Lord.

My soul hath relied on his word; my soul has hoped in the Lord.

From the morning watch even until night, let Israel hope in the Lord.

Because with the Lord there is mercy, and with him plenteous redemption.

And he shall redeem Israel from all his iniquities.

INTROIT.

Grant them eternal rest, O Lord; and let perpetual light shine on them.—*Ps.* A hymn becometh thee, O Lord, in Sion: and a vow shall be paid to thee in Jerusalem. O hear my prayer: all flesh shall

come to thee. Grant them, O Lord, eternal rest, and
let perpetual light shine on them.

AT THE KYRIE.

Lord of clemency, give to the soul (or souls) of
thy servant (servants) departed, a place of comfort,
a peaceful repose, and the light of glory.

AT THE COLLECTS.

O God, whose pleasure it is always to show mercy
and to spare, we humbly present our prayers to thee,
in behalf of the soul of thy servant N. (or of thy
servants,) whom thou hast called to thy judgment;
beseeching thee not to forget it forever, but command
it to be received by the holy angels, and carried into
paradise; that as it believed and hoped in thee, it
may be delivered from the pains of Purgatory, and
inherit everlasting life.

EPISTLE.

1 Thess. iv., 12–17. *Brethren :*—We will not have
you ignorant concerning them that are asleep, that
you be not sorrowful, as those who have no hope.
For if we believe that Jesus died and rose again,
even to them who have slept in Jesus, will God bring
with him. For this we say unto you in the word of
the Lord, that we who are alive, who remain unto
the coming of the Lord, shall not prevent them who
have slept. For the Lord himself shall come down
from heaven with commandment, and with the voice
of an archangel, and with the trumpet of God; and
the dead who are in Christ shall rise first. Then we
who are alive, that are left, shall be taken up together
with them in the clouds, to meet Christ in the air,
and so we shall be always with the Lord. Where-
fore, comfort ye one another with these words.

THE SEQUENCE OR PROSE.

Dies iræ, dies illa,	The '*day* of *wrath*,' that dreadful day,
Solvet sæclum iu favilla,	Will the whole world in ashes lay,
Teste David cum Sybilla.	As David and the Sybils say.
Quantus tremor est futurus,	What horror will invade each mind,
Quando Judex est venturus,	When the avenging judge shall find,
Cuncta stricte discussurus.	Few venial faults among mankind.
Tuba mirum spargens sonum,	The last loud trumpet's searching sound,
Per sepulcrum regionum,	Shall through the rending tombs rebound,
Coget omnes ante thronum.	And wake the nations under ground.
Mors stupebit, et natura,	Nature and death will in surprise,
Cum resurget creatura,	Behold the pale offender rise,
Judicantir responsura	To see his Judge with conscious eyes.
Liber scriptus proferetur	Then shall with universal dread,
In quo totum continetur,	The seven-sealed mystic book be read,
Unde mundus judicetur.	To prove the living and the dead.

Judex ergo cum sedebit,

The Judge ascends his awful throne,

Quidquid latet apparebit,

He makes each secret sin be known,

Nil inultum remanebit.

And all with shame confess their own.

Quid sum, miser! tunc dicturus?

Ah, wretched! what shall I then say?

Quem patronum rogaturus?

What patron find my fears t'allay,

Cum vix justus sit securus.

When e'en the just will dread that day?

Rex tremendæ majistatis!

Thou mighty, formidable King,

Qui salvandos salvas gratis,

Of mercy, inexhausted spring,

Salva me, fons pietatis.

Save me! O save! and comfort bring.

Recordare, Jesu pie,

Forget not what my ransom cost;

Quod sum causa tuæ viæ,

Let not my dear bought soul be lost,

Ne me perdas illa die.

Mid storms of guilty terror tost.

Quærens me, sedisti lassus,

Thou, who for me didst feel such pain,

Redemisti, crucem passus

Whose precious blood the cross did stain;

Tantus labor non sit cassus.

Let not thy sufferings now prove vain.

Juste Judex ultionis,

Thou whom avenging Powers obey,

Donum fac remissionis,	Cancel my debt, (too great to pay,)
Ante diem rationis.	Before that sad accounting day.
Ingemisco, tanquan reus,	Oppressed, o'erwhelmed with doubts and fears,
Culpa rubet vultus meus	Whose load my soul in anguish bears,
Supplicanti parce, Deus.	I sigh and weep; accept my tears.
Qui Mariam absolvisti,	Thou, who wert moved at Mary's grief,
Et latronem exaudisti,	Who didst absolve the dying thief,
Mihi quoque spem dedisti.	Hast given me hope, O grant relief.
Preces meæ non sunt dignæ.	Reject not my unworthy prayer,
Sed tu bonus fac benigne,	Preserve me from the awful snare,
Ne perenni cremer igne.	Which death and gaping hell prepare.
Inter oves locum presta,	Give my immortal soul a place,
Et ab hædis me sequestra,	Among thy chosen right-hand race,
Statuens in parte dextra.	The sons of God, the heirs of grace.
Confutatus maledictis,	From that insatiate abyss,
Flammis acribus addictis,	Where flames devour and serpents hiss,
Voca me cum benedictis.	Deliver me, and raise to bliss.

Oro, supplex et acclinis,	Prostrate, my contrite heart I rend,
Cor contritum quasi cinis,	My God, my Father, and my friend;
Gere curam mei finis.	Do not forsake me in the end.
Lacrymosa dies illa,	Well may they curse their second birth,
Qua resurget ex favilla, Judicandus homo reus.	Who rise to a surviving death.
Huic ergo parce Deus;	Thou great Creator of mankind,
Pie Jesu Domine, dona eis requiem. Amen.	Let all thy faithful mercy find.

AT THE GOSPEL.

John xi., 21–28.   At that time: Martha said to Jesus: Lord if thou hadst been here, my brother had not died.   But now also I know that whatsoever thou wilt ask of God, God will give it thee.   Jesus saith to her: Thy brother shall rise again.   Martha saith to him: I know that he shall rise again in the resurrection at the last day.   Jesus said to her: I am the resurrection and the life, he that believeth in me, although he be dead, shall live.   And every one that liveth and believeth in me, shall not die forever.   Believest thou this?   She saith to him: yea, Lord, I believe that thou art Christ, the Son of the living God, who art come into this world.

OFFERTORY.

Lord Jesus Christ, King of glory, deliver the souls of all the faithful departed from the flames of Purgatory.   Deliver them from the lion's mouth, lest hell swallow them, lest they fall into darkness: and let the standard bearer, Saint Michael, bring them into the holy light; which Thou didst of old promise to Abraham and his posterity. We offer thee, O Lord, a sacrifice of praise and prayers: accept them in behalf of the souls we commemorate this day: and let them pass from death to life.

SECRET.

Look down with favor, we beseech thee, O Lord, on the sacrifice we offer for the souls of thy servants; that as thou wast pleased to bestow on them the grace of the Catholic Faith, thou wouldst also grant them its immortal reward.

THE PREFACE.

It is truly reasonable, just and salutary, that we should always and in all places, give thanks to thee, O holy Lord, Father Almighty, eternal God, through Christ our Lord, who didst effect the salvation of mankind on the wood of the Cross: that from whence death came, thence light might also arise; and that he who overcame by the tree, might also by the tree be overcome. And, therefore, with angels and archangels, with thrones and dominations, and with all the hosts of Heaven, we sing a hymn to thy glory, saying: Holy, Holy, Holy, Lord God of armies, heaven and earth are full of thy glory; Blessed is he that cometh in the name of the Lord, his blood pleads for mercy, and his voice rises to the Throne of clemency.

DURING THE CANON.

Almighty God, whose Providence extends over all creatures, because thou art their Father, cast a look of mercy on the souls that love thee, and whose

2

keenest anguish is separation from thee. Remember, O God, that they are the work of thy hands, and the price of thy sufferings, death and infinite merits of thy divine Son, Jesus.—At this Name, we know that thou wilt mercifully incline thy ear in their favor, we offer thee for their happiness the precious blood of the Heart of Jesus, the powerful intercession of the Heart of Mary, and the humble supplications of all the Saints, and the works, and prayers offered on earth for the repose of the faithful departed.

AT THE ELEVATION.

O sacred Host, immolated for the salvation of the world, be propitious to our prayers. Precious Blood of the Saviour, shed for the remission of sins, sanctify us, and obtain mercy for the Faithful departed. Heart of Jesus, salvation of those who trust in thee, have pity on those souls who implore thee through the Heart of Mary.

CONTINUATION OF THE CANON.

O Heart of Jesus, source of mercy, and devoted to the salvation of mankind; we implore thy intercession in behalf of our brethren, relations, and benefactors, who are departed this life, that by the intercession of blessed Mary, ever a virgin, and of all thy saints, thou wouldst receive them into the enjoyment of everlasting peace.

PATER NOSTER.

Recite the "OUR FATHER," slowly, dwelling upon each petition.

AGNUS DEI.

O Lamb of God, who takest away the sins of the world, have mercy on our souls, now, and at their departure.

O Lamb of God, who takest away the sins of the world, grant us thy peace.

O Lamb of God, who takest away the sins of the world, have mercy on the souls of the faithful departed, (especially on *N.*)

O divine Jesus, at whose patience in suffering, and blessed death, many lamented their offences, and beat their breasts in token of contrition, by thy bitter passion, by the blood of thy pierced Heart, and by thy last agony, give me grace to grieve for my sins, and never more offend thee. Thou, who for love of me wast buried in a new tomb: grant me a new heart; that dying in thee, I may participate in the glory of thy resurrection.

O true light, enlighten my eyes that I may never sleep in eternal death. Thou art the physician of the soul, healing its infirmities by thy sacred Blood, O heal my soul, for I have sinned against thee. Let my soul, O Lord God, be sensible of the happiness of thy presence. Let me taste how sweet thou art; that being allured by thy love, I may never more go in search of earthly joys, for thou art my joy and my portion forever. What canst thou deny me, that hast given me thyself.

May the participation of these heavenly mysteries, O Lord, I beseech thee, obtain eternal light and rest for the souls of the faithful departed, through the merits, death, and resurrection of our Lord.

JOHN vi., 37–49. *At that time:* Jesus said to the multitude of the Jews: All that the Father giveth me shall come to me; and him that cometh to me, I will not cast out. Because I came down from heaven, not to do my own will, but the will of him that sent me. Now this is the will of the Father that sent me : that of all that he hath given me, I should lose nothing, but should raise it up again in the last day. And this is the will of my Father who sent me; that every one who seeth the Son, and believeth in him, may have life everlasting, and I will raise him up at the last day.

A PRAYER AFTER MASS.

And now, O God! having recommended to thy mercy the souls of thy departed servants, grant we may ever remember that we are most certainly to follow them. Give us grace to prepare for our last hour by a good life, that so death, however sudden it may be, may not find us unworthy of admittance into eternal glory. Open likewise the eyes, and soften the hearts of those who have the misfortune of being at variance with thee; inspire them, we humbly beseech thee, with a true sense of their dreadful danger, that by a timely consideration of the uncertainty of life, and the certainty of death, they may be sincerely converted, and obtaining pardon for their sins in this life, be happy with thee forever in the next. Amen.

THE WAY OF THE CROSS.

(From the Mannel de Piete.)

Pious souls, who love to meditate on Jesus suffering, by following that *"man of sorrows"* in the way to Calvary, you will derive consolation in your trials, strength in your weakness, courage in your temptations, and confidence when apparently abandoned. Ah! if you be faithful in following Jesus in this painful journey, if you study his interior dispositions, he will load you with graces, and you will be so happy as to console his agonized Heart.

CONDITIONS REQUISITE FOR GAINING THE INDULGENCES.

The Indulgences attached to the Way of the Cross are most abundant, and exceedingly precious; and are applicable to the souls in Purgatory. The essential conditions are: 1. That the Way of the Cross, receive a blessing from a Priest, who has received the power from the Pope. 2. That the person performing this devotion, go actually from one station to the other, however near they may be placed. 3. That they dwell upon each mystery, either mentally or vocally. It is customary to add to these pious considerations, a Pater, Ave, Gloria Patri, and the versicles "Miserere nostri," etc., "Fidelium," etc., and when concluding, five times Pater, Ave, and the Gloria Patri, according to the intentions of the Church, and then one additional for the Sovereign Pontiff.

When the Way of the Cross is performed in solemnity, it will suffice to kneel at each Station, turning towards the place it occupies.

If one is lawfully hindered from going to the place in which the Stations are erected, according to custom; it may be performed with one Cross only, indulged to this effect. This Cross can only suffice for one person, and must be held in the hand during the 14 Stations. The same number of " *Pater*," " *Ave*," and " *Gloria*," with one for the Pope's intention, must be said.

Preparatory Prayer

AT THE FOOT OF THE ALTAR.

O Jesus! our adorable Saviour, behold us prostrate at thy feet, imploring thy divine clemency for us, and for the souls of the faithful departed. Reject not our hearts, humbled and confused in thy presence, but deign, O most merciful Lord, to apply to them the merits of thy sacred passion, on which we are about to meditate. As thy love towards us is infinite, grant that we may love thee more and more, and that our hearts may be so penetrated with contrition, in contemplating this road of sorrows, consecrated by thy sufferings and blood, that we may receive with perfect resignation all the troubles and afflictions of this life. And thou, O pure Virgin, who, at the foot of the cross, becamest our Mother, and didst teach us the road to Calvary, we beseech thee to guide us in this path of grief, and teach us to follow it with the recollection and compunction that filled thy afflicted soul. Vouchsafe, O Mother of sorrows, to present to the adorable Trinity, the pious sentiments we experience during this holy exercise.

First Station.

JESUS IS CONDEMNED TO DIE.

℣. We adore thee, O Lord Jesus Christ, and bless thy Holy Name.

℟. Because, by thy Holy Cross, thou hast redeemed the world.

Let us consider the admirable submission of Jesus Christ, when he received his unjust sentence. He who was innocence itself, condemned to the most ignominious torments. All his sufferings were for our sins, and to redeem us from hell. The crimes of the world inflicted on him such terrible torments. Let us then, at least be grateful to him for his infinite mercies, and being penetrated with grief, exclaim, O most adorable Jesus, to what an excess didst thou love us, since thou didst permit thy sacred body to be torn with rods, and thy divine head to be crowned with thorns; and all this to excite the insensibility of our hearts. O amiable Jesus! since our crimes reduced Thee to this state, grant us the grace sincerely to detest them, that by repentance and penance we may obtain the pardon thou hast merited for us, by thy death.

Our Father, etc.

Hail Mary, etc.

Glory, etc.

℣. Jesus Christ crucified.

℟. Have mercy on us.

And may the souls of the faithful departed rest in peace. Amen.

Note.—The introductory and terminating Versicles and Responses and Prayers are the same at each Station.

Second Station.

JESUS IS LOADED WITH HIS CROSS.

Let us contemplate the resignation and meekness, with which Jesus received on his bleeding shoulders, the weight of the Cross, how admirable is the patience with which he bears the cruel instrument of his passion. By this he instructs us how we should receive all the troubles and afflictions of this life. Ah! have we not just cause to blush at our want of patience, when the least pain causes us to complain. O most innocent Jesus, we were guilty, and deserved the torturing punishment for our innumerable crimes and iniquities. Bestow on us, we beseech thee, strength to imitate thee in bearing with resignation the ills of this life, since they are ordained by thy providence as the means of satisfying thy justice, and preparing us for eternity.

Pater. Ave, etc.

Third Station.

JESUS SINKS UNDER THE CROSS.

Let us follow Jesus Christ on his way to Calvary, and contemplate him in this painful road; exhausted by the loss of blood, and the weight of the Cross, he falls beneath it, this enrages the monsters who accompany him, they strike him with redoubled fury, and utter against him the most horrible and impious imprecations. And Jesus, the meek Jesus, utters no complaint. In this manner he suffered to expiate our frequent falls into sin, likewise to teach us to submit to Providence in all the evils we have justly merited by our repeated offences. O, sweet Jesus! amiable Redeemer, how often do we fail in the fulfillment of our duties, and how many times have we not returned into that abyss of misery, out of which thou hadst compassionately drawn us. Ah, deign once more to stretch towards us thy helping hand, that we may avoid sin, and follow with constancy the road to Calvary, to be one day eternally happy with thee in heaven.

Pater. Ave, etc.

Fourth Station.

JESUS MEETS HIS HOLY MOTHER.

Let us conceive, if it be possible, the excessive grief that pierced at the same time the heart of the Son and Mother, when they met on the road to Calvary. Jesus perceived Mary overwhelmed with sorrow and drowned in tears, and Mary saw her only and beloved Son, dragged to execution by a troop of ruffians; loaded with every species of agony and almost dead by repeated sufferings. At the afflicting sight, her maternal heart was peirced with *"the sword of grief,"* she would willingly have sacrificed her life to deliver him from his executioners; but she knew that lost man was to be redeemed by his death, and her compassion for sinners triumphing over maternal tenderness, she united her sacrifice to that of her divine Son, and courageously remained with him throughout. O Mary, most desolate of Mothers, we were the cause of the sorrows into which thou wert plunged; but, O most pure Virgin, deign to regard us with compassion, and obtain for us a share of that contrition and ardent love, with which thou didst accompany Jesus to Calvary, that we remain as thou didst, firmly attached to the Cross of Jesus crucified.

Pater. Ave, etc.

Fifth Station.

SIMON ASSISTS JESUS TO CARRY HIS CROSS.

Let us consider the excessive kindness of Jesus

Christ towards us. If he permits us to share the
Cross with him, it is to teach us to unite all our sufferings to his, and courageously to imitate our adorable model.

O dear Jesus, thou didst drain the chalice of
affliction; and left us only a small portion. Do not
allow us to be the enemies of thy Cross by refusing
it, on the contrary, grant that we may accept it cheerfully, and mingle our grief with thy blood and tears,
so that loving daily more and more thy Cross, we may
at length become worthy of beholding thee in thy
kingdom.

Pater. Ave, etc.

Sixth Station.

A PIOUS WOMAN WIPES THE FACE OF JESUS.

Let us admire the heroic action of that pious
woman. She advanced through the crowd of soldiers,
to look on her divine Master; she perceives him
covered with dust and blood; at such a sight melts
her soul, and with courageous love, she prostrates
herself before him and wipes his adorable face.
That face, the brightness of which the angels cannot
support, and the impression remains on the hand-
kerchief of the compassionate Veronica. O Jesus,
the most beautiful of the children of men, to what
a state of misery thy love for us reduced thee.
Never wert thou more worthy of our love and adoration. We, therefore, adore thee with our whole souls,
and prostrate before thy infinite majesty, we implore
thee to render us pure in thy sight. Imprint deeply
in our hearts thy cross and sufferings, that we may
receive with pleasure, every occasion of mortification,
as the means of bearing some resemblance to thy
divine Majesty; may the remembrance of thy passion

and love, be the continual meditation of our lives, and make us each day increase in gratitude towards thee for thy amazing goodness.

Pater. Ave, etc.

Seventh Station.

JESUS FALLS A SECOND TIME.

Behold thy Saviour falling a second time under the weight of the Cross, again he is exposed to the impatience of his murderers, and the cries of a vile populace, O, then what torments suffered his body, and what afflicting thoughts endured his soul, at the view of our relapses into sin; have we not just cause to be ashamed of our many broken promises, and reiterated offences against his infinite goodness? Our divine Jesus by his second fall, wishes to teach us, that we should never lose confidence or be discouraged if we find the road to Heaven planted with thorns and briars. Jesus has pursued it first. If we walk in the path he has traced out for us, it will in the end conduct us to the kingdom of his glory. O Jesus, our strength and only hope, preserve us from the misery of again falling into sin. Do not permit thy sufferings to be in vain; we conjure thee by thy precious blood to save us, and at length render us worthy to view thee in thy glory.

Pater. Ave, etc.

Eighth Station.

JESUS CONSOLES THE DAUGHTERS OF ISRAEL.

Let us consider the admirable generosity of Jesus Christ, he forgets his own sufferings to console the grief of those pious women who follow him, shedding tears of compassion. He tells them not to weep over him, but to shed their tears for themselves and children, thereby giving us to understand, that sympathy for his torments, without a detestation of our sins which caused them, is of little avail in his sight. O amiable Jesus, the true comforter of our afflicted souls, cast on us an eye of pity, let our hearts be overwhelmed with regret in contemplating the torments we brought on you. Give to our eyes a fountain of tears to bewail our past offences, and grant, that being truly penitent, we may in the end like the daughters of Israel, hear from thy lips words of consolation and salvation.

Pater. Ave, etc.

Ninth Station.

JESUS FALLS A THIRD TIME.

Jesus draws near to the mountain of Calvary, his enemies transported with rage and joy, urge him cruelly on, so impatient are they to complete their deicide. The heart of Jesus at this moment was filled with grief, he saw that his sufferings would be useless to many sinners who would obstinately persevere in crimes. This terrible thought overwhelemed his soul, and the agony he experienced was so excessive, that he lost all power, and fell exhausted with his face to the ground. O Jesus, victim to love, thou art then arrived at the place where thou art to be immolated for the salvation of man, deign we beseech thee to look on us with mercy, and apply to us the merits of thy passion, that we may be enabled to offer thee, a tribute of praise and thanksgiving, during all eternity.

Pater. Ave, etc.

Tenth Station.

JESUS IS STRIPPED OF HIS ROBES.

Let us consider the pains Jesus Christ endured,

when the executioners tore away his clothes, the wounds he had received caused them to adhere to his body, so, that by tearing them away, they renewed the cruel pains of flagellation, the blood ran down in torrents, the flesh came away by pieces, his sacred mouth was filled with gall, and thus was he exposed to the view of a barbarous multitude, who loaded him with every species of insult. O most meek and innocent Jesus, to what a state have our sins reduced thee. Thou who wert the Holy of Holies, endured this cruel misery, whilst we who are the cause of all seek only consolation. Thou wert stripped to expiate our loss of grace, we implore thee to aid us in recovering it, that being once more adorned, in a manner pleasing to thee, we may persevere in thy love to the end of our lives.

Pater. Ave, etc.

Eleventh Station.

JESUS IS NAILED TO THE CROSS.

Let us adore Jesus Christ, extended on the Cross, offering his divine limbs to be pierced by the executioners. What torments he must have endured, when the nails pierced his hands and feet, parting the bones, bursting the veins, contracting the sinews and covering him with blood; add to all these sufferings his excessive thirst, augmented by the vinegar given him to drink. O most amiable Jesus, how often have we by our sins lacerated thy sacred body, and wounded thy divine heart, by our misguided and evil inclinations. O, may sincere penance and mortification, henceforward crucify in us all that opposes thy Holy law. May our hearts renounce all guilty gratifications, and sincerely attach themselves to thee and thy Cross. Grant this desire, O most compassionate Jesus.

Pater. Ave, etc.

Twelfth Station.

JESUS DIES ON THE CROSS.

Behold Jesus Christ, the God of sanctity expiring between two thieves, and suspended as a victim to appease heaven and reconcile it to the guilty earth. Listen to the last words pronounced by his dying lips. He supplicates from his father, the pardon of his executioners. He recommends us to his blessed Mother. He complains that heaven has forsaken him. He expresses the desire he has for our salvation by this exclamation, "I thirst." He commends his soul to his eternal Father. He announces that all is consummated, his strength fails, his head droops, his lips send forth the last sigh, and Jesus dies for us. At this instant all nature is in confusion, and can we alone be insensible to the sight? Ah! behold to what a state sin has reduced thy Saviour, yet he offers pardon to the penitent sinner, his arms are extended to receive him, his head is inclined to bestow the kiss of peace, and his divine heart open to shed grace on him. Let us hasten to the Cross and live henceforth only for Jesus.

Pater. Ave, etc.

Thirteenth Station.

JESUS TAKEN DOWN FROM THE CROSS, AND PLACED IN THE ARMS OF HIS MOTHER.

Let us penetrate into the heart of this most afflicted Mother, and conceive, if it be possible, the grief she felt on receiving in her arms the dead body of her dear Son. She contemplates his face discolored, his lips pale, his body cruelly torn, his feet and hands pierced, and his heart opened by the lance. Then indeed, was her heart truly drowned in bitterness, and her soul encompassed by misery, the extent of which was only known to God. O Mary, Mother of grief, we were the cause of thy affliction, our sins wounded thy heart, and nailed Jesus to the Cross. When shall we be worthy, by sincere repentance, to compassionate thy sorrows. Permit us, incomparable Virgin Mother, to adore in thy arms, our crucified Redeemer. Impress in our hearts a lively remembrance of the sorrow thou didst experience at the foot of the Cross, and by thy powerful intercession with thy divine Son, make us more worthy of blessing his adorable heart.

Pater. Ave, etc.

Fourteenth Station.

JESUS PLACED IN THE SEPULCHRE.

Here then, O my Saviour, is the tomb where thy adorable body reposes; precious pledge of our salvation! Permit us to join our sighs and tears, to those of thy blessed Mother, the disciples, and the holy women. Grant that we may be occupied continually in meditating on thy passion and ignominious death. Let our hearts constantly find a refuge from the vain pleasures of the world, in thy sepulchre, and there learn to lead a life in God. Dear Jesus, thou didst cause thy sacred body to be deposited in a new tomb, to give us to understand that our hearts ought to be regenerated, when we receive thee in the holy Communion. Deign, we beseech thee, dear Saviour, to give us pure hearts, formed after thine own; humble, mild, charitable, ardently zealous for the glory of God, and detached from all the perishable things of this earth, that each day becoming more and more like unto thee, its divine model, they may at length be found worthy to adore and praise its crucified Lord and Saviour, throughout eternity.

Pater. Ave, etc.

Prayer on returning to the Altar.

Divine Jesus, after having contemplated thy torments and humiliations, by following thee on this painful road to Calvary, we kneel to acknowledge our gratitude for thy infinite love, in delivering thyself to such excruciating sufferings. After such a sacrifice made for us, what dost thou require? Doubtless, that we should live according to thy precepts, and conform our desires to thy adorable heart, the centre of thy love for sinners. O adorable Heart of Jesus, crucified, mayest thou be daily more loved and honored. I resolve henceforth to do all in my power to honor thee. O pure Virgin Mother, our hearts belong to thee, Jesus gave them when he bequeathed us on that sorrowful mountain of Calvary, offer them to him this day, he can refuse thee no request, beg of him to convert, to bless, and sanctify them, that they may become worthy of adoring and glorifying him during eternity. Amen.

OREMUS.

Respice quasumus Domine super hanc, familiam tuam proqæ Dominus noster, Jesus Christus non dubitavit, manibus tradinos centium et crucis subire tormentum. Per Christum Dominum Nostrum.

[Terminate by six Pater and six Ave.]

WAY OF THE CROSS,

To honor the Sufferings of the Sacred Heart of Jesus.

PREPARATORY PRAYER.

Adorable Heart of Jesus, I prostrate myself before thee, in grateful admiration for thy sufferings in the mysteries of the Way of the Cross. O loving Heart, consider *my* necessities, those of my brethren, of the holy Catholic Church, and of all mankind; and at the remembrance of thy interior anguish on Calvary, dilate and bedew us with the rain of thy mercy.

Holy Spirit, visit my soul by contrition, render me capable of gathering, like a heavenly harvest, the Indulgences bestowed on the road in which I am about to follow my Saviour.

Heart of Mary, and all ye Saints, that during your exile here below, most assiduously frequented Calvary and watered it with your tears, assist me in this pious exercise, by your inspirations and salutary suffrages.

First Station.

℣. Adoramus te Christi, et benedicimus tibi.

℟. Quiæ per sanctum crucem turem redemiste mundum.

JESUS IS CONDEMNED TO DEATH.

Jesus became the friend of all men; in recompense for his infinite bounty, he is condemned to an ignominious death, and He consents to die in order to save us. Can there be greater love than to give life for a friend? O my soul, love the Heart of Jesus, for it first loved us! Jesus condemned in order that I may receive absolution from thy Father; condemn to death in me the miseries which lead me to wound anew thy Heart?

Pater Noster.

Ave Maria.

Gloria Patri.

℣. Miserere nostri Domine.

℟. Miserere nostri.

℣. Fidelium animæ, etc.

Note.—The introductory and terminating Versicles and Responses and Prayers are the same at each Station.

Second Station.

JESUS IS LOADED WITH HIS CROSS.

Jesus courageously takes up his Cross, and advances to death! Hear, O my soul, the words of thy Saviour: "Come to me all you who are weary, and heavy laden with sorrows, and I will give you relief; take my yoke for it is easy, and my burden for it is sweet." Heart of Jesus, grant me thy love and I will follow thee whithersoever thou goest—I wish no other guide than thy Cross, through the stormy sea over which I am sailing to eternity. Cross of Jesus govern all my thoughts, words and works, that they may be conformed to those of the Sacred Heart which was opened for love of us while attached to thee.

Pater. Ave. Gloria, etc.

Third Station.

JESUS FALLS FOR THE FIRST TIME.

Arrived at somewhat more than a third of the way, the Saviour falls, exhausted with suffering, and crushed by the weight of the instrument of his torture. Ah! how excessive are thy sufferings, my Heavenly Spouse! Ah! it is for thee that I suffer, O sinner! because thou art dear to my Heart! for thee, ungrateful soul, and for thy offences, I suffer, to win thee to eternal bliss!

Heart of Jesus, deign to apply to my soul the merits of thy mysterious meekness—quicken me by thy omnipotent falls. My Saviour, what shall there be in Heaven for me, or what shall I desire on Earth but the God of my heart, and my everlasting inheritance.

Pater. Ave. Gloria, etc.

Fourth Station.
JESUS MEETS HIS BLESSED MOTHER.

Recount to us, O Mary, what Jesus suffers while burdened with his humiliating Cross; thy sacred Heart alone can estimate his interior anguish. There is no sorrow like unto his—and this grieves thy maternal Heart—*well* art thou styled " Compassionate Mother." Aid me to share in thy sufferings, and in those of the Heart of Jesus, for when thou dost find a generous soul that loves while suffering, and suffers while loving, thou dost forget thy own heart-breaking grief.

Pater. Ave. Gloria, etc.

Fifth Station.
SIMON ASSISTS JESUS.

At the birth of Jesus, shepherds hastened to pay him homage, and adore him as their liberator, but on this day no one befriends him or shows him respect—there is none but a Pagan that consents to carry his Cross! Yet, Jesus said to more than one soul, "you who are my friends take pity on me." I hear thy voice, O divine Master, thy Heart shall no longer suffer without sympathy, thy sorrows shall be my sorrows, and the Cross planted in thy adorable

Heart, shall be my badge and the object of my complacency.

Pater. Ave. Gloria, etc.

Sixth Station.

A PIOUS WOMAN WIPES THE FACE OF JESUS.

Those whom God calls to the blissful society of heaven, He wills should be conformed to the image of his Son. A pious woman pities the sufferings of Jesus, and he immediately rewards her with the significant token of his blessed portrait. O Jesus, imprint in me thy resemblance—thy spirit—thy dispositions—thy virtues—the image of thy adorable Heart; in order that the Father may love me, bless me, and receive me into his kingdom.

Pater. Ave. Gloria, etc.

Seventh Station.

JESUS FALLS A SECOND TIME.

Jesus advances, his adorable body bending forward, his knees trembling, and at length he falls! This second fall must have been far more painful than the first, as our Lord's strength was failing, and his sufferings had become more excessive! And yet that Divine Saviour complains not, he is mute as the Lamb led forth to slaughter, he scarcely heaves even an interior sigh! Grant me, O patient Heart of Jesus. when I am so unhappy as to fall into sin, immediate sorrow for having offended thee, but banish from my soul all the trouble which arises from self-love. If we have sinned, thou art "our advocate with God the Father," let us not offer thee the cruel injury of despairing of a cause which is in thy hands. In sickness and in interior trials, I will recall thy patience, and this remembrance will help me to be submissive and courageous.

Pater. Ave. Gloria, etc.

Eighth Station.

JESUS CONSOLES THE WOMEN OF JERUSALEM.

Daughters of Jerusalem, you are affected to tears by the sorrows of Jesus, but are you not more deeply moved by his divine patience? Consider the calmness and meekness of his sacred Heart, breathed forth in the words "Weep not over me." Alas! when *we suffer*, our words are impatient and sharp, and every contradiction irritates us. And yet *our* sufferings are justly due to our sins. O Heart of Jesus, help me to penetrate the exterior, and discern all the ills that flow from sin. Change into tears some drops of thy precious blood, and distil them into my miserable heart, that I may mourn over my evil days. Thus I should draw good from ill, and my past life, hitherto sterile for salvation, will produce amaranthine flowers of a blessed eternity, flowers of penance, humility and love!

Pater. Ave. Gloria, etc.

Ninth Station.

JESUS FALLS THE THIRD TIME.

The heavy burden of the Cross has exhausted the remaining strength of Jesus, and he falls prostrate in the dust, amid the fearful imprecations of that brutal multitude. They shout, *"persecute him,"* *"oblige him to advance."* Yes, they who formerly enjoyed his kindness, now wish to triumph over him. O Jesus, by the merits of this third fall, voluntarily suffered for love of me, preserve me from that last and irremediable fall, from which the soul can never rise. Let me also learn from thy meek Heart, never to avenge myself on my enemies, for the petty sufferings their malice may occasion me, but docile to thy heroic teaching, help me even to rejoice in suffering for thy name.

Pater. Ave. Gloria, etc.

Tenth Station.

JESUS STRIPPED OF HIS GARMENTS.

A furious and pitiless troop fall upon Jesus, as vultures on their helpless prey, taking off his garments with shocking cruelty. Yet, Jesus is still patient, his features breathe naught but kindness, and he looks with sweetness on his rough persecutors. Ah! my soul, see our divine Saviour practices the admirable lesson taught in his sermon on the mount. Blessed are the poor in spirit, for theirs is the kingdom of Heaven. Let us not wait until the Angel of death and of judgment strip us with rude and inexorable hands, but let us imitate Jesus, born in a stable, and divested of all things on the Cross, by courageously removing from the heart whatever it possesses, or rather that by which it is possessed.

Pater. Ave. Gloria, etc.

Eleventh Station.

JESUS IS NAILED TO THE CROSS.

Approach, O my soul, and admire the patience of Jesus. They stretch him on the Cross, they pierce his hands and feet, they number all his bones, but he suffers no murmur to rise in his Heart. He practices the teaching of his gospel, they ask of him his right hand, and he also presents them the left. O Jesus, each bird of the air builds its nest according to its instinct, one on the lofty poplar, another on the humble shrub, and another on the earth. My soul also will build hers, or rather thou hast built it for her. In thy *sacred wounds*, she will seek shelter from the storm, and there exhale in pious sighs her love, her repentance, and her hope.

Pater. Ave. Gloria, etc.

Twelfth Station.

JESUS DIES ON THE CROSS.

On the cross, in the hour of death, the Heart of Jesus suffered both interior and exterior obscurity—first the three hours' *"darkness that was spread over all the earth,"* secondly, (at the ninth hour,) when uttering that piercing cry of anguish, *"my God, my God, why hast thou forsaken me,"* thus proving that his eternal Father had concealed from him, that serene countenance of loving mercy, by which he testifies to the celestial hosts, that he accepted the sacrifice of his only begotten SON. Our souls must also submit to the double night of Calvary, if we desire to enjoy the never fading light of heaven—we must *"see naught, in order to behold all!* We must sacrifice to the Heart of Jesus, and to the justice of God, (thirsting for expiation,) the delicious sentiments that divine love may awaken in our souls.

O Heart of Jesus, let me cast myself into thy wound, that from that abyss of mercy, I may enter the realms of eternal bliss.

Pater. Ave. Gloria.

Thirteenth Station.

JESUS TAKEN DOWN FROM THE CROSS.

Contemplate now, my soul, thy Jesus *dead* in the arms of his blessed Mother; his countenance is pale and livid, yet the serenity which ever reigned in his

Heart, still beams upon his stiffened features. And thou, O sorrowful Mother! who would recognise in thee, *her* whom the Angel saluted, blessed among all women. Alas! to-day thou who wert styled *full of grace*, art full of suffering. "Call me *afflicted*, and not *beautiful*," mayst thou say with Nöemi, for thy beauty has disappeared in a sea of tears; it is no longer visible except to the eye of God; but in his sight resignation makes thee more beautiful than ever! Obtain for me, O Mary, that calm in the midst of trouble, which springs from faith, hope and charity, and let me learn that those whom God intends receiving into his Heart, he tries in the furnace of humiliation.

Pater. Ave. Gloria, etc.

Fourteenth Station.
JESUS IS LAID IN THE SEPULCHRE.

O Jesus, deposited in the tomb, you teach me that we must die, not only a natural death, which I cannot ignore, for every hour sounds its knell, but also a daily and momentary death to myself, to the world, and to my passions. At the sepulchre thy sufferings and humiliations terminate. A grave also awaits me, and there too my combats must end. But after the tomb will come eternal light and glory. Grant that I may be of the number of those who shall be raised to glory. This hope will encourage me to walk in the royal way of the Cross, and this expectation will assist me to obtain final perseverance. Heart of Jesus, perseverance of the just, salvation of those who trust in thee, and delight of the Saints, have mercy on us.

Pater. Ave. Gloria, etc.

STATIONS OF THE AFFLICTED MOTHER.

N. B.—Pope Pius VII. granted to those who would consecrate an hour, or at least a half an hour, to honoring the sorrows of Mary, after the death of her Son, from three o'clock on Good Friday, P. M. until Holy Saturday at ten, A. M. a Plenary Indulgence, applicable to the souls in Purgatory.

First Station.

THE BLESSED VIRGIN AT THE TOMB OF JESUS.

How deep must have been the affliction of Mary on seeing the lugubrious preparations for the interment of her beloved Son. She compared in spirit the happy time in which she enveloped the body of the Infant Jesus in swaddling clothes, with this painful moment, in which she beholds him in the arms of Joseph and Nicodemus. Impossible to turn her moistened eyes from the dear object of her grief, but the stone that closes the entrance to the sepulchre soon deprives her of this last mournful consolation. Mary, then, with her head reclining on the tomb, with her lips sealed to the stone that conceals from her sight the only object of her love, addresses a final adieu to the Body of Jesus, inundating with her tears the earth which has received him into her bosom.

Second Station.

MARY RETURNS TO JERUSALEM.

Night approaches, and Mary, resigned—arises, bends her suppliant knee, once more kisses the holy sepulchre, and then raising her languid eyes towards Heaven, she departs; but leaves her heart inhumed with the body of her Son. The pious women kindly

drew her veil closely round her, and all descend in a
silence, interrupted only by sobs and deep drawn
sighs. Mary, as she retires, casts one lingering look
of tenderness on the spot of earth that encloses her
life and love.

Third Station.

MARY PASSING MT. CALVARY, PERCEIVES THE HOLY CROSS.

Into what a sea of bitterness must the Heart of
Mary have been plunged, when obliged to pass over
Mt. Calvary to re-enter Jerusalem, she again saw
that place in which a frightful deicide had just been
committed on the body of her Son! She sees the
Cross yet erect, and stained with the precious blood
of Jesus; she approaches reverently that wood lately
so ignominious; she kisses it with respect—presses it
to her heart, and waters it with a gush of agonizing
tears.

Fourth Station.

MARY RE-ENTERS JERUSALEM.

On again beholding that ungrateful and unhappy
city, in which the Holy of Holies had just been
treated as a criminal, John and the pious women give
free course to their lamentations. Mary heaves
sighs of such bitter grief, that hearts the most insensible are excited to tears and moans of sympathy.
Every advancing step into Jerusalem, is a new sword
of grief to pierce the Heart of Mary. The streets,
the public squares, and the Pretorium, each recall to
her some new insult that was offered to Jesus; *here,*
he was bound as a vile criminal; *there,* he was
scourged, on yon sacred spot his blessed face fell
upon the hard ground; through *that* street he passed
when going to the house of Herod. *Ah! my Son,*

Jesus, my beloved Son, what didst thou not endure?
O holy Virgin, may the affliction in which I
behold thee, penetrate my soul with compunction
and sincere regret! Engrave in my heart a tender
recollection of what thy maternal heart suffered, on
seeing Jesus' Passion through the love of sinners.

Fifth Station.

MARY IS RECEIVED AT THE HOUSE OF JOHN.

How great must have been the consolation of
St. John, when he received at his own dwelling the
Mother of his kind Master, now become also his
mother! But what a chilling contrast for Mary—
she no longer enjoys the presence and conversation
of her amiable Son, his gentle tones no longer salute
her ear, she feels the want of his gentle and filial
attentions. The sight of St. John recalls the thought
of her lost one, and thus revives her grief and tenderness. Her tears flow day and night, and naught
can console her, so absorbed is her mind in the remembrance of his cruel death, and the crimes of
men which were its cause.

I partake of thy affliction, O most forlorn of
mourners! but since thou hast adopted me as thy
child, in the person of St. John, suffer me confidently to cast myself into the arms of thy mercy;
disdain me not though I am unworthy of thy maternal love.

Sixth Station.

MARY IS EVER OCCUPIED WITH THE SUFFERINGS OF HER SON.

What tongue can describe the excess of grief
which overwhelmed the Heart of Mary, during the
two nights and days that elapsed between the burial
of Jesus and his resurrection! Dwelling continually

on his passion, that desolate Mother hears anew the seditious and inhuman shout of the Jews: she enumerates the blows of the thongs and scourges; she contemplates the ignominious buffets, and her son's beautiful countenance covered with vile spittle; she hears their impious mockeries and raileries—assists at the Crucifixion, and when in expiring agony she perceives him exhale his last breath, her Heart breaks asunder with grief.

O Mary, holy Virgin, overwhelmed with sorrow, engrave in my heart such a profound recollection of the opprobriums of Jesus Christ, that I may never lose sight of him, until my last moment of life.

Seventh Station.

MARY IS AFFLICTED AT THE SINNERS' LOT.

Mary had offered her dear and only Son to the God of vengeance, for the salvation of all *men*, of whom she was to become the protecting mother; yet her soul already wrung with sore anguish, was filled with a new degree of sadness when she foresaw the multitude of immortal souls that would perish for having abused the precious Blood just shed for their redemption. This painful vision, the last ingredient in her cup of thrice bitter sorrow, rendered her Queen of Martyrs.

O the most amiable of Mothers, suffer me not to be of the number of those ungrateful ones who increase thy grief by abusing the sacred and atoning Blood of thy divine Son. Deign to obtain its application to my soul in life, and in the hour of my death.

Eighth Station.

MARY AT THE RESURRECTION OF JESUS.

Absorbed in painful thoughts, quite occupied with

the unhappy destiny of numerous sinners who would be condemned eternally, although Jesus had given himself for their ransom.   Mary was lost in these painful reflections, when suddenly they make known to her the resurrection of Jesus! Cease thy mourning, O holy Virgin, yield thy soul no longer a prey to consuming grief, dry up thy tears! thy Son has risen, behold his glorified Body: contemplate the majesty of the royal vanquisher of death: admire the Angels and Saints that surround him, and let me unite with them in their salutation of O! Queen of Heaven, rejoice!   Allelulia! Allelulia!

CONSECRATION TO OUR LADY OF SORROWS.

Holy Virgin, Mother of my Saviour, I choose thee this day for my sovereign, protectress, and advocate with thy divine Son, Jesus: imprint in my soul the sorrows thou didst undergo at the foot of the Cross, and receive me forever in the number of thy children; assist me at every moment of my life, above all at the hour of my death, so that united to thy dolors in this valley of tears, and living henceforth in constant fidelity to thy service, I may merit by the imitation of thy virtues, the crown of glory that God bestows on his elect.

O God, who during thy sacred Passion, didst behold the most tender soul of the glorious Virgin, thy Mother, transfixed with a sword of sorrow, in fulfilment of the venerable Simeon's prophecy, grant us by thy goodness, that whilst celebrating with respect the memory of her Compassion and grief, we may gather by the merits and intercession of all the Saints, who were faithful in their attachment to thy Cross, the blessed fruits of thy Passion. O thou who livest and reignest world without end.   Amen.

TEN DAYS' PREPARATION

FOR THE

Festibal of Pentecost.

BY FATHER FELIX, S. J.

(Translated from a French Manuscript.)

SS. C. J. M.

FIRST DAY.

Veni Sancte Spiritus.	Holy Spirit! Light of light!
Et emitte cœlitus	From the Heaven's empyreal height,
Lucis tuæ radium.	Let thy radiance cheer our sight.

Meditation.

FIRST POINT.

The Holy Spirit is GOD, the God of all majesty. I am but a poor, miserable creature, and yet, O infinite condescension! that Omnipotent God, that divine Comforter, abases himself so far as to come to me, if I invite him. Still more, how many times in his infinite mercy and charity, has he not presented himself at the door of my heart, requesting a hospitable reception? And shall I be so coldly indifferent as not to invite him to enter! Shall I not on the contrary, imitate the Disciples of our Lord Jesus Christ, and his own blessed Mother, who remained enclosed in the retreat of the Cenacle, after our Saviour's ascension, awaiting the Divine Comforter that had been promised to them? Rise, my soul! awaken thy confidence, animate thy desires. Repeat frequently, as did they: "COME, HOLY SPIRIT."

SECOND POINT.

I am inviting the Holy Spirit, *but*, have I prepared an abode for him? Where is the Temple of my God? Is my heart truly ready, and is all within it in perfect order? Ah! I must undoubtedly dispose it during these days for receiving his divine Light; but this Light descends from above; it is a heavenly, supernatural, and divine operation, and demands from us dispositions proportioned to such great effects. Hence, let us elevate our thoughts, our affections, the whole heart towards Heaven. Let us withdraw somewhat from the dissipation excited by creatures, if we desire in earnest to unite our souls to the Creator. Recollection, Silence, Prayer and vigilance over the Senses, with mortification, are the means which I should adopt to dispose my soul for this inestimable favor.

THIRD POINT.

It is evident that I am in great need of a ray of that divine Light! for alas! how frequent are my falls! Either because the light reflects not on my steps, or because I close my eyes to its benign radiance? Why do I commit so many sins? Why is my heart so destitute of Charity towards him, whom I should love supremely? Because, that heavenly light does not illuminate my path. Ah! let us close our eyes, perhaps hitherto too widely opened in gazing on worldly vanities, and let us fix them on the light which emanates from the Holy Ghost. Thrice blessed if one ray reach our benighted souls! Come, Holy Spirit, deign to pronounce over this abyss of misery and darkness, the fiat, "*Let there be light.*"

At thy word Light will instantaneously descend. Come then, O Holy Ghost.

EXAMEN. RECOLLECTION.

Am I not of the number of those dissipated Christians who seldom or never examine seriously the state of their souls? Who rarely listen to the reproaches of their consciences? Have I nothing to reform relative to useless discourses or visits, and distracting conversations, in which the spirit of piety is dissipated or entirely destroyed.

When God favors me during prayer, or in my other pious exercises, by bestowing on me some light, some excellent thought, or devout sentiment, do I not evade it, by yielding to presumption with a crowd of other faults?

REFORMATION.

My Soul, let us examine, *am I well with God?* Can I justly be satisfied with my manner of life? Let us consider *deeply*, my soul. It was after salutary reflection that the poor prodigal returned to his father. Amid our daily occupations, let us endeavor to raise our thoughts to God.

ASPIRATION.

"Holy Spirit, Light of light!
From the Heaven's empyreal height,
Let thy radiance cheer our sight."

—

SECOND DAY.

Veni Pater pauperum	Come, O Father of the poor,
Veni dator munerum	Bring us treasures that endure.
Veni Lumen cordium.	Come, O Light of hearts made pure.

Meditation.

FIRST POINT.

I am poor, perchance nothing is wanting to me as regards the goods of *earth*, but alas! how paltry are these in comparison with the riches of Heaven, and how useless will they prove at the hour of Death. Real riches are those of the soul, those which will endure to all Eternity. When I would number my virtues, measure the extent of my piety, and compute my good deeds, how destitute do I find my soul. What profit have I derived from God's sanctifying grace. Wretch that I am, has not *mortal* sin reduced me to the lowest depth of misery. Ah! my soul, it is high time to draw aside the veil and undeceive ourselves—let us not dread making an humble, sincere, and candid avowal of our negligence, of our extreme indigence, to the Great Dispenser of every good. Banish pride, for it is excessively unsuitable to mendicants such as we.

SECOND POINT.

Let us hasten to come forth from this deplorable state of poverty, behold the divine Dispenser of all good is advancing. He can, in a moment, change us from being paupers, to be "*immensely wealthy;*" for his treasures are inexhaustible, and his liberality knows no bounds. If we unhappily remain in our state of destitution, we need impute the blame of this wretchedness to none but ourselves, to our own negligence and lukewarmness in prayer.

THIRD POINT.

I am not only poor, but I am blind. What an unfortunate condition! However it is only too real. *Within,* what darkness regarding all that concerns the weighty interests of my soul, the important affair of my salvation! Is not a heart cold, nay, icy towards God, a proof that I live without an acquaintance with that God who is so worthy of my best and highest affections? Is not the neglect of my duties towards God, even so far as to commit grievous sin, an indubitable proof that I have never understood the malice, blackness and hideousness of Sin? Had I been, even once, fully convinced and penetrated by this great and terrible truth: "There is an

Eternal Hell," would I have so frequently exposed myself to the danger of losing together with the grace of God, my eternal beatitude. How numerous and pressing are the motives that induce me to lift up my eyes towards the Spirit of Light, and to cry aloud with the blind man in the Gospel, "Lord that I may see!" And with the devout King David, "Lord enlighten my eyes." Give light and understanding, O my God, to my blinded soul.

EXAMEN. IRREGULAR AFFECTIONS.

Am I not too much attached to money? Are my expenditures always necessary, useful and reasonable? Do I not frequently go in search of all that can flatter the senses, and satisfy my delicacy? Am I not captive to self-love, vanity, self-esteem: and at the same time ever prompt and merciless in censuring, and judging harshly of others.

REFORMATION.

In order to eradicate the ill-regulated affections which spring from avarice, sensuality and pride, I will daily perform some act of mortification, of humility, and charity, during this Novena.

ASPIRATIONS.

Wash my soul which is soiled by its iniquities.
Bedew it, for it is arid. Heal it, for it is wounded.

THIRD DAY.

Consolator optime,	Thou of all consolers best
Dulcis hospes anima	Visiting the troubled breast
Dulce refrigerium.	Dost refreshing peace bestow.

Meditation.

FIRST POINT.

I would desire to experience nought but sweetness and consolations in the service of my God. But what! is this life therefore destined for enjoyment? Is it not, on the contrary, a time of combat and of trial? Ah well! my soul thou mayst, notwithstanding, seek consolations here on earth. But beware, ask them not of the world. Its promises are deceitful, and the delights it offers are either base or empty; *Consolationes mundanæ, aut turpes sunt aut vanæ.* The demon and sin, also present their cup of pleasures; but what perfidious poison lurks in the depths of that draught, apparently so delicious. An illusion of an instant's duration will produce an eternity of tears! *Gustans gustave paululum mellir et ecce morior.* (1. *Kings,* 14.) No, the Holy Spirit alone can give me lasting and real consolations, and He gives them solely to such as generously renounce the pleasures and enjoyments which the world and sin offer to allure them. Let us henceforward, O my soul, contemn those false consolations: let us never again be seduced by their gilded bait.

SECOND POINT.

Several guests strive for the mastery in my heart, and desire to take up their abode in it. Satan, Vice, the World, and the HOLY GHOST. Each says to me, "Son, give me thy heart." *Præbe, fili mi, cor tuum mihi!* (*Prov.* 23.) To which of these candidates shall I yield the preference? Can I hesitate? No, no; it belongs solely to thee, O Divine Spirit, O amiable guest, O guest dearest to my affections.— The others, I am well aware, in order to be received, spare no captivating promises nor beguiling flatteries;

but I should scarcely have admitted them to my heart, ere they would become its cruel tyrants, rending it with every species of anguish, remorse, and soul-withering dread. O my soul, hast thou not already been the victim of this experience. Awake, shake off dull sloth, banish far from us all that is not God, and let us offer to the Holy Spirit this miserable heart, for an everlasting habitation. O God of my heart, thou art my portion forever. *Deus, cordis mei, et pars mea, Deus in æternum.* (*Ps. 72.*)

THIRD POINT.

Have I not frequently experienced the delicious relief arising from a gentle, refreshing breeze, wafted towards me amid the scorching heats of summer? Too feeble image of what the soul experiences, when the Holy Spirit deigns to visit and re-create it with that divine breath which Holy Scripture describes as "the murmur of the sweetest zephyr." *Sibilus aræ temus.* (*3d Kings,* 19.) But alas! my soul, we comprehend nothing of these spiritual delights! Perchance, we even regard them as chimeras of the imagination. Well, then, let us to-day act as did those holy souls who have tasted them. Let us occupy ourselves seriously with the reception we intend to give the Holy Spirit. Mayhap the moment is coming, in which we shall at length taste how sweet is the Lord! *Gustate et videte quoniam suavis est Dominus.* (*Ps. 23.*)

EXAMEN. INDOLENCE.

1. When I awake in the morning, or during the night, do I take care to raise my heart to God, by reciting some prayer?

2. Am I exact in acquitting myself fervently of all my daily spiritual exercises?

3

3. When I am more strongly tempted, or have had the misfortune of falling into sin, has it not happened that I lost courage, and neglected my pious exercises, whilst I should on the contrary, have had more frequent recourse to prayer?

REFORMATION.

In the principal actions of the day I will carefully renew the uprightness and purity of my intentions, so as to accomplish God's holy will in all things, and recall his sacred presence.

ASPIRATION.

Lord for *Thee*, and in *Thy* presence.

FOURTH DAY.

In labore requies
In æstu temperies
In fletu solatium.

Thou in toil art comfort sweet;
Pleasant coolness in the heat,
Solace in the midst of woe.

Meditation.

FIRST POINT.

It is impossible that I should not also have my trial and my Cross—for who can be exempt from either here below, since we are born to trouble. (Job. 5.) Were there none, besides the constraint which fetters my liberty, the subjection and fatigue consequent on my employments, the solicitude inseparable from my condition, these are already a continual source of wearisomeness and fatigue. Hence, I often sigh for relief; but there is no other repose for the wearied heart but to offer to the Holy Spirit all these trials which are incident to human life, declaring to him that I will endure them cheerfully, because it is his holy will and pleasure. Let us accustom ourselves, O my soul! to a frequent renewal of this intention, and it will not be long ere we shall experience the truth of the divine saying: "My yoke is sweet, and my burden is light."

SECOND POINT.

Temptations! ah! among many occasions of sorrow and tribulation these, without doubt, afflict us most keenly! But what to do with them? Is there any one on earth exempt from temptations? who is disfranchised from those interior combats which exist between the flesh and the spirit? (Job. 7.) Have not the greatest of the Saints endured temptation? Consequently, very far from losing my peace of soul amid these trials, I should on the contrary think of opposing them with a generous, magnanimous resistance. But, if perchance the temptation attacks with too great violence, if my heart is, as it were, scathed by some sparks which have escaped the furnace of the infernal depths—ah! without delay an ejaculation, a cry of the heart towards the Holy Spirit must be my immediate and prevailing resource! His divine virtue will stifle the flames of every impure temptation; and the fire of love will temper the fire of concupiscence. "Inflame, O Lord, our reins and hearts with the fire of thy Holy Spirit, that we ever serve thee with a chaste body, and love thee with a pure heart."

THIRD POINT.

The Holy Spirit is the God of consolation. He loves particularly to console those who endeavor to please him. Therefore, he is styled *Paraclete*, which is to say, COMFORTER. Alas! whence is it that amid the tears that I had occasion to shed every day, that divine balm has never yet been perceptible to my soul? To whom must I attribute the cause? In my painful hours, amid my tears, have I understood how to incline my heart to the Holy Ghost, the Comforter? Is it of Him or of creatures I have implored relief, when bending under the weight of poignant affliction? And then, what is, after all, the subject of my weeping? Is it not, alas! everything else except my sins? Let us, O my soul, commence to mourn over our transgressions, and we shall soon discover that there is nothing in the wide world sweeter than the emotions attendant on true compunction. It is only with such as shed this species of tears, that the Holy Spirit desires to act the part of Comforter. "Blessed are they that mourn, for they shall be comforted." (Matt. 5.)

EXAMEN. HUMAN RESPECT.

1. Do I not sometimes refuse to take the counsel of others, fearing that I may appear scrupulous or ignorant?

2. Have I not delayed going to Confession, or have I not frequently changed my confessor, solely on account of the shame I experienced for continual relapses into similar faults?

3. Through dread of exciting ridicule, or by complaisance towards the weakness of others, have I not omitted certain good works, or even, perhaps suffered myself to be led to the commission of evil?

REFORMATION.

I will carefully make known to my Director in future, all the good and all the evil that I perform. At least once a month I will render him an account of my conscience. I will adopt his advice on all occasions and in every circumstance; and, believing that he represents my divine Saviour to me, I will resign myself without reserve to his direction.

Grant me the joy which springs from thy salutary assistance, and strengthen me by thy holy Spirit.

———

FIFTH DAY.

O lux beatissima,	Light immortal! light divine
Reple cordis intima,	Visit now these hearts of thine,
Tuorum fidelium.	And their inmost being fill.

Meditation.

FIRST POINT.

The Holy Spirit is God, hence he is *light*. *Deus lux est.* (1. *Ep. Jno.* 1.) Sins on the contrary are darkness: *Opera tenebrarum*, (*Rom.* 13.) Now it is impossible for light and darkness to reign in the same place: *Quæ societas luci ad tenebras?* (2. *Cor.* 6.) I implore the Holy Spirit to come into my heart, and indeed I cannot act more wisely. But is not my heart obscured by the thick darkness arising from its vices, its bad or ill-regulated affections, its grovelling inclinations? Alas! if unhappily this darkness predominates in my soul I must first of all dissipate it by sincere repentance, by an honest confession and by mortification of the senses. Without these I should vainly hope that the Holy Spirit will be propitious to my prayer: *could* he come and occupy the darksome abode of Sin?

How delightful, if on the Day of Pentecost, I should find myself *"filled with the Holy Ghost,"* my *will* imbued with a holy fervor! Ah! blessed day! O wonderful change! to find myself no longer what, alas! I have been hitherto! But could it be possible, that being indifferent to this desirable, beautiful change, I might prefer to remain in my old habits, and in the criminal attachments of my heart. Ah! may God preserve me from such blindness! O my soul, have recourse to prayer; asking earnestly of the Lord the petition of the Royal penitent. "Create within me a pure heart, O God, and renew an upright spirit within me." (Psalm 50.)

THIRD POINT.

Who may therefore hope for the plenitude of the gifts of the Holy Ghost? Faithful hearts. *Tuorum fidelium.* But these hearts that are faithul to the Divine Spirit, are they who live in accordance with the teachings of the Faith; who faithfully keep their baptismal vows, of renouncing the world, and having no fellowship with the Prince of darkness.

How many reflections have I to make on the subject of these three obligations? Have I ever dwelt upon them seriously? Do I discover in my soul and in my exterior conduct, a correspondence with this triple promise? Am I faithful to the Holy Spirit? Have I characteristics that give evidence of it?

EXAMEN. INCONSTANCY.

1. Am I not subject to leaving the practices of devotion which I have undertaken, without a sufficient pretext?

2. Am I faithful to the good resolutions that I

take, and to the promises I so frequently offer to God, particularly when I go to confession?

3. Do I take care to examine what is the source of my inconstancy? May it arise from the natural fickleness of my dispositions? from negligence in accomplishing my pious exercises—or may it not spring from a cowardly respect for creatures? It is not enough to enter into engagements with Almighty God; we must soar above the judgments of men, so as not to be forced to blush in their presence, on account of the change we are resolved to effect in our conduct.

REFORMATION.

I am determined in future to exert a greater vigilance over my eyes, my tongue, my ears, and over all my senses. Has not too great freedom in my looks, and in my conversations, frequently proved, both to myself and my neighbor, a fruitful source of temptations and sins?

Every morning and evening I will recite an AVE MARIA, in honor of the Immaculate Conception of B. V. M., to implore her to obtain for me the precious gift of purity.

ASPIRATION.

If thou take thy grace away
Nothing pure in man will stay;
All his good will turn to ill.

SIXTH DAY.

Sine tuo numine,
Nihil est in homine,
Nihil est innoxium.

If thou take thy grace away,
Nothing pure in man will stay;
All his good will turn to ill.

Meditation.

FIRST POINT.

Let us examine, O my soul, how far the assistance of the Holy Spirit is necessary to us. It is of Faith, that without the assistance of the Holy Ghost, I cannot pronounce the Holy Name of Jesus meritoriously. (1. Cor. 12.) A dead body, a corpse, would sooner be able to *act*, to *feel*, and to *walk*, deprived of the aid of a soul, than a soul could be capable of performing any good action without the help of the Spirit of God. Let us, therefore, acknowledge with humility to that Divine Spirit, our extreme need of receiving him; and let the sentiment of our weakness serve as a stimulus in preparing our hearts more carefully for his reception. But, we must remember that even *to do that*, our efforts would be powerless without his assistance. Let us then invoke the Holy Spirit, and let us pray with unbounded confidence that if we perform all that is requisite on our part, he is ready on his side to help us with his grace.

SECOND POINT.

A body without a soul, is incapable of acting; it will only become corrupt and spread infection; so without the Holy Spirit, my *soul* can perform no good action, and is alas! only too capable of accomplishing every kind of evil. It may yield to temptations; it may plunge into the miry pits of sin, and obstinately stay there: it may in fine destroy itself, and do all this just as a multitude of others have done, and continue daily to do. I am fully aware of this. I admit it. How then is it possible for me to remain in indifference and inaction, without desires, without supplication for the assistance of the Holy Spirit, and without preparing my soul for his coming.

On the other hand, if the Divine Spirit of God deigns to assist me, I shall be capable of all good, *yes, all absolutely all.* I can resist the most violent temptations; I can live in continual innocence; I can practice the most heroic virtues; I can become a Saint: (Phil. 4.) *I can do all things in him who strengthens me;* and let us say boldly, not only I can do all, but I can also do it with facility. O my soul, canst thou sufficiently condemn those past distrusts, or dost thou dare to say: "No! I cannot always live thus! no, impossible for me to live without vain pleasures, in such continual restraint!" What canst thou fear if thou hast the blessed privilege of possessing the Holy Spirit? All fear, all discouragement is an injury to him.

EXAMEN. OBSTINACY.

1. Am I not guilty of the sin of Obstinacy, that is to say, do I not deliberately persevere in some sin, or in the immediate occasion of committing it.

2. After unfortunately falling into sin, have I not deferred, (through indifference or false shame,) confessing it? Because it does not cost me more to confess several sins, than to acknowledge one, have I not authorized myself to multiply the number of my falls, as though each sin were not a new offence of God, and as if it were not independent of confession, to be expiated either in this life or the *"life to come."*

3. Perchance I have already gone so far as to commit sins without any dread, and without any restraint: I may have even boasted of committing them, and boldly endeavored to persuade others to do the same? Am I so fatally blinded as to live

joyfully in the midst of my sins, knowing at the same time that I have the *"living God"* for my enemy?

REFORMATION.

I am resolved to determine, and commit to writing, what kind of life I should adopt, or rather a regulation for my future course, with such resolutions as the Holy Ghost may inspire, and my Spiritual Director approve.

ASPIRATION.

Come, thou Father of the poor,
Come, with treasures that endure,
Come, O Light of all that live.

SEVENTH DAY.

Lava quod est sordidum,	Heal our wounds, our strength renew,
Riga quod est aridum,	On our dryness pour thy dew,
Sana quod est sancium.	Wash the stains of guilt away.

Meditation.

FIRST POINT.

I ought to have preserved my Baptismal innocence —how delightful would it be, were I as pure as when I came forth from those cleansing waters! But, alas! God alone knows the number of sins with which I have unworthily defiled my soul. Could I possibly shed tears bitter enough for the loss of that brilliant, that enviable innocence. However, if I will, it depends wholly upon myself, to recover a degree of purity similar to that primitive cleanliness. The Holy Ghost like limpid water, has power to wash away the stains of sin. Mingled with my tears of contrition, this divine water would prove a healing bath to me.

SECOND POINT.

I continually complain of feeling no attraction to Holy Communion, of having no relish for pious books; no tears to weep over sins as I would wish, of being, in a word, hard hearted as adamant; arid as the desert sands, and as earth that is scorched and withered by a torrid sun. Since it is so, why not expose to the Holy Spirit these different necessities of the soul, and do it with unlimited confidence in his power and willingness to relieve me. Do not his beneficent and penetrating rains soften and refresh the withered, sterile heart. Why not say to him continually: "Come, Holy Spirit, and take possession of my soul, it is as earth without water to thee." (Ps. 142.) Why not implore him to grant a greater attraction to the things of God; without, however, forming this petition, through attachment to consolations, but solely in order to be able, with the divine assistance, to produce more abundant fruits to salvation.

THIRD POINT.

The Holy Spirit is also a balm that heals every wound. Ah! would it were given me to perceive the wretched state of my soul! Ah! what a number of wounds should I discover? Perhaps some inflicted by mortal sin; and, alas! how many could I count made by venial sin? The latter less in size, not so deep, indeed, but almost past enumeration. Am I not like the unfortunate traveller in the Gospel, "*all covered with wounds.*" What shall I do? except prostrate humbly before the Holy Spirit,

as we see often at the gates of temples, the unhappy
beggars who, infected with disgusting ulcers, supplicate the pity of benevolent men; and in that
posture, with a profound sorrow and true confusion,
show the injuries done to my soul, to this charitable
Physician: he will, no doubt, take compassion on my
state, so pitiful—and pour on my soul a healing
balm.

EXAMEN. TEPIDITY.

1. Do I never omit reciting my morning and evening prayers? and when I say them do I acquit
myself of these pious exercises with diligence, respect and attention.

2. Do I assist at the Holy Sacrifice of the Mass
when my duties will allow me to do so? When in the
church am I never wanting in the respect and
modesty due to the House of God? Have I never
scandalized my neighbor by a dissipated air, and
have I performed my exercises of devotion with a
real interior recollection.

3. Have I not adopted a custom of approaching
the Sacraments with languor, with wearisomeness;
or else through human respect? Have I always been
careful before going to confession, to excite my soul
to contrition for my sins, and to a firm determination
of amendment, through the supernatural motives of
the goodness of God in my regard, and my ingratitude towards him, with similar incitements calculated
to render these necessary acts more perfect.

REFORMATION.

I resolve to impose on myself some small penance,
by performing on every occasion whatever I have
omitted, through negligence, in exercises of piety—or

even when I have performed them in a lukewarm spirit.

ASPIRATION.

Wash my soul for it is soiled—
Bedew it, for it is in aridity:
Heal it for it is wounded.

EIGHTH DAY.

Flecte quod est rigidum,	Bend the stubborn heart and will,
Fove quod est frigidum,	Melt the frozen, warm the chill,
Rege quod est devium.	Guide the steps that go astray.

Meditation.

FIRST POINT.

Docility is a mark of predestination. (Job. 6.) But, on the contrary, it is an index of unfortunate obstinacy in evil, and even of final reprobation, to be unwilling to listen to the counsels and advice of such friends as are animated with a discreet and laudable zeal, and are also appointed to conduct us. Have we a sincere wish to be directed in all that concerns our salvation? Do we give to our Spiritual Director the full and entire knowledge which he should have of our souls? Do we follow with ease the inspirations of grace, the good examples also that are placed before us, to incite us to virtue? If, on the contrary, there is a stiffness and indocility in the soul, let us endeavor to render it pliant and docile to the operation of grace, and let us repeat frequently the prayer of the wise man: Give to thy servant a submissive heart. (Kings 3.)

SECOND POINT.

These are the days in which heaven spreads abroad over the earth the fire of Divine Love. (Luke 12.) The christian world is inflamed with the light of the charity of God, which the Holy Ghost is shedding in the hearts of the faithful. Ah! one must be very insensible to remain in the midst of the world, surrounded by such a strong heat, and rest as cold as marble, or even indifferent in the service of our blessed Lord!

My soul will be in this state unless I prepare it beforehand to be enkindled by this lovely, heavenly light. But, as green wood cannot burn until after having lost its excessive humidity, so I must first liberate my heart from all those terrestrial affections, (which being inordinate,) will only serve to extinguish the fire of divine love. Come, my soul, awake! and let us *prepare* for the coming of our Lord. (1 Kings, 7.) Those Saints, who have most excited our admiration at the marvellous effects they have experienced from this sacred fire, did nothing else in order to prepare themselves to be consumed in its divine ardors.

THIRD POINT.

The most melancholy mistake I could possibly make, would be to deceive myself in the choice of a state of life. For in this there is question of my eternal salvation. God forbid, that I may not have formed designs already for my future course, without any other guide than the caprices of my will, the desires of ambition, or any other equally bad counsel, and thus have already strayed from the ways that divine Providence had marked out for me. On this point especially, I make protestations the most sincere, not to wish to accept any other guide than him, in an affair of such vital importance. I will implore during these days of grace, the assistance of his Light, and beseech him in mercy to indicate to me the path in which I should walk. But it is his divine pleasure that I also recur in humility, to the advice and lights of those persons whom he has charged to direct me.

EXAMEN. PRESUMPTION.

Does it not sometimes happen that I trust too much to my own strength, by exposing myself openly to the occasions of sinning, without dreading their unwholesome influence, nor my own frailty? Do not all my devotions prove mere exterior practices—and do I not neglect self-denial, the correcting of my faults, the eradicating of bad habits, and the overcoming of my passions Do I not presume too much on the longanimity of God and on his mercy, by incessantly falling into the same sort of sins that have been so often pardoned, without fearing that their measure may not now be full, and that wearied with my ingratitudes, the Lord may not decide on forsaking me.

REFORMATION.

What is to be done if we have had the misfortune to fall into mortal sin? Immediately humble yourself before God, make a good, fervent act of contrition, and go to confession as soon as possible, so as not to remain in that state of death, and in the danger of speedy condemnation for eternity.

ASPIRATION.

Grant, Lord, that I may at least learn to fear thee, if I have not learned to love thee.

NINTH DAY.

Veni Sancte Spiritus.	Holy Spirit! Light of light!
Et emitte cœlitus	From the Heaven's empyreal height,
Lucis tuæ raduim.	Let thy radiance cheer our sight.

Meditation.

FIRST POINT.

Among the seven-fold gifts of the Holy Ghost, which he bestows on his faithful servants, three especially seem to me to be of peculiar necessity.— The first, is the *gift of Fortitude.* "Be strong in combat," behold, the war-cry that we are daily bound to repeat. And our Divine Master teaches us, that in order to gain heaven, we must not only employ force but *violence:* I should therefore, resist the attacks of my enemy with a *lion-like* courage. *Is* it thus I meet the foes of my eternal salvation? I, who on the contrary, am so timid, so cowardly! I, who give way at every temptation, even the weakest! I, who am disconcerted, and vanquished with the most trifling word! I ought to be unshaken as the *cedars,* and I am like a *reed* that a zephyr can bend and overthrow. Let the view of so much weakness confound us, O my soul, and induce us to petition for the *gift* of *fortitude,* so requisite for remaining firm and invincible in the hour of peril. But also, let us be particularly on our guard—for nothing would so soon render us powerless in danger, as the weak-minded *presumption* that precipitates us into it.

SECOND POINT.

The second *gift* is that of *Piety.* This virtue is to be chiefly exercised towards God, and parents. Every day I say *Our Father;* but if God is my father, *when* do I exhibit my filial gratitude to him? Have I not already shown myself in relation to him a prodigal son? Ah! if it be so, O my soul, let us cast ourselves into the arms of so tender and excellent a father, and let us say to him in tenderest accents: *"Father, I have sinned against heaven and before thee, and I am not worthy to be called thy child."* And then, addressing our prayers to the Holy Spirit, let us beseech him that we may be henceforth worthy sons of such a FATHER.

THIRD POINT.

Third, is *the gift of Fear* of God. To fear God and keep his commandments, is the whole of man: in these consist true greatness, in these genuine wisdom. If I *fear God*, I shall no longer *fear men.* Blessed is the soul that fears the Lord. Let us humbly implore the Spirit of God to bestow on us *this* gift, and to obtain it let us have recourse to the intercession of the blessed Virgin: she is the mother of "beautiful Love," the mother also of the *Fear of God.*

EXAMEN.

1. Which passion is it that predominates in my soul, and is the most ordinary source of my sins?

2. Have I so little self-control, as to allow myself to give way to anger and resentment, causing others perhaps to sin in the same manner?

3. Am I yet so subject to the empire of concupiscence, that a deal of trouble is the consequence, when any privation is imposed on me, in the indulgence of allowable pleasures, or in refusing those which are not such.

REFORMATION.

I wish at once and forever, to correct those nu-

merous sins that a too great *freedom in speech* causes
me to commit against *truth, charity* and *purity*.
And, as an efficacious remedy for extirpating, in a
short time, these unbecoming habits, I will impose
on myself the practice of some penance, every time
that I chance to fall into any fault of this nature.

ASPIRATION.

Thou, on those who evermore
Thee confess and thee adore—
In thy seven-fold gifts descend.

OR,

O incomparable Virgin, meekest of creatures, obtain for us—with the pardon of our faults—*meekness*
and *purity*.

TENTH DAY.

Da Virtutis meritum,	Give them comfort when they die:
Da salutis exitum,	Give them life with thee on high:
Da perenne gaudium.	Give them joys which never end.

Meditation.

FIRST POINT.

If I am so unfortunate as to lose my soul, all else
will be worthless to me. Noble origin, wealth, talents,
all would be absolutely nought! In effect, what good
will it be to have occupied an elevated position in the
world, if I am eternally condemned? What advantage will accrue to me from having revelled in
opulence and luxury, when I am burning in eternal

flames? What profit, to have shone by the extent of my knowledge, and dazzled by the brilliancy of my genius, when I shall have lost the crown of immortality! Indeed it is quite time for me to reflect seriously, and to attend, under the inspiration of the Holy Ghost, to the highly important affair of my salvation. I must protest by my *conduct* more than by my *words,* that my will to save my soul *at every cost* is firm and resolute. O my God, bless, fortify, and perfect in me the determination of my will, which has been hitherto so fickle and languishing.

SECOND POINT.

Do I really seize the meaning of these words, "to save my soul." To save one's self is to merit and acquire an unmeasured, endless felicity. Shall I then be so destitute of common sense as to sacrifice eternal bliss to momentary satisfactions, to the degrading pleasures of sense? It is known to my God, alas! as well as to myself, what degree of solid judgment I have hitherto exercised. What a subject, O my soul, for regret and confusion. Let us no longer delay concluding so advantageous a contract. For Him, and for love of him, let us generously sacrifice the illicit pleasures of this fleeting life, and in exchange, he assures to us eternal joy, and peace and blessedness.

THIRD POINT.

There is no room for choice. If I wish to have Paradise for my inheritance, I must purchase it by the practice of the christian virtues, in particular, by patience and mortification. Shall I dare pretend to buy it at a cheaper rate, than did the Divine Master himself? Now, was it not necessary that Christ should suffer, to gain an entrance into glory?

It is therefore, insufficient, merely to ask the Holy Spirit the grace of attaining to that reign of bliss and glory; we must in particular, petition him for a life, filled with virtues and merits. And since I enjoy the certitude that divine grace will never be wanting to me, (for God does not refuse it when we solicit it,) from this moment I will courageously begin the work, and will neglect nothing that may prove conducive to making these days preparatory to the festival of Pentecost, the beginning of a new and saintly life.

EXAMEN. PERSEVERANCE.

1. During what period of time have I been faithful to the pious resolutions that I have so often taken?

2. What method does the tempter employ, to lead me to relapse into faults similar to those I have been guilty of again and again?

3. What is the most ordinary cause of my falls?

4. May it not be the voluntary omission of some particular practices of piety, at first undertaken with courage, and soon after abandoned through indifference.

5. Might these frequently spring from the facility with which I listen to the first suggestions of Satan, and my passions. Nothing can be apparently less than a spark, and yet, nothing more is necessary for exciting a terrible flame.

REFORMATION.

I will commit to writing, in order to offer them to the Holy Spirit, the good resolutions that he has deigned to inspire me with during this Novena, and supplicate him to aid me by the assistance of his grace, to observe them with fidelity, so that they may thus operate a change in my soul, similar to that which was effected in the Apostles; that is to say, a total change—one generous, and permanent. I will also implore the all powerful intercession of the most blessed Virgin, whom the Church proclaims the Temple of the Holy Ghost, and when receiving Holy Communion on the day of Pentecost, I will remember that it was in the Cenacle itself, where our divine Saviour instituted the Sacrament of his love, that the Apostles, assembled with the blessed Virgin, received the Holy Ghost with the abundance of his gifts.

ASPIRATION.

Light immortal! light divine!
Visit now these hearts of thine!
And our inmost being fill.

MEDITATIONS

FOR

The First Friday of each Month.

BY THE REV. F. HUGUET,

Mariste.

(Translated from the French.)

SS. C. J. M.

FIRST FRIDAY OF JANUARY.

THE HOLY THOUGHTS OF THE HEART OF JESUS.

The thoughts of Jesus Christ were all, and in all things for God alone.

The *exterior* of things affected him only inasmuch as they conducted him to God. He saw reflected in all creatures, as in a mirror, the power, greatness and wisdom of Almighty God. Did he meditate any design, did he suffer himself to form any project; all was solely for the greater glory of God. Thence arose the facility his sacred Heart enjoyed, in conversing with God entire nights, without distraction and without disgust; of remaining united with God in the most dissipating occupations of his divine mission; of turning as easily from action to prayer, as others willingly pass from prayer to action. His mind, being in continual accord with his heart, never lost sight of his heavenly Father. His whole life was one continual exercise of the purest love for God, and when sleep closed his sacred eyelids, still his heart watched and prayed.

The first step in the interior life, is to endeavor to imitate the Heart of Jesus in this holy disposition. The multitude of your useless thoughts, and to which you voluntarily grant your admission, is the occasion of the tumult which continually agitates your mind, even when you wish to be recollected. Can we *love* God "*with the whole mind,*" if our interior sentiments dwell habitually upon what has no reference to him? Do we lose more time by *thinking* vainly, than by *speaking* uselessly?

Follow the counsel of the Apostle to the Philippians: *Brethren, think on whatever is true, whatever is modest, whatever is just, whatever is holy, whatever is amiable.* iv., 8.

Consider seriously, whether you have hitherto thought only on what is *true*. Have you not rather nourished the mind with all the errors that the world has presented you? Have you not wished to ally the prejudices of the world with the verities of the Gospel? *Think on all that is true;* but where find the truth, except in thee alone, O my God, and in Jesus Christ who is verity in essence. *Truth*, says Saint Augustine, is the life of the soul, and the love of God is its sentiment.

Think on whatever is pure. In this we find the sacrifice of all thoughts that can defile the soul, and which proceed from our sinful origin, or our corrupt nature. What will create this revolution in man if not the love of God? Augustine, previous to his conversion, was tyrannized by profane thoughts: but as soon as divine Charity triumphed in his heart, he thought only on the truth of God, on his mercy, and on his infinity. He saw God alone in all beings, he only interrogated creatures by way of inviting them to make him acquainted with God.

Think on whatever is just. The deepest injustice of our thoughts is to render us miserable. We forge while *thinking*, the chains which hold us captive; we chase from our souls the peace that Jesus Christ came to bring on earth; we make of our hearts a stormy sea, a labyrinth of illusions, a field covered with the enemies of our salvation. But, says Saint Chrysostom, let us love the Lord Jesus, and immediately all will be joy, delight, glory, light, and happiness in all our powers. Should it cost us any thing to make the sacrifice of what torments us? It is so delightful to love, and to think of good things.

Think of whatever is holy. That is, on whatever separates you from the world, and will unite you to God. The more we think of God, and discover his amiability, the more we love him, and the more we desire to love him. A faithful soul that desires to belong wholly to God, and who sincerely desires to love him, willingly thinks of him, and makes this her chosen occupation: she suffers with difficulty whatever withdraws her from it, and always returns to it with delight. In a word, nothing is so agreeable as to think on what we love, particularly when the object beloved is infinitely amiable in every respect, and that the heart finds in it all that is destined to fill it. It is so much the more natural and easy to think of God, because you ought not dwell upon aught besides, except on his account, and in reference to him. When it is in the order of God that you should think on certain things, when you have no other intention in thinking on them but to do his holy will, you are thinking of God, you are in his holy presence.

Think on whatever is amiable. That is to say, to employ all means of entertaining peace among brethren, to avoid whatever may wound others; in relation to self not to be occupied with melancholy and troublous thoughts; to bear in unalterable peace of soul, all the misfortunes of life, all trials from heaven; it is to overcome with a holy cheerfulness all the difficulties that arise in the way of salvation.

Ah! Lord, how powerful is the influence of thy love over our thoughts! It teaches us that thou alone art in possession of all beauty, sanctity, wisdom and liberality; that in thee all benefits reside; that with thee all the afflictions of life are pleasures, poverty a source of opulence, humiliations a title to glory, death a principle of life. Love performs in us, what thy omnipotence effected in the beginning over chaos; thou drawest from the bosom of confusion all the order and all the beauty of creatures; and he who but commences to love thee, assigns to each of his faculties its proper place. The thoughts enlightened, wander no more; the desires, regulated by thy holy law, no longer aim at things unworthy of them; the affections, directed towards thee, no longer lower themselves to the frivolous amusements of the world. Love always holds the soul in a condition of sacrifice, for it is its glory to be immolated for thee. O God! how blind we are when we repulse the hand of that amiable Sacrificator, even in the rigors exercised over us, through motives of beneficence.

COLLOQUY.

Grant, O divine Saviour, that we may love thee with the whole heart, making thee the sole object of all our thoughts, directing to thee our every intention, seeking on all occasions, thy honor, and endeavoring to be totally consumed in the service of thy love, both in the faculties of the soul and body.

Sacred Heart of Jesus, teach me to forget myself, since it is the only way by which I can find an entrance to thee.

PRACTICE.

Whenever the clock announces the hour, recite some prayer to the Sacred Heart of Jesus.

ASPIRATION.

If I forget thee, O Heart of Jesus, let my right hand wither.

FIRST FRIDAY OF FEBRUARY.

OF THE SACRIFICE OF THE HEART.

The Heart of Jesus is a perfect model of sacrifice.

In the old law, the Sacrificator when immolating the victim, spared himself. But in the august Sacrifice of the law of grace, the priest and victim are blended on the same altar. Continual sacrifice of a God to a God, for the love of men, which the Heart of Jesus has miraculously perpetuated!

Of all sacrifices, the one most difficult, most painful, and the longest in accomplishing, is the sacrifice of the heart, but it is the most agreeable to God, and the only one worthy of him. Giving the heart to God is much, but it is the latest of all sacrifices; it is more, it is the way of the perfect. Oh! "sacrificing the heart" is of frightful latitude; happy the soul which shrinks not from apprehension, for she who embraces this devotedness, and casts herself with resignation on the altar of immolation, is infallibly predestinated! Oh! how sweet and pious is the death of her who has daily repeated to her God: "my God, I sacrifice myself!" and who in her last avowal can declare: I *have* sacrificed my *heart!* this is the whole man, therefore, our Lord demands absolutely the heart. *My son, give me thy heart!* This is the noblest and worthiest of offerings; for as the heart is the seat of life, the will which resides in it is the queen of the human faculties; hence, the great sacrifice of the soul to its God, is to be consummated in the heart. If nature is affrighted, grace rejoices; for the soul makes a true application of the words of the divine Spouse: *The world will rejoice, but you will be in sadness.* Delicious and holy sadness, which has nothing in it that is cowardly or

inordinate, nothing that wearies or dejects in the
exterior, since it is compatible with a meek and
amiable cheerfulness; we may, in this state, laugh
with moderation, participate in innocent mirth, and
be outwardly calm and serene; and in the secret of
the heart, in the very presence of God, and in the
silence of solitude, weep at the feet of Jesus, and
pour forth the trials of the heart into the bosom of
the divine Spouse.   Oh! what abundant occasions of
tears has he who loves God, and wishes to sacrifice
his heart to him, in sincerity.   No, the maxim: "to
suffer or to die," is not vain.   Oh! a life without sufferings is truly worthy of compassion, and I should
be almost tempted to believe it a road, more or less
direct towards the eternal abyss.

*A life without suffering is a life destitute of God,
and unworthy of him.*   But what means, to suffer
in goods, in health, in pleasures, in reputation itself?
Almost nothing, we must go farther, we must suffer
in the HEART, in its most legitimate sentiments, its
fondest inclinations, its deepest affections; for then,
according to the words of Jesus: *We lose the soul in
order to save it.*   There are four kinds of satisfaction
that must be sacrificed.   The *first,* that of the senses;
and verily, it must be a very imperfect soul, that
does not comprehend this absolute necessity; the
second, that of the mind; the *third,* that of the
heart; the *fourth,* sensibility to divine operations in
the soul.   Now, permit me to describe to you the
different sacrifices to be made.   As to the privation
of the pleasures of the senses, I find it so evident,
that I feel that it hardly needs a word; this sacrifice
embraces whatever flatters the hearing, the smell,
the eyes, and above all, the touch, which is the most
dangerous of the senses, and has been ever combatted

by the Saints, with the utmost constancy and zeal. O, how dangerous is an enemy, which continually accompanies us! Wo to him who slumbers, fatigued with contending, and believing that he may lay down his sword over the apparently slain victim: with the senses, there can never be peace and truce. Wo to him who dares to say: I have conquered, I am sure of myself;—he is on the brink of destruction.

The second kind of sacrifice attacks the pleasures of the mind, such as vain curiosity, pernicious anxiety to know, even things holy, as the mysterious ways of souls, the love of elevated thoughts, of noble expressions, elegant discourses, pompous sentences, ascetic books, the conversation of mystic authors, of persons versed in spiritual matters, in a word, what frequently feeds and strengthens the soul the least.

The third sacrifice cuts away even the gifts of God that are perceived and relished; it immolates in effect that attachment to the delights of contemplation, and even the joy that swells up in sweetness in the bitterness of the Cross; for even so far extends the purity of heart required by God, who wishes to be loved for himself alone, to sacrifice and resignation concerning the inspirations, lights, tastes, aridity and desertions, which might also seem to give a support to the soul.

The fourth, comprises the most legitimate affections, and the most allowable demonstrations of friendship, but which, however, wound the Heart of Jesus, for it is not possible to conceive how jealous that Heart is of its Spouses! Without the entire sacrifice of every satisfaction, there can be no union with God, for whatever sullies the soul forces the Beloved to withdraw, and nothing effects this so much as a divided heart; to love pleasure is an offence to

Jesus, who took for himself nothing but sorrows and trials; it contradicts the Gospel which preaches mortification only; it profanes the temple of the Holy Ghost, which is our heart, by giving entrance to pleasure which is the idol of the passions. Without self-hatred it is useless to call ourselves the disciples of Jesus—now to flatter self is not to renounce self. Hence it is in some manner sacrilegious, and an abomination for the soul that has given itself to God, to seek satisfactions. Does it not rob God of all the affections that it bestows on his creatures? yes, for pleasure dissipates and distracts, and God wants the undivided heart. The ancient philosophers would have condemned themselves to perpetual blindness, to unheard of labors, for a vain smoke; a pagan would have torn out his eyes in order not to be distracted in his calculations, or to avoid the snares of concupiscence. And shall we see the children of God seeking their satisfactions, whilst their father demands the privation of them? yes, I cannot conceive why a christian does not tremble at the sole mention of the word pleasure. Oh! the insidious poison, the perfidious serpent, it glides in without announcement and in secrecy, in order to strike its deadly blows more surely; its consequences are terrible, for but *one* satisfaction purposely indulged can disconcert the firmest soul, weaken it, and lay it open to new assaults, conduct it to new falls; and thence will arise a habit, and from habit DEATH.

COLLOQUY.

Oh! my God, thou art pure and holy! One pleasure indulged, suffices to destroy a soul, and do I fancy myself secure? Oh! yes, I would desire the word *sacrifices* every where, as a memorial of my weakness, and of the need I have of purification.

PRACTICE.

Wear a crucifix, and kiss it at night and in the morning.

ASPIRATION.

What shall separate me from the Heart of Jesus.

FIRST FRIDAY OF MARCH.

THE AGONY OF THE HEART OF JESUS.

After recommending his Disciples to his Father, and fortifying them against the scandal of his Passion, Jesus, perceiving that his hour approached, withdrew to the Garden of Olives, consecrated by his prayers.

Separated from his Apostles, alone in the presence of his irritated Father, humbly prostrate on the ground, Jesus endeavors in vain, to disarm him by his supplications. God has referred all the iniquities of mankind to him, a voluntary victim, and the great Apostle, inspired by the Holy Ghost, fears not to say, that he who knew no sin, became sin itself. His soul, holier and purer than the highest celestial intelligences, suddenly found itself covered with all our prevarications, so that, in the words of a pious Bishop, with the eyes of divine modesty, he saw it soiled with the most shameful abominations of sinners; with its eyes of clemency he beheld it blackened with their rage and hatred; with the keenest perception of religious sentiment, he perceived it tarnished with their impieties and blasphemies. In fine, with the eyes of virtue itself, he discovered himself sullied with all their disorders.

Full of the light and of the knowledge of God himself, Jesus penetrates the mysteries of evil, sees clearly present to his mind, all the past crimes, and all the disorders which were to desolate and inundate the world, until time shall be no longer; he numbers them and deplores each one in particular, because there is not one but what has its own peculiar malice; like those rapid rivers which discharge themselves into the sea, without blending their waters with those of the abyss that absorbs them, so all the different and various sins entering into the soul of the Saviour, offer it so many deadly assaults, which are felt in their individual force, without mixture or confusion.

On whichever side he casts his sacred eyes, he sees nought but torrents of sins, that descend upon his adorable person: *Torrentes iniquitatis conturbaverunt me.* Behold him prostrate and overwhelmed, not daring to raise his eyes to Heaven, and moaning beneath the disgraceful load, under that world of iniquities, a thousand times heavier than the earth which he sustains by the power of his word; for, says the scripture, he plays in sustaining the universe, while here he complains, by his prophet, that sinners had aggravated his yoke, that they had laid on his shoulders the burden of their crimes, and that he was unable to bear it.

One of the most poignant sufferings of Jesus, was the view of the numerous infidelities of privileged souls, whom he had chosen to be his Spouses, and who, after having given themselves to him without reserve, would by degrees, return to the spirit of the world which is so opposed to the Gospel. Who is able to recount the anguish of his heart, when he saw the inutility of all his designs over them, and the preference which they would not scruple giving to weak and miserable creatures.

We, being finite creatures, conceived in ignorance and iniquity, and continually inclined to evil, we can never know clearly the deformity of sin. But the holy soul of Jesus, united to the divinity, and endowed with more light and love than the Cherubim, experiences consequently, a greater horror of the smallest of our offences, than all of the most illustrious penitents have felt for the crimes of which they were guilty, and which have led them to die with sorrow and regret.

Our divine Saviour suffers the most cruel anguish without alleviation and without consolation. A susceptible heart inundated with grief soothes itself by disclosing its bitterness into the bosom of sympathising friendship; but if Jesus permits his fainting humanity to seek relief from the Apostles, he wills that it shall find none: ungrateful men! they sleep profoundly, while their divine Master is a prey to the horrors of agony.

Deserted by God and man, Jesus resigns his soul to the most profound affliction. His sorrow, says the Prophet, is great as a bottomless and shoreless sea, it would give him death a thousand times, did he not reserve himself to the rigors of a bloody immolation. *Tristis est anima usque ad mortem.*

In this state of abandonment he tremblingly addresses his Father, no longer presuming to supplicate him with that sweet and modest familiarity, that intimate confidence of a son assured of obtaining whatever he requests. *Father, if it be possible, let this chalice pass, yet not my will but thine be done.* He no longer employs the language of a tenderly beloved son, who formerly commenced his prayers with thanksgiving: *Father, I thank thee, that thou hast heard me, and I knew well that thy paternal goodness ever listens to me.* What constraint, what violence in the prayer of that only Son. *Factus in agonia prolixius orabat;* being in agony he prayed a long time. Formerly, *one word* was sufficient to obtain everything: Father, I will, *volo Pater;* now that the only Son is under the guise of a sinner, he no longer acts so freely: he prays, and prays with dread; he prays, and praying long, he drinks *alone*, in deep draughts, all the disgrace of a lengthened refusal.

And now an infinitely painful thought again redoubles his anguish, it is the inutility of his sacrifice to the greater portion of mankind. The future opens to them in vistas, and all the outrages that shall be offered to God, unfold themselves to his affrighted view, he sees the blood of the testament, that blood that he is about to shed for us, and which is destined for our sanctification, trampled under foot, and profaned by the greater number. He sees his prospective torments not only useless, but even pernicious to those for whom he is about to endure them. He cheerfully yields himself to death, and the souls that are so cherished by his heart, will perish forever; the scandal of his cross will be annulled for those very ones for whom he supported it; there is not one, even of the reprobate, whose salvation he would not have preferred a thousand times to his own life, and whose eternal punishment does not give him inexpressible pain. At this view, a sweat unheard of in the annals of grief, a bloody sweat, inundates his whole body, penetrates his garments, flows down on all sides bedewing the earth, and leaving him exhausted, pale, motionless and nearly lifeless. Nevertheless, there yet rests enough of animation to allow him to make an act of submission to the divine justice, and ratifying the engagement that he has just contracted, he signs it, so to speak, with that very blood, with which the earth around him is covered. *Non mea, sed tua voluntas fiat.*

Oh! how consoling for the afflicted, to contemplate Jesus in Gethsemane, in the mystery of his agony! How sweet, to incline to him when he deigns to condescend to us; to offer him our sorrows, for he also has wept, our sensibility which he justifies by his own example, and to let our tears fall upon his bosom, for he suffered his to flow!—God suffering and afflicted!—ah! it is God in this mystery that I need in my exile, it is he that my poor heart sighs for, *Ecce Deus noster iste.* It is not in heaven, but in the scene of his weakness that I will seek him; the distance is too wide between the eternal hills and this valley of tears; such splendor does not accord with wretchedness, the length of the way overcomes me: I must have Jesus, and Jesus acquainted with my infirmities and trials, *scientum infirmitatem*: ineffable mystery of mercy and love.

However, *an Angel comes to console him who from the height of heaven constitutes the joy and felicity of the Angels.* The Son of God was destined, under the appearance and form of a sinner, to be beneath the celestial spirits, and to *feel* that humiliation in the end that he receives from one among them, *qui modico quam Angeli minoratus est.* It was also intended to teach us not to seek the remedy of our woes, in vain discourses with men, but in our secret conversations with God. *Apparint angelus de cælo confortans eum.*

We can never form any idea of the sufferings of the Heart of Jesus in his agony, until after having undergone interior trials and sufferings. With what-

ever degree of good will we have consecrated ourselves
to God, and have accepted all the trials it may please
him to send us, when the hour of suffering and distress arrive, and the grief incident is carried to a
certain point; when also we are no longer sustained
by a species of ardor and courage, and are no longer
sensible to the operations of grace (though it is ever
active;) then we enter into a kind of agony provoked by a general rebellion of the passions, and
by the revolt of nature which cannot look upon
its own destruction without a convulsive shuddering
horror.

God causes us to undergo this painful state, in
order to humble us profoundly, and convince us that
our strength comes from him alone. In this violent
crisis, in which we seem to repulse with horror, the
cross that we had embraced with love, and in which
we become a prey to frightful temptations against
God, we must not think that we cease to be agreeable
to him, when we say to him: *My God, if possible,
let this cup pass from me:* provided we add as did
Jesus Christ: *Nevertheless, thy will and not mine be
done.* In this moment man has two wills: the one
of nature, which cannot be effaced, and which is
rather a blind instinct than volition; the other of
grace, which may be called a superior will, adhering
to the good pleasure of God, and which would not
for all the world be separated from him. We do not
always distinguish this superior will, because it does
not make itself perceptible, and we are not in a state
to reflect upon ourselves, and it would be a means of
support. But the proof that it exists within us, is
our constant and inviolable fidelity, and that were
the slightest mitigation of the cross proposed to us,
we would reject it with horror.

PRACTICE.

Interior contrition for all the sins and iniquities of the past life, which have contributed to render the agony of the Heart of Jesus more cruel.

ASPIRATION.

Heart of Jesus, abyss of mercy, pardon me.

FIRST FRIDAY OF APRIL.

HUMILITY OF THE HEART OF JESUS.

"*Learn of me that I am humble of heart*," are the words of our blessed Lord. The humility of our Lord was of quite another nature, and much more profound than ours. He possesses an eminent knowledge of the infinite distance that lies between the greatness of God, existing in himself, and the lowness of his creatures formed from nothingness; and as his soul united these two extremes in his person, it was continually absorbed with the liveliest and the most penetrating sentiment of the divine majesty.

The masters of the spiritual life have remarked, that our Lord did not teach *us* to be humble of heart, according to his example, but to learn that *he* is humble of heart. And why? Is it a virtue that his example may not teach us? Yes; we cannot be humble in the same sense as Jesus Christ was. If humility consists in debasing one's self below what we really are, Jesus Christ alone was, and can be humble, he who being God by nature, made himself man, and embraced whatever is vile and contemptible among men. He was humble, because he united

4

himself to a nature infinitely inferior to his; he was humble, because in the nature to which he united himself, he submitted to all the humiliations due to the haughty sinner, who deserves the derision of God and of men. He was humble of heart, because his humility was of his own choice, a humility sincere, and accompanied with its proper interior sentiments, and conformed to the condition of a voluntary victim of sin. The humility of Jesus Christ was generous and without effort; it flowed from its source as it were, because it was ever comparing the greatness of God with the nothingness of man.

It is impossible for us to be humble in the same sense as was Jesus Christ. *Nothing*, is the foundation of our being, how could we abase ourselves, and take any place below our origin? Sinners by our own will, deserving the maledictions of God, and the torments of hell, worthy only of contempt and abhorrence, and thereby less than nought, to what state could we be reduced, which could pass for a state of humility? Let us admit that in the natural order, and in the supernatural order, in this life and in that which is to come, there is no confusion, contempt or ignominy, which is beneath our deserts. And when we shall have acknowledged it in the rectitude of our heart, when we shall have submitted to all the humiliations that a guilty creature deserves, when we shall have avowed ourselves deserving of these humiliations, we shall be also obliged to acknowledge that to submit to all that is not humility on our part, is but the acceptation of a just chastisement.

Souls really humble comprehend that there is none but the Word of God who in becoming incarnate, abased himself beneath what he was; hence the

Scripture says that "*he annihilated himself*," and this is not said of any creature.

If that be true, if nothing is more evident among the principles of Faith, where are we, and what is the extent of our pride not to consent to suffer either from God or man the least shadow of contempt, nor the slightest apparent repulse? The sole idea of contempt excites a sentiment of revolt, troubles us, puts us beside ourselves; we cannot persuade ourselves that to despise us, is to render us our due, and that it is impossible to carry contempt in our regard too far. We avoid with the greatest care whatever can cause us to lose the false esteem of men; we sacrifice our duties, the divine inspirations, the strongest and most certain lights of conscience, to the fear of a raillery, or to a false and miserable judgment that may be formed of us. It appears to us, that the most painful effort of virtue is to appear in the eyes of men, such as we wish to be in the *heart* in the sight of God; and we are not capable of that effort, and on a thousand occasions we falsify our promises and our resolutions. What unjust and stupid pride! Again, did we but blush at this pride, did we humble ourselves for it on reflection; but we applaud ourselves for it; we think we have noble and elevated sentiments; we treat as folly and extravagance, the esteem that the Saints entertained for humiliations, and the holy eagerness with which they have embraced them.

Were we humble with the humility that becomes us, we would not value, either in ourselves or others, birth, wit, nor the graces of form, nor other natural gifts; and we should never consider them as a title to higher esteem for ourselves, and an authorization to despise such as are destitute of them. For all these advantages do not belong to us, *who are nothing;* God gave them to us through pure liberality, and it was not his intention that we should extract vanity from them. Still more, these advantages are not in themselves useful to salvation. Indeed, we have made an ill use of them, and they have proved occasions of sin to us. We have in no circumstance occasion to glory in them; and on the contrary, we have great reason to humble ourselves on their account.

Were we humble with the humility that becomes us, we should believe ourselves unworthy of the esteem of men, and we should refer all their praises to God, without reserving any to ourselves, lest we rob him of his glory. Neither would we dread contempt, because we merit it, as least as sinners. We would be glad to be covered with opprobrium in view of satisfying thereby the divine justice. Undoubtedly, we must do nothing which deserves blame, but neither must we take so many precautions for avoiding the judgments of men; and when virtue draws down any calumny upon us, any railleries, any contempt from them, we should congratulate *ourselves* and pity *them.*

If we were humble with the humility that becomes us, we should serve God without interest, convinced that we deserve nought, and also that he is too kind in supporting our services. We would receive his favors with gratitude; and far from appropriating them to ourselves and taking complacency in them, they would only serve to humble us at the sight of our indignity, and we would return them to him with the same purity as they came to us from him.

Thus the humble soul sees only what it justly merits in the hardest treatment that it experiences from God and from man. All that it asks is, to have strength to bear it, that is, that they promote God's glory. For it, it consents to its destruction most cordially, and takes not what happens to it as a trial, but as a chastisement too mild in comparison with its offences. Acquiescing thus in all that God grants it to suffer, it finds its peace, strength, and happiness in humility; it is ravished that God satisfies himself, and that at the expense of what it is, he acquits whatever is due to his justice.

But by what means can we attain this humility? By the total resignation of self to God, by remitting all our interests into his hands. We have it in our power to give ourselves. When this donation is made and without retracting, God fulfils his designs over us, and he bestows on us whatever we need for their execution. The first light that we receive from heaven, should produce humility in us, and this will eventually merit all others for us. It gives, above all, that profound, generous, peaceable, inalterable humility, which on the one hand, puts us in quality of sinners, far below nothing, and on the other, raises us above the world, the demon and ourselves, and renders us great with the greatness of God, strong with the power of God, holy with the holiness of God. This humility is infused; it increases in us in proportion to our temptations, sufferings and humiliations. It is possessed, while its possessor is not aware of having it, because to think one's self humble, one must believe himself to be placed beneath what he deserves to be, and this thought will never enter into the soul of a saint, who, on the contrary, is always intimately persuaded that God and men treat him better than he merits.

The more he thinks himself condescending, the more he is persuaded of his own elevation; whosoever *perceives* that he abases himself, is not yet in his place—which is beneath or beyond all abasement.

The more *pure* love is, the nearer to perfection is humility. Pure charity divests man of himself; it clothes him with Jesus Christ; and in this consists true humility, that we live no longer in ourselves, but that Jesus Christ lives in us.

COLLOQUY.

O humble and abject Saviour, grant me true christian wisdom, and a relish for self-contempt. O good Jesus, who didst suffer so many opprobriums and humiliations for the love of my poor soul, impress strongly in my heart the esteem of them, and grace to desire to practice them.

PRACTICE.

Watch over your heart, in order not to say or do anything which might attract esteem. And beware of excusing yourself.

ASPIRATION.

O Heart of Jesus, grant me grace to become truly humble.

FIRST FRIDAY OF MAY.

A SOUL CONTEMNED IS THE DELIGHT OF THE HEART OF JESUS.

In order to form a just idea of the truth that is to be the subject of this meditation, recall to mind that the state of abjection, and of humiliation, regards two conditions; either the occupations and employments of such as live in Community, when they are repulsed by every one, and treated as the refuse of the Society; or when persons entertain a low opinion of us, and when our reputation, that delicate flower, which even the most pious souls hold in such rare estimation, has faded in the minds of others. Now, whatever may be the trial sent us, let us be sure, that for a truly christian soul, this state is the most sublime degree of happiness that can be attained on earth.

In effect, a person held in contempt by the neighbor forms the real delight of the Heart of Jesus, because that divine Saviour, in opposition to the spirit of the world, takes complacency in whatever the world rejects and despises. The divine Master has no inclination to anything but the most profound abjection; he loves it so tenderly that he can scarcely find an appellation that expresses his satisfaction in it to give himself, nor what posture to select in order to be buried and lost in that precious state. He repeats that he is less than a man, styling himself a *worm of earth:* or if he be man, he says that he is man in the depth of opprobrium, and through love for this adorable abjection, he is always as it were covered with disgrace, says Isaiah, so as to testify the excessive fondness that he has for remaining in this humbled state.

You will now easily comprehend that a person who is in contempt, and placed in a mean position must be the delight of his divine Heart, because he finds in him subject for congeniality with his inclinations.

The Heart of Jesus does good to others in a concealed and hidden manner, so also souls that are consecrated to him should love to act, not performing their good works in a visible and apparent way, but privately, so that the glory be referred to him and not to themselves. They should be overjoyed that from what ever good they may be so happy as to accomplish, naught returns to them but sufferings, contempt, and humiliations, and that God alone receives all the honor.

Jesus takes pleasure in sanctity alone; now is it not evident that a soul becomes just and holy without difficulty, when everybody despises it and treads upon it as if it were so much dust.

This state works out its sanctification, and does it in so much greater proportion as its lowly state is more contemptible and shameful. Jesus rejoices in dwelling in the soul of his faithful Spouse, advancing in holiness of heart and life, as she is more and more humbled in the view and in the opinion of men.

It is of necessity that persons in a low and vile condition, give consolation and satisfaction to the Heart of Jesus; because he cannot help loving his own dear image: now a person truly humbled and despised, is the most faithful copy of the incarnate Word, who "annihilated himself" by taking the form of a slave.

It is, therefore, certain, that profound abasement is the characteristic of Jesus, that his intention was to become the last and the most contemptible among men. He could not do more, for to suffer, speaking in the absolute, is not so unworthy of a God, as to be debased in an ignominious manner; for suffering is conformable to the magnanimity of heroic souls, but humiliation and disgrace are only suited to mean and ignoble souls. Hence, the endurance of debasement and shame, is a noble and distinctive trait of his adorable character and person.

To set the last seal on the advantages of contemptuous treatment, we may declare, that Jesus becomes the unique possessor of a soul rejected and univer-

sally despised. Self-love deserts it, for abjection is
the death of pride. The esteem of men cannot swell
it, for the world only appreciates what creates a favorable display. It may be said of this soul, what
Pilate said to the Jews, concerning our blessed Lord,
when presenting him to them: "*What shall we do
with Jesus.*" So of the soul that is despised and in
contempt, we may say: "What shall we do with it"
—it is not required in any place! What shall we
do with it?—*Jesus* will receive it, take possession of
it, delight in it, and thus solve the mystery of its
apparent inutility!

It is said in the sacred writings that our divine
Master conducts the faithful soul into solitude, in
order to speak to her heart, and converse with her in
confidence; now abjection is a place so remote from
creatures, that it is generally shunned and even
abhorred.

How amiable then is the industry of the divine
Lover of our souls, who in order to enjoy them at
leisure, and become their sole possessor, reduces them
to a state in which creatures avoid and shrink from
them, so that being quite alone, he may possess their
love without a rival—heart to heart.

O state more desirable and more glorious than that
of the most sublime elevation, for by my meanness
and effacement in the opinion of others, by my seeming degradation, and by my insignificance, I can
contribute to the satisfaction of Jesus! This alone
is worth heaven itself—to be able to contribute to
the divine delight of that sacred Heart! How can
it be possible, that when perusing these things, every
soul that entertains the slightest affection for Jesus,
does not burn with the holy desire of seeing itself
humiliated and contemned by the whole broad world.

O Heart of my dear Master, if I am good for nothing in this world, either because I am destitute of talents, or because my person is contemptible, I can at least conduce to thy divine pleasure, in the depth of my littleness, unworthiness and obscurity: this is indeed, a too glorious ministry for *me!* Thou alone art my support, grant me grace never to seek any other reliance.

PRACTICE.

Make frequent and fervent acts of holy love.

ASPIRATION.

Grant me, O Heart of Jesus, thy love and thy grace, I shall be rich enough—I ask thee for naught besides.

FIRST FRIDAY OF JUNE.

MEEKNESS OF THE HEART OF JESUS, IN ITS MANNER OF TEACHING.

Let us admire the patience and meekness with which the divine Saviour instructed his disciples.

He taught them the whole truth, dissembling nothing, but with a degree of kindness, everyway suitable to throw us into self-confusion. He taught them not to follow him through any other than supernatural motives, not to expect from him any human advantages, relying solely on the bounty of heaven. How much the Heart of Jesus must have suffered from those untutored minds, and those hearts so little acquainted with spiritual things! Nevertheless, he always treated them with meekness and benevolence, and never gave way to discouragement because he could not succeed in healing them of their prejudices. He knew that that moment of success would arrive, and he waited for it patiently. He did not spare them instructions, although he did not gather any immediate fruit from his lessons, and even foresaw that they would remain unproductive. He explained to them in private, the sense of the parables which he employed in speaking to the multitudes; and if he sometimes reproached them with their little understanding, it was not to offend them, nor to show them that he was shocked himself, but to stir up their minds and render them more attentive. His condescension to them was extreme; and it appears inconceivable to us, when we consider the divine character of the master, and who were his pupils. How must he have been obliged to plane away, and reduce, and abridge his materials, to bring them on a level with their capacity! How many useless and indiscreet questions did they address him! what kind and delicate artifices must he have adopted, in order never to offend or discourage them! What constancy in repeating to them a hundred times, the same things, which frequently, they understood no better on hearing them the last time, than they did the first!

There is no virtue more necessary for those who are charged with the care and instruction of others than meekness. They are obliged to contend with the defects of mind, and temper, and against the bad dispositions of the persons to whom they are speaking. If they show humor, impatience, disdain, or an imperious air, they will excite prejudice against themselves, and their instructions; they will alienate minds, and will excite rebellious emotions or disgust.

Let them remember the examples of our divine Lord,
how he proportioned himself to each one's mental
capacity, enlightening them by insensible degrees,
seizing the favorable moments, dissembling or smooth-
ing the difficulties which might repulse his hearers.
And even now, such is his conduct towards men, and
Saint Peter calls it on this account *multiformis,* or
thousand forms in his grace—and as wisdom teaches
us that every one found in the manna the taste which
he desired, so Jesus varies his instructions according
to our differing necessities. The nourishment he
gives is adapted to every soul, according to its present
necessity, and according to its hunger. Does he not
tell us that he knows each one *by name?* His direction is therefore different for feeble and indolent
natures, different for firm and formed characters,
different for the perfect, and for those who are not
yet so: to each one he offers his necessary and suitable good, with a wonderful and tender beneficence.

From the abundance of the heart the mouth speaks,
and not only in what it says, but also in the manner
in which it is said. An humble master may teach
great things, but he will teach them with humility;
there will be nothing in his air, nor in the terms he
employs that savors of self-sufficiency or pride; he
will understand how to descend to the order of intellect he is addressing, and proportion his subject
and explanations to that degree of intelligence. If
he carries weight and authority in his declarations,
it will not be to aggrandize himself, but to exalt *him*
in whose name he speaks, and to make a deeper and
lasting impression on his hearers.

Such was the method of the divine Master in his
teaching. No affectation in his discourse, no parade
of eloquence, but an irresistible ravishing simplicity.

It is impossible to say lofty and divine things in a plainer manner. His expressions, without being low, contain nothing above the level of ordinary minds; and yet they enclose a meaning so profound, that the greatest geniuses discover it but imperfectly. He borrows his comparisons from the commonest objects, and his allegories contain nothing unusual or that is not familiar. It is the Heart speaking to the heart, filled with what it is uttering, it causes it to pass into the minds of the hearers. Read his conversation with the Samaritan woman at the well. See how, little by little, he instructs, touches her heart, and wins her, and then gradually leads her to acknowledge him as the promised Messiah. It was, without doubt, the work of grace; but his discourse was its instrument, and he proportioned it to this secret action.

Thus, in proportion, do those teach who have the interior spirit. They speak with assurance indeed, but at the same time with humility, because they do not speak of themselves. They enlighten the mind, but they affect the heart much more; they warm it, penetrate it, and fill it with a divine unction. They are simple, easy and familiar; but in their simplicity they have a benign and fascinating majesty, which captivates and enchants. To hearts well prepared, they carry an efficacious conviction, which springs only from the grace that divinely inspires and directs them.

COLLOQUY.

O Divine Heart of Jesus, inflame my heart with the fire that consumes thine, and endow my soul with that charity, meekness and heavenly prudence, that are requisite for gaining souls to thy service.

PRACTICE.

Invoke confidently, the Angel guardians of the persons whom we are obliged to instruct or govern.

ASPIRATION.

Heart of Jesus, grant us thy peace.

FIRST FRIDAY OF JULY.

THE HEART OF JESUS FORMS THE SOLE DELIGHT OF A SOUL IN ADVERSITY AND CONTEMPT.

If a soul in abjection and contempt becomes agreeable to the Heart of Jesus, we may say, that reciprocally, Jesus alone forms the delight of that heart.

Represent to yourself a soul without talents, without the esteem of any one, destitute of employment, and as it were, a mere cipher in the world or in a community. Because she is rejected by creatures, she feels the necessity of seeking satisfaction in the Heart of Jesus, and there she is received with kindness. Is it not natural to every one to seek an asylum and place of refuge, when he is banished from his country? Nature itself suggests it. Those who are in a mean and despicable position, are as it were, exiles from human life and the intercourse of their fellow beings, and thus they are driven to the blessed necessity of seeking alleviation and an abode in the divine Heart of Jesus, as they are rejected on every side.

O admirable method of that kindest of masters! For in order to oblige you to have recourse to him, and give yourself to him, he permits you to fall into contempt, so that being repulsed by creatures, you may be constrained to seek him, and cry out: If no one will care for me, I shall at least possess Jesus, who is my all.

Jesus can alone prove the delight of an abject and scorned soul; because it *cannot* find any enjoyment in creatures. It has been too frequently deceived to trust to them any more, or to hope for any satisfaction from them. And as the heart cannot exist without some source of pleasure, it must necessarily take it in Jesus, its only comforter. Like the Apostles on Mount Thabor, it sees naught but Jesus whichever way it turns, all earthly things having forsaken it; and that faithful Spouse is so kind, that he takes pleasure in receiving what no one desires, and in lavishing his most tender caresses on what every one considers worthy of scorn.

All satisfaction is in proportion to the subject or object which occasions it, and therefore it is extremely natural that he who has become the scoff of creatures should find his consolation and dearest delight in Jesus, the most abject of men.

But the crowning glory and happiness is, that God, finding no resistance in this oppressed soul, which is destitute of earthly pretensions, does with it whatever he will, he augments its confusions and humiliations, without ever hearing a single murmur from that soul.

It is so much the happier in this holy disposition, because having parted with all things, it is disfranchised from all the cares and solicitude that torment those who strive to please the world, and enjoys a calm and delightful liberty free from all apprehension of loss.

But this is not all; in this state of humiliation and desertion it enjoys the most sublime operations of grace, and other ineffable communications. As the grain buried in the ground whence it originated, springs up and flourishes beneath the summer sky; so this same individual in his low state is like a concealed and fruitful germ, which before God and in the sight of man, produces admirable fruits of life and immortality.

Thus the disadvantages which are the portion of a soul profoundly humiliated, and destitute of talents are the advantages of divine grace, which always seeks oppressed and rejected souls. The ruin of the soul in the vain opinion of men, is the principle of its elevation in the Heart of Jesus, which receives and caresses whatever the world refuses. Having fallen into the lowest deep into which tribulation can cast it, it enjoys invariable peace. Its virtue is in security, for no one covets or admires its condition, and being neglected, and forgotten by all creatures, it becomes easy for it to commune with the Heart of Jesus, the source of the sweetest and purest consolations.

COLLOQUY.

My divine Saviour, if I am in contempt and abjection because I am wanting in abilities, learning or other natural gifts which invite the applause of the world, did not God create me thus? And could I do otherwise than love the divine hand that hindered earthly advantages from conducing to my eternal loss? Can I complain on finding myself in company with thee my Jesus, my all, who for love of me chose to become the scoff of the multitude? Ah! I prefer ten thousand times to be contemned by all creatures with Jesus reigning in my heart, to all

the vain approbation of men without the Heart of
Jesus.   A thousand times blessed were it thus given
me to live and die rejected, scorned, and ignored by
the whole world.

PRACTICE.

Avoid thinking of yourself, uselessly—and take
no notice of what does not concern you.

ASPIRATION.

O Heart of Jesus, be thou all to me, and let me
be all to thee.

FIRST FRIDAY OF AUGUST.

HOW MUCH THE HEART OF JESUS LOVES PURITY.

The Sacred Heart of Jesus is the sanctuary and
model of purity.   Observe the countenance of the
Saviour; consider his modest looks, his reserve in
every gesture, his whole deportment so composed and
perfectly governed.   The words of Jesus are chaste
words; but the Heart of Jesus is purity itself, and
the plenitude of purity.   When the Son of God
came into this world, says St. Jerome, his first care
was to surround himself with virgins, so that being
adored in heaven by pure spirits, he might be similarly loved on earth, by souls as pure as angels.

"Virginal integrity is the portion of Angels," says
St. Augustine; "it is in a corruptible flesh, the preparation, and possession of eternal incorruptibility,
which is God.   Virgins are terrestrial Angels and
heavenly men."

Such is your beloved, such is he who feeds among the lilies, who marches attended by troops of virgin choristers; such is Jesus, that most pure LAMB, whom the virgins accompany withersoever he goeth. Jesus, who has in heaven a virgin Father, and virginal Angels; who has on earth a virgin Mother, a virgin nursing Father, and a beloved virgin Disciple; Jesus, the Spouse of virgins, a virgin himself, the splendor and perfection of virginity.

The divine Saviour deigned to place the most lovely and the most holy of all the virtues, in the number of the evangelical beatitudes, and to promise pure hearts the vision of God himself. Virgin souls enjoy familiarity with God; God enlightens and blesses them in an extraordinary manner; they are the Spouses of Jesus Christ. I have betrothed you, says St. Paul, to an only Spouse, JESUS CHRIST, in order to be presented to him as a pure virgin.

Ah! how much also are the riches of virginity augmented, in making it an evangelical counsel, a precept, an obligation, by a voluntary, inviolable and perpetual vow!

"Son," said the father of the prodigal to his friend that had always remained with him: "*Son, thou art ever with me, and all that I have is thine.*" What happiness is comparable to being continually with God, seeing, loving, serving, possessing and enjoying him. It is a foretaste of the bliss of heaven.— Meditate the other words—*all that I have is thine.* The pure soul is in possession of all the treasures and riches of God. God hides nothing from it; he shares all his gifts with it, all his graces, all his perfections—*himself.*

Chastity is a participation of the substance of God, spiritual and simple, but radiant with beauty.

A chaste soul is one that is resuscitated in spirit, and which is of the same nature as Jesus risen, who has no longer the weight and grossness of the flesh, who is spiritual like an Angel, and divine like God his Father. It enters with him in his perfect sanctity, and in all his divine qualities, which change him wholly and bestow on it the same inclinations and sentiments with which the Son of God is replete in the state of his resurrection.   It is a wonderful thing that a gross creature like man can possess the grace, even in this life, of being similar to an Angel, and of being able to enter upon a participation of God; but it is only after having long combatted in the spirit of our Lord.

Purity is as frail as it is beautiful : it is like a highly polished mirror that the lightest breath can tarnish ; a lily of brilliant whiteness which the slightest touch may wither : a lighted taper that the gentlest zephyr, the least imprudence can extinguish : in fine, it is a precious treasure which we carry in earthen vessels which may be shattered with a tiny shock.

In proportion as virginity is sublime, says Saint Augustine, do I dread the baneful breath of pride which slays it. God alone bestows and guards holy purity: the best means we can add for its preservation is humility.

The christian virgin, says Saint Basil, is easily discerned by her garments, in her deportment, in her every movement, so that those who meet her, perceiving in her the living resemblance of God, incline with respect, being edified by her modesty. The christian virgin, knowing that she can neither avoid the sight, nor hearing of her divine Spouse, conducts herself always as though she were in the presence of Jesus Christ, and continually heard by him.

A virgin that has consecrated herself to God by vow, should be pure and perfect. Her eyes should no longer open but to dwell upon heaven, her mouth, but to sing celestial hymns, and her ears to hear the wonders of the Lord, and the truths of eternity; her imagination should no longer be occupied by any but the purest images, and the visions of the world to come; the mind should only be occupied with the hope of future blessings, and the mercies of God towards her soul.

Worldly and vain objects, however innocent they may be, henceforth wound the purity of her looks. Worldly discourses, were they merely idle and useless, soil the sanctity of her lips; the recital of the affairs and amusements of the world, dishonor the chastity and innocence of her ears; the care of the body, if there enter into it any self-complacency, violates the purity of her consecration; and too natural attachments with even her sister religious, profane the sanctity of her heart. The faithful Spouse in the world is occupied with the care of pleasing her Lord; this division is allowed, because the obligation and tranquility of a sacred engagement render it necessary. But the Spouse of Jesus Christ should study to please him alone; whatever divides her heart is an infidelity; every care that does not tend to attract to herself the tenderness of the heavenly Spouse, and offer him marks of her affection, excite his jealousy, and wounds the fidelity she has sworn to him. In a word, all that is not holy, eternal, heavenly, sullies, degrades and debases her.

COLLOQUY.

O most amiable Heart of Jesus, I adore thee, because thou art my God. Receive my prayers in that

sanctuary of propitiation and divine purity.   Attract
me wholly to thy Heart.   O Jesus, more beautiful
than all the beauties of earth, render my heart pure,
wash me more and more from former faults, in order
that I may approach thee and dwell forever in thy
heart.

PRACTICE.

Examine seriously all the affections of your heart.

ASPIRATION.

Create within me a clean heart, O God, and renew
an upright spirit within me.

FIRST FRIDAY OF SEPTEMBER.

ON FIDELITY IN IMITATING THE ZEAL OF THE HEART OF JESUS.

Zeal is a consuming thirst for the glory of God,
and the salvation of souls.   Zeal is the perfection of
love; if the love of God is a fire, zeal is its flame.
The most exalted of all good works, says St. Denis,
is to co-operate with God in the salvation of souls.

The Heart of Jesus is a perfect model of that divine
zeal which ought to inflame the hearts of all such as
really love it.   Find, if possible, one single act in his
life not animated with its gentle flame.   The infinite
love with which he burns for God, was its measure,
and prompted him to say: "The zeal of the house
of God consumes me."   He devotes himself without
sparing himself in the least, even to exhaustion—
and when necessary, leaves his customary repose and
nourishment.   He would have given himself in particular for each soul, if one sacrifice had not have

been sufficient for all. For your perfection, for only one degree of sanctity, he would have sacrificed himself a thousand times, if these new merits could have added anything to infinite merits.

It was his zealous Heart, which, multiplying in some manner, his adorable person, sent apostles throughout the known world to announce the kingdom of God. In the adorable Eucharist, the Saviour continues exercising his zeal, his Heart is an ocean of light, of grace, of love, and of spiritual wealth, which he loves to spread throughout the mystical body of his church. In that sacrament of love, Jesus gives a new eclat to the glory of his Father, and makes his grace superabound in favor of souls. Now it is in the sweetness of the most secret intimacy that this two-fold wonder of his beneficence is displayed. Sometimes he sends his beloved children salutary inspirations: sometimes he gives them strong impressions which animate them with renewed activity. Here, it will be a privileged communication of his interior grace; there, some secret gifts which he bestows on prayer. Now, what the blessed Saviour does for you, you can do for others, faithful children of his Heart; yes, you can participate in the apostolical ministry of gaining hearts to Jesus, by an edifying manner of conversing, by good advice, fervent prayers, and the numerous other means that piety suggests. A simple word dictated by holy charity, a look of compassion alone, have rallied many a soul in the love and service of God.

Another means not less powerful, of which Jesus makes use in the Eucharist for promoting the glory of God his Father, and obtaining the salvation of souls, is the example that he gives us of all the virtues. His hidden life in the tabernacle is the summary of the practices and exercises which prepare, pursue and consummate the work of perfection.

But alas! his divine examples do not influence generally, because there are many who do not reflect, whilst yours, pious souls, immediately present to their eyes, are more suitable, on account of our weak nature, to act with fruit on the hearts of such as are so happy as to witness them. If you truly love the Heart of Jesus, be faithful *" to let your light so shine before men, that seeing your good works, they may glorify your Father who is in Heaven."* Forget not this important maxim, it is easier to conduct a soul to virtue by example than by words.

In fine, prayer is another means of exercising zeal, which the Heart of Jesus employs in the Sacrament of his love. Advocate and victim at the same time, he never fails to intercede for us, and immolate himself for our necessities. Faithful souls, children of his sacred Heart, redouble your wishes and your prayers, offer that Heart a holy violence, that violence which his mercy demands, constrain it to make itself beloved; hasten by your prayers, the triumph of that divine Heart, throughout the entire world.

Adopt the pious sentiments that filled the soul of the venerable Margaret Mary, when she said: "I cannot express the joy that I experience at the increase of devotion to the sacred Heart of my Saviour; it seems to me that I only breathe for that." She says also: "Our Lord discovered to me treasures of grace and love, for those persons who will consecrate themselves to it, and then devote themselves to rendering and procuring to that sacred Heart, all the love and honor of which they are capable; but treasures so vast, so desirable, that it is impossible for me to express them! Our Lord, showed me the

names of a multitude of persons that were inscribed
in his sacred Heart, on account of the desire that
they possess of causing it to be loved and venerated,
and for this reason, he said that they should never
be effaced."

PRAYER.*

"Would that all creatures were changed into
tongues and mouths, to bless and love thee, O Heart
of my adorable Saviour. Would that the heavens
and the earth were filled with thy praise."

PRACTICE.

Offer all you may suffer to-day, for the conversion
of those who do not know, or refuse to know the
Heart of Jesus.

ASPIRATION.

Heart of Jesus, consumed with zeal for the salvation of souls, take pity on us.

---

* M. Olier.

FIRST FRIDAY OF OCTOBER.

THE HOLINESS OF OUR PRAYERS WHEN THEY ARE UNITED WITH THE HEART OF JESUS.

When we pray and implore the favors of God, in
union with the Heart of his divine Son, our prayer
is always just; for who can be better acquainted with
our soul's necessities than the mind of Jesus, since
he alone can descend into the depths of our hearts,
and discover all their windings, recesses and motives?
And if he possesses a knowledge of us so very in-

timate and so profound, is it not a proof that we always pray for precisely what is requisite to the welfare of our souls, being inspired and conducted by such an enlightened mind?

The Spirit of God, says the Apostle, compassionates our weakness; for we know not what we should ask, neither the manner of asking; but the same divine Spirit prays for us with ineffable sighings and lamentations. God, who sounds the heart, is conscious of what the Spirit desires, and knows that he asks nothing which is not conformed to his holy will. Hence, you need only unite yourself to that divine Spirit, and our Lord who lives in you, will supply whatsoever may be wanting.

By this union we shall acquire an admirable disposition, so that we shall never request but what Jesus has inspired us to do: *Erunt docibiles Dei.* It is therefore, true, that when united to the Heart of Jesus, we shall never go wrong in relation to the substance of our prayers, and we shall always solicit what is most becoming to our spiritual wants.

But it is no less certain that the manner of praying is always holy in this same union with the Heart of Jesus. For then whatever prayer a soul addresses to God, it no longer desires but Jesus alone, it does not multiply itself in a hundred good things which it might petition, it does not even dwell upon the more holy gifts, because being united to Jesus, what can it desire more than Jesus in whom are eminently included all good and perfect gifts?

One of the greatest advantages that we reap from uniting all our prayers with those of the Heart of Jesus, is that we are infallibly heard. Therefore, whatever be your miseries and imperfections, unite yourself to Jesus; pray and you will obtain what you ask; for here there is no longer question of that unfaithful soul which merits the wrath and chastisements of God, but only of Jesus, to whom the divine Father can refuse nothing. However troubled and guilty your conscience may be, you will not be considered, because being united to Jesus, and offering your sighs and devout supplications to heaven, the eternal Father will not hear your voice, but the voice of Jesus praying and sighing in you. True you are that wicked Esau, but being united to Jesus the voice that issues from your mouth is the sweet, persuasive voice of Jacob, which ever arises with favorable acceptance to the eternal Father.

Though you were not to pronounce one word, but remain like a wretched criminal whose mouth is closed by shame, your prayer will not prove less acceptable, provided you remain faithfully united to Jesus, and by favor of this union become clothed with him; for then, the eternal Father will only descry the coat of his son Joseph, *tunica filii mei est*, which will serve you as mantle, and thus his divine eyes will rest upon you with love and complacency. But though you dread that he may fix his divine sight upon your miserable person, lose no confidence in the efficacy of your prayer, so long as your soul remains lost in its intimate union with Jesus, for he will not think of your soul, sinful as you may be, except as it is purified and shielded by the precious blood of his divine Son, and then he can no longer resist your prayers which will be accompanied by that voice of the blood of the innocent Abel, dead for the expiation of your faults and the satisfaction of divine justice provoked against you.

Having become, according to the expression of Saint Paul, rich in Jesus Christ, we ought to regard the adorable Heart of the Saviour as his treasure. Thence he draws every species of good: *De bono thesauro cordis sui profert bonum.* In this august sanctuary we find all necessary graces prodigally lavished: graces of expiation which reconcile us, graces of sanctification which perfect us, and graces of intimate union which do us honor. The old man reformed and regenerated, the new man spiritualized and in some sort divinized are the marvellous effects of divine bounty for which we are indebted to the Sacred Heart of Jesus.

COLLOQUY.

Hail, O Sacred Heart of Jesus! source of eternal life, infinite treasure of the divinity, burning furnace of divine love, thou art my refuge and the place of my repose. Grant that my heart may be so united with thy sacred Heart, that thy will be mine, and mine eternally conformed to thine.

PRACTICE.

Perform all your pious exercises in union with the Heart of Jesus.

ASPIRATION.

Incline unto my aid, O God, O God make haste to help me.

FIRST FRIDAY OF NOVEMBER.

OF THE MEEKNESS OF THE HEART OF JESUS.

Meekness is the daughter of humility; every humble heart is so much more meek as it is more humble. What therefore must be the degree of

meekness of the Heart of Jesus! and how well might
he be authorized to say; *Learn of me that I am
meek.* The principle of that ineffable meekness was
in his Heart; he had but to follow its movements, because his soul was always under the dominion of the
Word which governed and directed it in all things.
It is however, just to add, that no soul ever possessed
a susceptibility so keen and exquisitely delicate; no
trait of injustice and malice from his enemies escaped
him, and he felt towards their evil dispositions all the
aversion that could animate a Man God.

Jesus Christ treated familiarly with the lowly and
insignificant, with the poor and with children. He
associated with plain, uneducated men, and bore their
weaknesses with unalterable meekness, as well as
their indiscretion, ignorance and inconstancy. He
repeated for them again and again the same discourses,
he developed his thoughts to them, and elevated them
gradually to the knowledge of the most sublime
mysteries; he animated their confidence, encouraged
their good dispositions, corrected their ideas; and
finally, he did not disdain to call them his friends and
brethren. He lived with them more like a father
than a master; he treated them almost as though
they were his equals, and when we think what he
was, how much their superior, not only according to
his divinity, but even according to his humanity, we
are ravished at his meekness and condescension.—
His doctrine was sublime and his teaching quite opposed to their prejudices, and to all the passions of
the human heart. But his discourses were accompanied with such grace and insinuation, that he
persuaded, moved and captivated every heart. His
meekness appeared chiefly in the contradictions that
he experienced during his public life, and in the

manner with which he justified himself against the odious reproaches which were made him.

What meekness during the course of his dolorous Passion! After rendering an account modestly, and in a few words, of his conduct and of his doctrine, he remains silent; and he accomplished to his latest breath, what had been predicted of him, that he should be slain like an innocent lamb, without opening his mouth to complain.

This virtue accords perfectly in him, with zeal and firmness. When there was question of defending the interests of his Father, and of truth, of rebuking hypocrites, he spoke with fire and vehemence; he testified a holy indignation; he even displayed his divine authority.

But when there was only question of himself, either he repulsed not the injuries and the calumnies with which they loaded him, or he defended himself with great moderation, never showing the least alteration in his looks and words, and employed, without warmth, invincible reasons, which left his enemies without the power of replying.

The meekness which springs from virtue, does not resemble that which arises from the natural temperament. Souls naturally meek are often weak, easy, indifferent, and carry their indulgence to excess; but such as become so in order to imitate Jesus, are strong, firm, full of sentiment, indulgent when necessary, and without failing in their obligations.— The person who is naturally mild, will not rebuke, for fear of being moved and driven from his usual calmness; the soul meek through virtue, will reprove forcibly, but always with self-possession. *One* will dissemble through timidity, the other will speak through a motive of charity. *One* will be frequently exposed to omit fulfilling his duty in this respect, the other will discharge it on all occasions, *faithfully*, without human respect. The one will transact his affairs through interest for himself, the other will do it solely with the intention of pleasing God, and doing more good.

In performing works of zeal, in the government of others, imitate the ineffable meekness of the Heart of Jesus. Let there be no violent ways, no harshness, no sharp reproofs, nor bitter and too sensitive words; break not the bruised reed, and quench not the smoking flax. Consider how our blessed Lord behaved in regard to sinners when they gave him cause of offence. Does he immediately display his justice? No, he meekly represents their infidelities to guilty souls, he invites them to repent, he waits patiently for them to return to him, and if they be chastised, it is always in a paternal manner and with views of mercy. In a word, he adopts every means of gaining and changing the will, and up to the last moment, when final impenitence is consummated, it is not permitted to presume that God has totally abandoned the sinner without hope of pardon.

You cannot feel more deeply interested for the glory of God and the salvation of the neighbor than does the Heart of Jesus: you cannot employ more efficacious means than his. Act therefore outwardly as it did inwardly. Let your advice, your invitations, and your reproaches second his; labor in obedience to grace, and to that end let grace animate, direct and sustain you in the exercise of your zeal. If we are not on our guard, there will be much personal feeling in our zeal for God and the welfare of souls. We consider ourselves; our self-love is what we wish to content; it is not God's reign that we desire to establish but our own. There is an art of preparing minds, of insinuating ourselves sweetly, of managing them, of not insisting on more than is necessary, so as to win them efficaciously and put them in the way of cure, which none but God can teach, and he only teaches it to such souls as he himself has in entire possession.

PRACTICE.

Present all your words to the Heart of Jesus, that they may be filled with its meekness.

ASPIRATION.

Jesus, meek of Heart, render my heart like to thine.

FIRST FRIDAY OF DECEMBER.

LOVE OF THE HEART OF JESUS FOR OBEDIENCE.

Obedience is a virtue that inclines us to follow God's will, and submit to it on all occasions.

The great obstacles to this virtue, are attachment to creatures, and above all, love to ourselves, because these are seeming goods, which arrest us and hinder us from running in the way of God's commandments.

For this reason, in the order prescribed for religious vows, poverty and chastity are named first, so as to arrive at obedience, for it is necessary to be disengaged from the exterior goods of the world, and sensual pleasures, that we may be free in the ways of our Lord JESUS CHRIST.

For this reason, St. Paul warns us to offer our bodies as victims, and after, to render a reasonable obedience, pre-supposing the death of the body, and all its pleasures, as necessary to the perfection of this virtue.

There is yet a third obstacle to obedience, which is still more baneful, it is an attachment to self-will, which hinders us from sacrificing our noblest faculty to God. When we obey any superior, we should always place before the eye of Faith the divine Being, who is represented to us, by the creature who speaks to us and governs us. When we hear any command given to us, or obey any regulation made for us, we should consider in them the voice of God that is calling us.

We are children of God. In this capacity we should delight to obey him, or those who represent him to us. Our Lord, as the perfect Son of the Eternal Father, obeyed him from the commencement of his life, until his death. He lived thirty years under the direction of St. Joseph, and of his holy Mother, considering each as the image and representative of his Father, God.

The Gospel does not mention any virtue of Jesus Christ during all that time, but his submission and obedience. He dies also and leaves the world as he entered and lived in it, by the order of obedience. Our Lord in regenerating us, fills us with his own spirit and life; *he lives in us* so as to effect the glory of God in us, in the same manner as he accomplished it in himself. During his life, our blessed Lord always kept his eye fixed on God his Father, and awaited precisely the moments of the divine will. Now, he continues in us the same exactitude, and desires that we should follow the orders of his Father with similar punctuality.

We are servants redeemed from the slavery of sin, and the bondage of Satan. Our Lord in redeeming us, delivered us from that unhappy and cursed captivity; he subjected us to his Father, and remitted us under his dominion. We therefore belong to Jesus Christ, as to him who has ransomed us. *You are no longer your own,* says the Apostle, because you belong to Jesus Christ, who redeemed you by the price of his blood, and made you his. The christian should, therefore, by the inclination of his spirit and his grace, be in subjection to the laws of Jesus Christ, his king, and should glory in being his vassal.

Another motive is our *quality* of *victims,* for at the same time that Jesus Christ acquired us for himself, he offered us to God, gave us and consecrated us with himself, as victims of his Father. Hence, as victims consecrated to God, and destined to sacrifice, have no right over themselves, so we have no longer dominion over ourselves; for at the moment that our Lord bound us to him, and incorporated us in him by baptism, we are consecrated to him on the altar of his Father; *we are dead to ourselves, and living to God in Jesus Christ.*

We are therefore no longer ours, but belong solely to God, expecting the period of our immolation and sacrifice, in the same manner as victims await from the high priest, the moment of their death and sacrifice.

God alone has a right over all that belongs to us, and a power to use it as he wishes for his own service. We are *his* by a special consecration, and he alone is the high priest who possesses the right of disposing of us.

Still more, *we are the temples of the Holy Ghost.* He alone is our soul and our life, and should move and direct us. We should consequently obliterate

our own will and views in order to let him occupy
their place, so that by his supreme power he may
vivify and direct the members of Jesus Christ.

The Heart of Jesus chasing the evil spirit from
his temple and its members, filled them with his
divine Spirit, so that he may dwell in his house and
be the faithful governor of the place. The Christian
becomes a new creature by means of the Holy Spirit;
hence that same Spirit destroys and consumes the
human self-will in order to introduce and establish
himself in its place. As he is the personal will of
God, he wills also to fill the human will with his presence in order to render it divine, and thus annihilate
that detestable faculty which defeats and ruins the
Christian.

Consider also the title, DEAD, *which we bear as
Christians.* You are dead, says the Apostle Saint
Paul. We ought, therefore, to be dead to our own
being, and especially to our self-will, which is the
source and root of the life of Adam in us. The
Christian's care should be to suffer himself to be
possessed and governed by a spirit of uprightness
and sanctity. He should let his will be filled and
replaced by the will of Jesus Christ dwelling in him
and vivifying his soul.

COLLOQUY.

Receive, Lord, my free-will, I am nothing, I possess nothing which comes not from thy munificent
liberality. I restore the whole to thee that thou
mayst do with it and with me as seems to thee good.
Grant me conformity and union with thy sacred
Heart, and my highest desires will be satisfied for
time and eternity.

PRACTICE.

Resolve to obey, through a spirit of faith, whatever authority, temporal or spiritual, it is our duty to recognise—and never dispense ourselves without previous prayer and counsel.

ASPIRATION.

Thy will, O my God, be done now and forevermore.

—⁂—

For the Festival

OF

THE SACRED HEART OF JESUS.

THE LOVE OF THE HEART OF JESUS.

The Heart of Jesus possesses in itself a power of love so great, that were all the Saints and Angels of heaven to concentrate the fire of their charity in one only heart, it could never equal it. Every time that an act of charity emanates from the secret depths of the Heart of Jesus, it requires all the omnipotence of God himself. The flame of its love differs not from ours, but the spirit of the Eternal Word animates it with its divine breath. The omnipotence of Him, who with a word created the universe from nothing, is employed in raising to its highest degree of heat the burning furnace of a human heart. Under the influence of the strong affections which agitate it, every pulsation of that heart reveals to us in all their power, the raptures of the Son of God who dwells in it.

The Heart of Jesus experiences all the sensations that comport with human nature, without however

experiencing its violent transports. In that Sacred
Heart shines, in all its native splendor, the purest
eternal light, and the holy ardors that consume the
Seraphim are cold as polar ice when compared with
the love that animates it. O wonderful love of the
virginal Heart of Jesus, it is not infinite, because it
did not always exist; and yet the Angels themselves
have never sounded the depths of that fathomless
Ocean. Like eternal love, it ignores all progressive
development; for from its earliest pulsation in the
breast of the Infant Jesus, it was as ardent as it is
now in the Heavens.* Pure as in created love, it
burns towards men with all the vehemence of a real
passion; its force springs from the power of God,
while its tenderness is maternal.

Therefore, though Jesus sleep, his faithful Heart
never ceases to love us, and continually thinks on us,
his poor creatures. Of him it is said in the Canticle
of Canticles: *I sleep, but my heart watches.* His
slumber was not like ours, for it is said, that when
his senses were buried in sleep, he was always conscious of what he was doing, and the acts of love to
God and man, which palpitated in his whole being,
never suffered any interruption.

Our Lord calls himself in several places of the
sacred writings, a jealous God. But of what is he
jealous? Of one sole thing, of the homage of our
mind and *heart;* not an homage sterile and of mere
speculation, but one that influences our whole
sentiments and conduct. The homage of the mind
consists in acknowledging God to be all; the beginning and the end of every thing, and that beside
him there is nothing. It consists, particularly, in
humbling our minds before him, in submitting our

*Dalgairns.

lights to him; or rather, in being well convinced
that he is our light in both the natural and supernatural order; that we neither see nor judge rightly,
but inasmuch as we see as he sees, and judge as he
judges; which implies an absolute dependence of the
mind on his, a continual death to our intelligence to
consult his alone, a constant fidelity to act according
to his views, and not according to ours.   This homage
he exacts, he has a right to exact it, and he is infinitely jealous of it.

The homage of our heart, consists in establishing
our Lord the centre of our every affection, in loving
him with all our strength; in loving ourselves in him
and in reference to him; and in loving no creature
but in a subordinate and subjective disposition, towards that principal love that we owe to him.   When
we reflect a moment on what our Lord is, and what
we are, can we doubt that all our affections belong to
him, that he exacts their homage, that he is essen-
tially jealous of them, and that he cannot suffer
disorder in them, without reprehending them and
punishing it.

The delicacy of his jealousy may be seen in the
Gospel.   Although Martha is busy and eager for
him and in his service, yet he is jealous of it, because she is occupied with what is *for him*, rather
than with *himself*, and with what is *totally of him*,
as was Magdalen.

But why is the Heart of Jesus so jealous? because
he is God, infinitely holy, and loving order supremely;
because his love, such even as he communicates to
the blessed, is incompatible with self-love.   No one
can with his own strength combat his self-love; but
he can yield himself to the Heart of Jesus, he can
suffer the jealousy of our Lord to act against that

5

inordinate love; with the help of grace he can second that jealousy; and when there is question of giving the last blow to that unfortunate human *me*; he can consent to suffer, and not disturb the hand that is immolating it. Many a combat and many a trial are necessary to arrive at it, but a faithful and a generous soul, which resigns itself into the hands of Jesus Christ, and never resumes its own reign, no matter in what way it is treated, will infallibly attain it.

To give ourselves then, to the Heart of Jesus, to render it love for love, we must renounce ourselves, forget and lose our own petty interests and embrace his; have no will, glory or peace but those of that loving and adorable Heart, in a word love God and not ourselves.

COLLOQUY.

May the Heart of Jesus be the only retreat of our hearts, living with the flames of its love. My supreme Good, I love thee above all things; would that I were capable of producing infinite acts of pure love. Would that I could love thee more ardently than the whole of Paradise: my dearest, most cherished consolation is, the hope of loving thee eternally. Ocean of bounty, abyss of mercy, boundless LOVE, let me lose myself in thee.

PRACTICE.

Spend the day in retirement from the world, in self-examination, and forming holy purposes of denying self, and devoting the homage of the mind and heart to the Sacred Heart of Jesus.

ASPIRATION.

O Jesus, I desire but one thing—it is to dwell in thy Heart forevermore. Immaculate Heart of Mary, conduct me there.

NOVENA

PREPARATORY TO THE

Festibal of the Sacred Heart of Jesus.

BY FATHER BORGO, S. J.

(Translated from the French.)

SS. C. J. M.

Father Borgo's Novena.

Pope Pius VII., in his desire to increase the devotion of the faithful to the Sacred Heart of Jesus, granted, by a decree of his Eminence, the Cardinal Pro-Vicar, of March 15, 1809, (kept in the *Segretaria* of his court,) and a Rescript of the S. Congr. of Indulgences of Jan. 13, 1818, to all the faithful who should make, with contrite hearts, the above named Novena, before the Feast of the Sacred Heart.

I. The Indulgence of 300 Days, each day of the said Novena, and

II. The Plenary Indulgence, to be gained either on the Feast of the Sacred Heart, or some one day in the Octave, when, after having assisted at every day of the Novena, having Confessed and Communicated, they shall pray for the intention of the Sovereign Pontiff.

This Novena may be used any one other time in the year, with power to gain these Indulgences on the same conditions as above.

Any of the faithful who are not in possession of F. Alphonso Rodriguez's book on Perfection, which F. Borgo's Novena assigns as spiritual reading during the Novena, may, by the permission of the same Pope Pius VII., use any other book of devotion or spiritual reading they like.

FOR THE DAY WHICH PRECEDES THE NOVENA.

Meditation.

PREPARATORY PRAYER.

An act of Faith in the presence of God.

OFFERING OF THE MEDITATION.

Ask God to grant you the grace of being attentive, to enlighten you and touch your heart.

First Prelude.—Represent to your mind Jesus Christ at the very instant in which he was instituting that Divine Sacrament. He is seated at the table with his Apostles, and holds in his hands that same bread which he blesses, and changes substantially into his own body. Consider him raising his divine eyes towards heaven, radiant with a brilliancy, the softness of which is ineffable. Contemplate that countenance of a God burning with a more than ordinary love towards us. He is in an extacy of love.

Second Prelude.—Ask him to assist you with an extraordinary light, that you may comprehend the intentions of his love in that august sacrament, and grant you the grace of being profoundly penetrated, in order that you may personally concur in their accomplishment.

FIRST POINT.

Jesus Christ instituted the sacrament of the Eucharist, in order to appease the ardent desire he felt, of communicating his every blessing and benefit to us. No other means of sharing these with man had appeared to him adequate. Consider, O pious soul, how insatiable this liberal heart was in loving you.

This is not a new gift that he would bestow on souls that he loves; it is an assemblage of all possible gifts; in this heavenly boon all graces are concentrated. Whatever may be the necessities of a soul during this life of vicissitude and trial, in this, she may find assistance, remedy and resource. Souls whom temptations are trying, disgrace afflicts, misfortune intimidates and dejects, *souls*, that are uncertain and wavering, poor, infirm and languishing souls, learn how to have recourse to this divine remedy, and to use it in a proper manner. In this, whatever kind friends, the most enlightened counsellors, examples, and the most sage reflections, could offer—whatsoever indeed, all the devotions of universal Christianity could present, are included. It is in this treasury of all conceivable benefits, that an infinity of souls have found their sanctification. Other means are frequently denied us. But in this sacrament, Jesus Christ is ever present, ever ready; everywhere, and accessible to each and all. Why then, O lukewarm soul, do you languish in the ways of God?— Why yield to such guilty sloth? How is it possible that you can despise a blessing so universal?

But again it is not simply a compendium of all divine gifts; it is a gift entirely new, it is the grandest of all gifts. Those are only the fruits that arise from the boundless charity of the divine Saviour; but here we have the mother plant that yields all these fruits—your divine Redeemer himself, who gives himself wholly to you. In giving you himself, he presents you all, absolutely, his sacred humanity with all the merits of his mortal life; he gives you his divinity with its countless treasures of wisdom, his infinite power and beneficence. In fine he places no bounds to your desires of spiritual wealth, but those which you create by your disposition and capacity.

Ponder well, this excess of love, O worldly soul, who art so susceptible of the friendships of this transitory, perishable life. A present calms your anger, warms anew your indifference, interests and engages your heart; and is it credible! for your God alone, that ungrateful heart ceases to be sensible? Ah! put on the confusion of repentance, shed tears of tenderness, and resolve upon what you should think, feel, and do, in order to satisfy that divine Heart which lavishes its benefits upon you.

SECOND POINT.

The liberality of Jesus Christ induced him to institute the sacrament of the Eucharist in order to unite our souls with his. He is himself the merchant in the Gospel who sells all his wealth to acquire a rare and extremely valuable Pearl. O Jesus, Son of God, are we indeed of ourselves, and is the possession of our hearts also, so very precious in your eyes. Comprehend, O degraded and ungrateful soul, the extent of the grandeur of this mystery—if possible. The only Son of the Father aspires with ardor to become one with you in the most intimate union which can be formed between the Eternal God and a mortal, and by an effort of his wisdom and power, he has found means to identify himself in some manner with you by being converted into your very nourishment. He desires to belong unreservedly to the creature, provided that, by a reciprocal and loving offering of its whole self, the creature consents to become entirely His. Reason would revolt at such a belief, did not faith impose it. Yes, **my Jesus and my God**, I believe it.

But how can I be insensible to such magnanimous love—am I acquainted with its characteristics, as I should be? Alas! how have I delayed knowing thee and knowing myself! The more I admire thee O my God, the greater is the horror, that I entertain for myself! How often have you thus lovingly united yourself to my soul! But, O divine Lover, to what a monster did you find yourself united! to what a monster of unworthiness, of impurity and of ingratitude! My soul has been so often immersed in the sea of an unapprehended felicity—one instant of which would not have been too dearly purchased by the last drop of my blood! Blind, insensate, unfortunate guilty *soul*, how many such moments thou hast forever lost—how many ineffable delights thou hast not known how to enjoy. The very seraphim envied thee and me. Ah! contemptible and loathsome senses! Ah! deceitful world! Ah! perfidious and treacherous passions, what have you bestowed on me in exchange for such unspeakable blessings!

Pause here a few moments, O devout soul, and compare so intimate a possession of a God of LOVE, with those frivolous causes of your lukewarmness which have deprived you of the taste and knowledge of these great blessings. Form generous resolutions, implore great lights and powerful graces, and making an act of entire renunciation to self-love, offer your heart without reserve to the desires, the designs and the burning affection of the infinitely amiable, and infinitely loving heart of your divine spouse.

FIRST DAY.

LIFE OF BEATITUDE OF THE HEART OF JESUS CHRIST IN THE BLESSED SACRAMENT.

Meditation.

The truth expressed above, is a verity incomprehensible to your self-love, which discovers the Heart of Jesus Christ in an absolute deprivation of all the tangible goods of earth.

PREPARATORY PRAYER.

A fervent act of faith in presence of God.

OFFERING OF THE MEDITATION.

Implore our Lord to give you the grace of being attentive, to enlighten your mind and touch your heart.

First Prelude.—Imagine you perceive Jesus Christ in the Blessed Sacrament, disclosing his Heart, enthroned on his sacred Breast, and radiating an ardent fire, amid a soft, mild light.

Second Prelude.—Ask him to give you a share of that mild light, and a participation in that divine fire, that your heart may be undeceived and enlightened, and inflamed with his love.

FIRST POINT.

Seek in the Heart of Jesus Christ, what idea you should entertain of temporal grandeur, beauty and felicity. In the circumscribed ciborium which contains Him, that divine Heart enjoys an infinite happiness, without, however, delighting in any manner in what the world esteems, nor in what your self-love leads you to believe essential to your happiness. Instead of those diversions in which the world finds its aliment, Jesus has no other company than solitude.

and silence. Instead of pearls and precious articles of furniture, the tabernacle in which he dwells is often poor, and destitute of even such ornaments as would be less unworthy. In those very moments in which He is not left entirely alone, he has generally none but the most miserable and the most uncouth persons in attendance on him. But how frequently does he find himself in the presence of his declared enemies? how often is he insulted, mocked and profaned? How deplorable is his condition in the eyes of self-love! Nevertheless, that divine Heart, in the midst of this solitude, reduced to such society, and satiated with contempt, loses nothing of its ever infinite happiness. But *you*, you so often lose your repose, and for infinitely less cause! Heart, blind and weakened, by attaching yourself to sensible things, you make your happiness depend on them: these have hitherto been the objects of your search. Yet your heart possesses the same nature as that of Jesus Christ; neither his divine Heart nor your heart was made for the goods which seduce the senses.— Recognise your error—O Heart infinitely happy, give me grace to know the emptiness of that happiness, the illusions of which abused my self-love and led my reason astray—and give me an unfathomable contempt for all that the world esteems and loves.

Now, examine by what particular propensity your self-love is most prone to be flattered, and adopt resolutions quite opposed to it—and pray.

SECOND POINT.

Study in the heart of Jesus Christ, the idea you should form of the greatness, beauty and happiness of spiritual blessings. The love and possession of God constitute the beatitude of the Heart of Jesus Christ;

that Heart being personally united to the Divinity, its happiness is infinite, as are also its love and union with God : for this reason, that happiness can never undergo the slightest diminution, on account of a deficiency in those sensible benefits, to which you attach such immense value. That poor ciborium is to him as acceptable as his throne of glory. Gaze at the sun a few moments, you will be incapable then of perceiving aught else; the impression produced upon your vision is such, that it is no longer susceptible of any minor impression.

O blessed insensibility to the goods of this life—this alone, can render your heart happy. Say therefore, interiorly : "My heart has the same nature as that of Jesus Christ; whatsoever renders that divine Heart happy, can alone form the happiness of mine." Recall those days, or rather those hours of your life, during which your heart was inflamed with love for your God. O sweet and yet bitter recollection!—What then was wanting to your contentment? Compare with its actual condition, the peace which then pervaded your soul. Compassionate yourself—love yourself sincerely—be angry with yourself.

O Heart of my Lord Jesus, infinitely contented and happy, when will you have compassion on me? From that tabernacle, Jesus answers me. Insensate soul, when wilt thou take pity on me? And what will you then answer? Humbly implore pardon of him for having suffered that sacred fire which he kindled in your soul, to be extinguished; form a courageous resolution, a practical and special resolution, to detach yourself absolutely, from whatsoever offers an obstacle to the rise and increase of divine love in your soul, and consequently raises an impediment to your happiness even in this life.

Spiritual Reading.—Christian Perfection of Rodriguez. I Part, 1 Treatise, chap. 14 and 15.

VISIT TO THE BLESSED SACRAMENT.

On this day, consider Jesus Christ as the only object which can render you happy, and his Sacred Heart as the place in which your felicity is deposited. Form an act of desire. Supplicate God to grant that his love alone may always form your delight.

ASPIRATION.

Grant me thy love and thy grace, I shall be rich enough: I pray for nothing more.

PRACTICE.

Reflect during the performance of your several actions, in what manner and in what dispositions of heart, Jesus would have accomplished them, and let this reflection serve to correct and sanctify your usual manner of performing them.

SECOND DAY.

OF THE LIFE OF GRACE OF THE SACRED HEART IN THE BLESSED SACRAMENT.

Meditation.

Preparatory Prayer.—As usual.

First Prelude.—Represent to your mind, in the blessed sacrament, Jesus Christ drawing aside his sacred vestment, and pointing to you his Heart, whence gushes forth a torrent of limpid waters, emblem of the graces which he desires to shed with abundance into your heart, and into the hearts of all who come into his presence.

Second Prelude.—Go into his presence, as a poor diseased individual, covered with leprosy and languishing with a mortal thirst; petition him for grace to heal, and purify you and repair your enfeebled strength.

FIRST POINT.

Jesus Christ, in this august sacrament leads a life of grace. If a man dwells in a foreign country in order to traffic there, or to acquire information, it is justly said of him that he leads a commercial life, or a life devoted to study. Jesus Christ deigned to reside on this earth, all unworthy as it is of his glorious state, in order to become an Agent in our regard, and to take care of the interests of Divine Grace. Hence we may style the life that animates him in our midst in the blessed Sacrament, a life of grace.

What compassionate sentiments must have been excited in his Heart, when residing among us, he healed, and in order to heal, himself sought the sick; when he bestowed sight on the blind, raised the dead to life, and his love for us inspired him to perform so many prodigies? All these sentiments of pity, of tenderness, mercy and liberality he experiences now simultaneously in this state which is an epitome of all his wonders. How disinterested must his sentiments have been, when in the plentitude of his will, he submitted to so many foreseen fatigues, contradictions and vexations? All this charity, all that infinite love, he still experiences in this adorable Sacrament, in which he daily renews the work of our redemption.

Similar to the violence and activity of a great flame when restricted within a narrow furnace, is the burning love of his divine Heart. Yes, that infinitely loving Heart, *experiences a species of inexplicable torment at the excessive plentitude of graces which it contains,* and from which it cannot unburthen itself, for want of subjects proper for receiving them. The Saviour one day declared to a soul whom he cherished, showing her his Heart, resembling an abyss of fire. "My Heart is consumed with the desire of communicating itself to souls. Aid me, my daughter, in subduing this ardent flame; publish abroad, and induce others to publish universally that I will pour forth my graces without measure on all souls who will implore them from my sacred Heart."

But you are one of those cold hearts, quite insensible to the impassioned love of the Heart of Jesus. Have you weighed and comprehended the sentiments of that Heart? Now, that you are acquainted with them, what think you of it and what think you of yourself? O Heart, infinitely liberal and charitable, why did I not know you earlier! This is the cause of my being hitherto so destitute of graces, so feebly confident in thee, so timid in prayer, so reserved in my petitions.

Admiration. Thanksgiving. Confidence. Resolutions.

SECOND POINT.

What are the sentiments that Jesus expects from you in this life of grace, in which his Heart deigns to exist in that Sacrament?

1. You should consider that divine Heart as your sole place of refuge in all the necessities of your heart. This you have not done hitherto, because that loving Heart was the last help to which you had recourse. Had you believed practically that in that divine Heart, you would find the true remedy for your temptations, your sadness, doubts,

and moments of weakness, you would not have sought it, in your senses, in creatures, nor in your own passions. Examine with sincerity what injuries you have offered by this to the most tender, and the most powerful of all hearts, and begin a reparation without further delay.

2. In having recourse to that divine Heart, you should entertain a sincere and ardent desire for all the graces which are necessary to you. That divine Heart has an unlimited knowledge of the most hidden sentiments of yours: he perceives your want of earnestness in loving him in the very moment in which you are imploring some grace. He sees that you dread that grace which should detach you entirely from creatures, and that, whilst you pray with the lips, you experience a secret horror of self-hatred, of love of humiliations, and of entire renunciation to your own tastes and inclinations. However you cannot render yourself worthy of the graces of Jesus Christ, but by the sincerity and ardor of your desires. Meditate upon those which Jesus forms for you, and compare them with yours. Blush for them, in the depth of your heart, ask his pardon, and supplicate him to accorl that the first of all his favors be a strong desire of being healed by his grace, and of being rendered worthy of the desire that he has of communicating them to you.

3. You should have recourse to the Heart of Jesus not only with humility, but also with a loving confidence—that is, with a kind of amicable familiarity which God allows, and even desires that you should hold towards him in this Sacrament of love. O Soul, who hast hitherto mistaken your real good, consider this prodigy. The God of majesty and glory, before whom the Angels of Heaven tremble

with a holy fear, abases himself so low as to be willing to converse on earth familiarly with men. You yield your heart without reserve to creatures, very often more vile than yourself, and who perchance dishonor and betray you: and your heart removes, is shut—when a God designs to descend even to you! Ah! humility is not the barrier that restrains you, it is your feeble love for him, and the too weak persuasion of the love which he bears to you. Ah! Divine Heart, infinitely loving and amiable, it shall be so no longer.

Open to the Heart of Jesus, therefore, your whole heart; make known to it your troubles, discover to it your wounds; expose to it your necessities. He knows not how to resist an oppressed heart, which solicits relief with ardor and confidence.

Spiritual Reading.—Rodriguez. Part I., VII. Treatise. Chap. 8 and 9.

ASPIRATION.

Thou art my sole refuge and reliance.

VISIT.

Recall the Preludes and the fruit of the Meditation.

PRACTICE.

Perform some act of charity, politeness or friendship, towards some one for whom you may have experienced an aversion, with the intention of doing penance for your prolonged coldness to the Heart of Jesus.

THIRD DAY.

JESUS CHRIST IN THE MOST BLESSED SACRAMENT LEADS A LIFE OF SACRIFICE.

Meditation.

First Prelude.—Imagine that you behold Jesus in

the Sacrament, as a Lamb ready to be immolated on the altar, and flames issuing from his Heart, which consume him as a victim.

Second Prelude.—Entreat him to give you grace to understand fully the value of his Sacrifice, and to bestow on you the courage to imitate him, by an entire and generous sacrifice of your whole being to his love.

FIRST POINT.

The love of Jesus Christ for his divine Father and for us, was the principal motive of the sacrifice of the Cross, but the hatred and envy of his enemies, and of those who crucified him, participated in it also.

Here love effects the whole—this is a novel invention of a Heart inflamed with love, it is a work which belongs entirely to that Heart, which can never grow weary with loving. The essential interest of God's glory, and redemption of mankind, was infinitely satisfied by the sacrifice of the Cross.

Then, why this prolonged and continual renewal of that same sacrifice? Because what sufficed to appease the infinite justice of the Father, was not capable of sufficing to the infinite love which the heart of the Son indulged for men. To accomplish *that our divine Saviour be sacrificed*, it was enough that his enemies should ignore him, for had they known him, they would never have crucified the Lord of glory. The sacrifice of the Cross endured but a few hours; Jesus Christ renews it every instant in the Eucharist, for no moment of time elapses, in which the Holy Sacrifice is not offered in some locality of the revolving world. Hence the life of Jesus Christ may justly be denominated a life of sacrifice, himself being the victim and the sacrificator. But in order to immolate himself anew in this sacrament, he must conceal his sacred humanity from those who are dearest to him.

Why again, did he not think it sufficient to have this sacrifice renewed annually, as the other mysteries which the Church commemorates? Why did he not at least, provide in this new sacrifice, for the exterior glory that should accompany it, and not allow it to be offered in an obscure and hidden manner, which would expose it to irreverence and even to sacrilege? Why again? ah! the difficulties which his grandeur and our degradation opposed were infinite; they were insurmountable, except by a Heart insatiable with love for us.

Now, blind and icy soul, have you comprehended what participation the Heart of Jesus Christ has in the sacrifice of himself, which he continually offers for us, ungrateful as we are? Admire, give thanks, and form the desire of corresponding to so much love.

SECOND POINT.

The life of sacrifice which the Heart of Jesus lives for us in the sacrament, is an invitation which he presents you, to lead a similar life of sacrifice for his sake; if you wish to correspond with his love, you have only to imitate it. It is his love for you, which moves him to sacrifice himself daily for you; love him, and it will cost you little to immolate yourself for Jesus. Ah! did you know how he repugns those vain and futile sacrifices which are so frequently offered him! Think deeply on this, they are tokens of a feeble love. Whence is it, that retirement, poverty, and obedience are so burdensome to you? Why do you find it so difficult to overcome a resentment or an antipathy, or to moderate a friendship?

It is, alas! because after so many years passed in the service of God, you have never even tasted the smallest drop of that ineffable joy, that loving souls find in suffering with Jesus. Unhappy soul! Begin at once to offer your sacrifice, and you will learn how to love him.

Every trifling sacrifice will awaken in you a new degree of love which, filling you with courage, will conduct you to a still grander and more noble oblation. However little the soul persists with constancy in these feeble efforts, the Heart of Jesus, impatient to communicate by degrees the fire which consumes it, will place it in an opportunity least expected of offering to it a heroic sacrifice. Let this soul only dispose itself for it, and Jesus will kindle in her heart one of those flames of love, which will enable it to accomplish this heroic act, the principle of its sanctification. Such is the ordinary way of the sanctification of souls; consider it attentively, it is less difficult than it appears.

Compare the sacrifices of Jesus Christ with that which he demands of you on the present occasion. If your sacrifice be small, how shameful to refuse it! If it be great, fortunate soul, ah! behold the day in which Jesus Christ wishes to begin your sanctification; behold your day of prosperity. Look upon this tabernacle—within it resides your Supreme Good, your Spouse, your God who is immolated for you. Speak to that adorable Heart with that confidence and that familiarity which should have been produced by yesterday's meditation, and take your resolutions.

Spiritual Reading.—Rodriguez. Part II. Treatise 1st. Chapters 14 and 15.

Frequently say to your senses, your inclinations, and your will: *Eamus nos, et moriamur cum illo*—Let us go and die with him.

VISIT.

Go before the Blessed Sacrament as though you were to assist in spirit at the Crucifixion of Jesus Christ, at the instant in which his side was pierced with a lance that penetrated his Heart. Admire—even to ecstacy—humble yourself; excite yourself to generosity; offer yourself, and implore fervently the grace of constancy in the holy resolutions that you have just adopted.

PRACTICE.

When beginning this day, examine diligently what inclination, repugnance, or what defect exists in you which would prove most displeasing to the Heart of Jesus, and faithfully sacrifice it on this very day.

FOURTH DAY.

HONOR THE SACRED HEART OF JESUS, FOR HIS LIFE OF HUMILITY, IN THE BLESSED SACRAMENT.

Meditation.

First Prelude.—Here, consider attentively that Jesus Christ appears without any parade of majesty in this tabernacle—and strive to form some conception of the pomp which surrounds him in heaven. Compare the difference of these two states.

Second Prelude.—Supplicate him to disclose to you the secret intentions of his Heart, in a state so far beneath his infinite grandeur, and that he may render this state pleasing to you, by inspiring you with a desire of imitating it.

FIRST POINT.

"Learn of me that I am meek, and humble in heart." Self-abasement and the love of whatever may contribute to it, constitue the distinctive traits of humility. Consider the abasement of Jesus Christ in the Eucharist. He allows nothing, absolutely nothing, to appear of any thing which might attract honor to him. What signs do you perceive of his divinity? The splendor, majesty, throne of glory, and attendant Angels—where are they?— What signs do you perceive of that Omnipotence that sustains the world, of that Omniscience that governs it, of the Supreme sovereignty which reigns in heaven and on earth? Could he conceal himself more studiously, if he *dreaded* being honored as God? Could he subject himself more completely, if he willed effectively to be neglected and despised? His abode is nought but a narrow, inconspicuous nook, formed of wood, or at most of marble; and if we except a small number of altars, provided with ornaments, He is everywhere lodged in so simple, so miserable a way—so uncleanly indeed, that the lowliest artisan is accommodated better than he. He might have exacted from Christians a tribute of gold and precious stones, offered to his tabernacles, as formerly he did to the temple built by Solomon. But fully aware of what would take place at some future day, he resigned himself to the indolence, avarice, irreligion and ingratitude of men. Where is there a more striking example of humility of heart? Necessity does not compel him; a free and voluntary choice prompts him to prefer that condition of abjection, and such contemptible exterior appearances.—Here then is a Heart which loves humility, with a sincerity beyond suspicion; and this is the type of that humility which he gives you to practice.

Examine now, whether your words and deeds of humility that you occasionally perform, are as voluntary and as loving. Are you as neutral in your desires, as is the Heart of Jesus in the sacrament, to honorary or to contemptuous treatment? Do you, like him, leave your honor and reputation to the free will of others? Ah! what a model—what a lesson! How wide is the difference between a Spouse enslaved, and a Spouse that is a king. Reflect—resolve—pray.

SECOND POINT.

Consider two remarkable circumstances in the humility of the Heart of Jesus, in the blessed sacrament.

1. A Heart less enamored with humility, would have thought that the glory of God requires a boundary line to the degradation in which he appears in this sacrament. Almighty God would have been far more easily recognised and respected, had he sometimes permitted some sensible indices of the divine majesty to transpire. But the Heart of Jesus thought not so: he wished his example of humility in the adorable sacrament, to be infinitely perfect. Reflect, devout soul, your secret vanity often deceives you! If I am silent, say you, if I yield, my honor, my innocence, justice itself will be compromised.—Ah! know you not the highest honor of innocence is to be unjustly contemned; that justice finds its glory in supporting an unjust oppression? It is the favorite maxim of the humble Heart of Jesus; and

in the hidden recesses of the cloister, opportunities are not wanting, in which, even on very small occasions, pious souls having adopted this maxim, have performed deeds of heroism.

2. A heart less passionate towards humility, than was that of Jesus Christ, would have believed that he could have exerted greater influence to the advantage of souls, had he made himself known to men in a manner at least, in some degree more evident to the senses. O loving Heart, incarnate for our sakes! which of us would have been able to resist the splendor of the sweet, and all-divine beauty of your sacred humanity, had we enjoyed but one glimpse of it, and *that* fleeting as the lightning's glare? But the Heart of Jesus thought not thus; he believed, in his infinite wisdom, that it would prove more advantageous to us, to set before us, in the adorable Sacrament, the highest example of humility.

Hence it is certain that your pride, your vain self-esteem, the arrogance so natural to you, O devout soul, Jesus Christ reprobates, and looks upon them as *your* greatest enemies and his. In order to undeceive you wholly by his own example, he renounced in thus concealing his real glory, the facility of winning all our tenderness to him. But O Heart wonderfully humble! O my divine Saviour infinitely humiliated! you are so much dearer to me, as for my instruction you have more profoundly humbled yourself: *Quanto pro me vilior, tanto mihi carior.**— Examine the particular circumstances of your life; take special resolutions, and earnestly implore proportionate assistance.

---

*St. Bernard.

Spiritual Reading.—Rodriguez. Part II. Treatise III. Chap. 19 and 22.

ASPIRATION.

The deeper thy abasement for my sake, the dearer my affection for thee.

VISIT.

Retrace the tableau of the first Prelude.

PRACTICE.

Avoid ambitioning praises, and excusing yourself.

FIFTH DAY.

HONOR THE LIFE OF LOVE OF THE SACRED HEART IN THE BLESSED SACRAMENT.

Meditation.

First Prelude.—Make an act of faith in the real presence of our Lord in the Holy Eucharist, and imagine that Jesus addresses you from the tabernacle these words which he addressed to his Apostles: "Lo! I am with you always, even to the consummation of ages."

Second Prelude.—Entreat him to infuse into your soul the degree of gratitude which he expects from you, for the love and tenderness exhibited to you in this promise.

FIRST POINT.

Jesus Christ might have accomplished our sanctification by communicating himself to us solely under figures, and not *really*; but a love infinite as his could not be satisfied with giving us aid at a distance; he prefers doing it, himself being personally present.

But why was he not satisfied with coming in reality in the blessed Sacrament, as at the celebration of the holy sacrifice of Mass? Would not this august sacrifice have proved sufficient to ensure a great number of personal visits from his elect? No, this is not enough for his affectionate Heart—it desired to reside without interruption in the sacramental species, *that is,* to become our fellow citizen, and as it were an occupant of our very dwellings. He could have selected one single city in every province, and one sole temple in each town, as a residence. But no, his intentions were widely different—he would be omnipresent. In the immeasurable space of heaven, his humanity exists but in one locality; on earth, his humanity becomes in some manner immense, and is found wherever a few christians are assembled. It is therefore true, according to the language of several Saints, that the Heart of Jesus, is burning with love for men. But pause here, and reflect that this perpetual and universal presence among men, is one of the greatest miracles of his omnipotence, for his most holy humanity is multiplied infinitely in so many localities; and what is even more remarkable is, the multitude of affronts to which the multiplication of his presence continually subjects him. Do you respond with an equally inflamed desire to the passionate love of the Heart of Jesus for you? Examine—what does he require that is painful or inconvenient in a visit to his tabernacle? Enumerate if possible the expenses, embarrassments, and cares, attendant upon the ceremonious presentation of subjects before the powers of earth? Compute the ceremonies, ablutions, practices, and observances of the Jewish law, when God's people were to appear before the tabernacle of the Ark of the Covenant! But to approach God in the dispensation of love, neither poverty, deformity, nor low condition, nor insignificance, nor simplicity of garments offer any obstacle. Only love him and your love gives the right of a reception from him, accompanied with an unspeakable affability, as with an equal, as with a friend on terms the most intimate. O incomprehensible love! What countless benefits, what an abyss of tenderness! But, O religious soul, how many reasons for secret remorse, and for the futile motives which have easily prevented us from visiting him.

Consider some new proofs of the attraction of Jesus Christ to reside among us. He experiences so much pleasure in dwelling with us, that if we cannot go to him, he causes himself to be brought to us, and then the testimonies of his love are truly excessive. In what localities does he allow himself to be borne? In places which would prove for your refinement and delicacy abodes of disgust and horror— in low and miserable huts, in rooms filled with fetid odor, even in frightful dungeons. Again, consider the hands that sometimes carry him, often they are those of unworthy Priests. Yet such is the love of God, such his tenderness towards us, that apparently he perceives it not. In the primitive ages of christianity, the christians were allowed to take the Body of Christ on the holy table, carry it away with them, and preserve it with them in their residences, and during their journeys, and had not the Church, (indignant in reference to the disrespect that the relaxation of faith and diminution of charity would produce eventually,) forbidden it, Jesus Christ would have endured this treatment to this very day. What reply do you offer, devout soul, to these reflections? Have you hitherto considered, what degree of love his divine Heart manifests, in thus establishing himself among us.

But once again, a new evidence of his love even more admirable. However ardent the desire that he experiences of being always with you, he does not hinder you from acquitting yourself of your temporal duties, nor from attending to your temporal interests in the world.

If you are obliged to attend to your affairs, to the duties of your state, he is never impatient at being left alone; he waits until you are free and can return to him. He does not even require you to desist from your allowable diversions: he suffers you most willingly to go at your ease, either to the table, to your recreations, or your permitted amusements. Can a more wonderful love be conceived? It seems that in his excessive desire of gratifying you, he takes the most delicate precautions not to be burdensome or wearisome to you. Besides so many hours of the day during which he is forsaken, he passes long nights, wholly alone in his ciborium, and whilst you slumber, his Heart watches in your place; he remains awake, and supplicates his Father for you; he wakes, and defends you against the dangers that surround you; he watches, in fine, like a faithful sentinel over the well-being and safety of your abodes. Ah! if your heart is not penetrated with a love so tender, so discreet, so timid, so constant, so beneficent, so perfect, acknowledge that you have no faith, or that you possess a heart unworthy to live. Offer yourself just reproaches, mourn over your neglect in becoming acquainted with God, and take a resolution worthy of the gratitude which you owe to Christ, who, in the excess of love, forgets himself and immolates himself to passing his life with you.

Spiritual Reading.—Rodriguez. Part I. Treatise V. Chap. 1 and 2.

How amiable are thy tabernacles, O Lord of Hosts! why can I not dwell forever in thy presence, O divine Spouse! (Ps. lxxxiii.)

VISIT.

Recollect the ideas of this meditation, and resolve to repair your past coldness.

PRACTICE.

When absent from the church, frequently return there in the secret of your heart, offering all you do, as acts expressive of gratitude.

SIXTH DAY.

TO HONOR THE ACTIVE LIFE OF THE SACRED HEART IN THE BLESSED SACRAMENT.

Meditation.

First Prelude.—Represent to your mind, Jesus Christ in the blessed sacrament, under the figure of the Good Shepherd, who carries in his bosom a wounded and dying sheep, he heals and restores vigor to him, by pressing him to his divine Heart.

Second Prelude.—Beseech him to impart to you an ardent zeal for contributing with all your capacity, to extending his knowledge and love.

FIRST POINT.

If you possess sincere love for Jesus Christ, it will

be impossible for your heart to avoid feeling a deep interest in all that concerns him. That affectionate Heart does not remain in idleness in the blessed sacrament, he is laboring therein with an activity that equals his love. The glory of his heavenly Father and the salvation of souls are the grand motives which retain Christ in the Eucharist. From that silent tabernacle in which he has fixed his abode, Jesus Christ governs and directs his Church. At that divine table, he nourishes and invigorates the sheep of which he is the pastor, and those sheep are holy souls, of whom he has become the master, the physician, and the protector. There, like a skilful preceptor and attentive tutor he instructs and comforts them, and strengthens their weakness.— There, sometimes with the authority of a master, sometimes with the mildness and benevolence of a friend, he invites souls to him that are infirm, dying, or dead to his love, and mingling like a true father, frightful threats with the most tender promises, he gives them a new life, health and youth. In a word, all the benefits we receive, come to us from that source, his Heart is the immense ocean of light, love, health and spiritual riches which are dispersed over the whole mystical body of the Church.

If then, devout soul, you desire to belong to that amiable and adorable Heart, clothe yourself with its spirit, participate in its labors, let its interest become yours. You are the slave of Jesus Christ, he purchased you at a great price: your duty, therefore, is to charge yourself with whatsoever your strength will allow you to undertake for his relief. You are his daughter; you should therefore conceive a heart-felt interest in the concerns of your Father. You are his Spouse; how disgraceful to you, if, contenting yourself with the quiet repose of his love, you do not exert every effort to contribute to his glory? Nothing, therefore, can dispense you from laboring with all your powers, for the glory of God and the welfare of souls. You will, ere long, perceive how the work is possible to you: for the moment be convinced that it is your positive obligation. Take a rapid glance over all your thoughts, words and actions that are past, and observe whether you have ever directed any one towards the grand object of glorifying your Master, your Father, and your Spouse, by promoting the love of God in others. *Ah! it is verily impossible to love Jesus Christ, without acting for him!* Here form your resolution. Blessed is that religious community in which all will simultaneously adopt the above resolution.

SECOND POINT.

The active life of the divine Heart in the Eucharist is a model of the *active life that you are capable of observing.* The great works of his glory are here accomplished silently, without the renown that accompanied the fulfilment of his functions during his mortal life, intending *them* to serve as examples to apostolical men. *Here,* all is the effect of a peaceable, interior grace: thoughts, counsels, salutary emotions which he creates in the heart with an ineffable sweetness, and a patience proof to every trial, and which he afterwards fructifies and fortifies with an abundance of secret graces in those who approach him.

Behold, O Spouse of Jesus Christ, the portion of the apostolate which may be yours. It is not necessary for you to ascend the pulpit; a pious conversation, a prudent advice, a friendly prayer, a word pronounced in a tone of interest, a look of tenderness and compassion toward your equals, may accomplish much for God. Ah! we sometimes employ artifice and address, to insinuate ourselves in the favor of our companions, even so far (occasionally) as to make little scruple of displeasing God: why should not the love of Jesus Christ adopt a similar industry in reconciling two persons, in preventing a fault, or disregard of rule, or to save some simple and imprudent soul from danger?

The second means of the active life of Jesus Christ in the sacrament, is example. The secret life of Jesus Christ in the same sacrament is the compendium of all the divine examples of his mortal life, to numerous souls the fruitful source of the most sublime perfections. But your holy examples, work, so to speak, still more fruitfully than those of Jesus Christ in this sacrament. His examples are not effectual in all persons because all do not attach themselves to considering them; but yours will strike such of your companions even, as would not desire to see them. Hold it as certain, that the greatest difficulty in introducing a holy practice into a monastery, consists in finding one who will set the first example. Dare, when such an occasion presents, to aspire to so enviable a distinction and to such great merit before the Heart of your God.

Finally, *prayer* is another means of the active life of Jesus Christ in the blessed sacrament. He is therein constantly as our advocate and victim, offering for us, to God the Father, both his powerful mediation and his own person. Therefore employ prayer, that efficacious and indeed infallible means of promoting God's greater glory. Use this mild method, while practicing all the others: it is the supplement of the whole; for the employment of other methods is not always in our power. Ah! did you but know what a multitude of souls owe their salvation to the fervent prayers of holy persons who are consecrated to God! Unite your heart to the Heart of Jesus. Offer yourself secretly with him as a victim for the salvation of souls; let that be the principal object in the good that you are able to perform, as in the evil that you will be forced to endure. From this moment and forever offer yourself to the *active Heart* of Jesus, and consider this as a certain means of obtaining the greatest favors from his love.

Spiritual Reading.—Rodriguez. Part III. I Treatise. Chap. 9 and 10.

ASPIRATION.

Amiable Jesus, may thy holy name be sanctified throughout the wide universe; may every soul perform thy adorable will.

VISIT.

Offer to God, the Father, the divine Heart of his dear Son; offer it to him for the Holy Church, for the conversion of all sinners, and for the perseverance of the just. Let it be your particular intention in this offering, with that of your good actions, to intercede for the special sanctification of the persons belonging to your community.

PRACTICE.

From the beginning of the day, and several times during the day, you will offer your actions for all persons who have given you any occasion of suffering.

SEVENTH DAY.

HONOR THE HIDDEN LIFE OF THE SACRED HEART IN THE
BLESSED SACRAMENT.

Meditation.

First Prelude.—Recollect yourself profoundly; banish every worldly thought, forget the broad universe itself, and imagine that you are alone in that wilderness, to which he withdrew during forty days. You are there, *not* to receive instructions that relate to christians in general, but *such* as particularly concern persons in your state.

Second Prelude.—*Now*, redouble your fervor, and supplicate him not to hide nor refuse you any of those lofty virtues to which he called you when giving you a religious vocation—and that he may grant you lights proportioned to the sublimity of his graces.

FIRST POINT.

The hidden life of Jesus Christ is one of the most sublime examples that God presents us in the blessed sacrament. Who would say, on seeing Jesus Christ, hidden beneath the lowly appearances, that it is nevertheless he who moves and governs the firmament—the sun, the stars, angels, men, and all other creatures? Nothing is here displayed of that prodigious exercise of his providence, wisdom and power; Jesus Christ remains here solely to promote the secret interests of his Heart with souls. His life is one of silence, solitude, humility, patience and obscurity; a secret and interior life. In such models, we must consider that *hidden life* in which he so solicitously desires that we should imitate him.

The foundation of this *hidden life* is the *interior spirit*, which should be the soul of all your deeds, a spirit which never acts at hazard, nor through human motives, but which has God alone in view; a spirit, which judges of nought by appearances, but upon reality and real substance, and before which, all that is not God is but vanity and emptiness; a spirit, which seeks not to do much, but to do well; a spirit, which regards nothing as insignificant when there is a question of pleasing God; a spirit, consequently, which springs from God, and which, (the pure love of God being its sole guide,) *asks him alone for its recompense.* You will easily comprehend how necessary this INTERIOR SPIRIT is to your perfection.—Commence from this moment to form practical resolutions; for, if your first efforts do not tend to the acquisition of this *interior spirit*, you will never arrive at that *life hidden* in Jesus Christ, concerning which St. Paul, and so many succeeding Saints, have uttered such wonderful things.

In this hidden life, the religious soul, having by means of the spirit that animates her, banished the world completely from her heart, loves to conceal from the world, all the good that this spirit may accomplish within her, and to be hidden even to herself. This is not a soul under illusion, which, guided by a deceitful spirit, withdraws from usual and general duties and obligations; but, ever submissive to whatsoever charity and her holy rule require from her, she nevertheless loves and seeks silence, solitude and recollection. She dreads seeing and being seen by the world without, lest human considerations might stealthily intrude into the motives, or into some circumstances of her actions. She desires and wishes no other witness of her virtues or her sufferings than God; for this reason she renounces all the vain consolations of the world, from which she endeavors to

hide as much as she can, whatever might discover to
it either her interior joy, or her secret trials. She
fears nothing so much as those singularities which
commonly result from illusions. Unless an indispensable necessity exacts it, she carefully avoids discovering those virtues, even for which she feels most
attraction, and that she would practice with the highest perfection. She would wish that no one ever
thought of her. She never interferes with what
does not concern her; and were it possible, she would
choose in all things, whatever would prove most
mean and obscure, and what the others would not
wish to have. Obedience alone has all the keys of
her soul, and whilst this virtue does not oblige her,
she could pass entire years in a religious house, without giving occasion to speak about her.

Compare this style of *life*, with that of Jesus
Christ in the sacrament; it is the same kind of life.
Compare it with that which you daily lead, and consider the difference; but however great it may be,
beware of allowing yourself to become dejected.—
Entreat the divinely hidden Heart of your Spouse, to
excite in yours a desire full of confidence and courage.

SECOND POINT.

The fruits of this *hidden life* are as much more
precious, as that life is the most excellent.

1. It is a sure and easy means of arriving at great
purity of conscience and a great detachment from
the world and self. What is the source of your defects? They most frequently arise from occasions
presented to your senses and bad habits, by exterior
objects. This happens in acts of impatience, of
curiosity, of vanity, etc. The study of this *hidden
life* by exciting within you a love of retreat and the

withdrawal from all superfluous cares, takes from you an infinite number of occasions. This study, also, leads you insensibly to reflect often upon yourself and observe the dispositions and emotions of your heart: and these considerations induce you to avoid a countless number of faults, which you do not perceive, until after their commission. Hence, attachment to the world and to ourselves diminishes by degrees, because the custom of thinking on the former objects of our attachments, on our tastes, our irregular habits, and the danger of taking complacency in them, diminish at the same time by rapid degrees.

2. Peace and repose, at least in the *superior* part of the soul, are infallibly the fruit of the *hidden life.* In what has been said above, you may easily perceive many causes of this interior tranquility. Whence come, (says St. James the Apostle,) so many tempests which rise in your miserable hearts? is it not from your passions? You see, therefore, what an amount of aliment the study of this hidden life removes from your passions, and what progress it causes you to ensure towards that immutable peace of soul, which you so much desire.

3. The *hidden life* is indispensably requisite to a spouse of Jesus Christ for acquiring THE SPIRIT OF PRAYER. The spirit of mental prayer can never be accorded to a soul who is during the time allotted to that exercise filled with herself, occupied with a crowd of frivolous thoughts, and absorbed with distractions during the remainder of the day. Here then is the genuine method of putting an end, once and forever, to the complaints which you form concerning the imperfection of your prayers; it cannot fail of being conformable to the manner in which

you pass the day. How often has experience taught you this verity.

4. In the order which God commonly pursues, interior consolations and divine favors of the most signal excellence accompany this *hidden life*. He who knows it not, fancies it a life of melancholy; he who is acquainted with it finds in it, if not immediately, ere long, pleasures eminently superior to such as the world offers. Recall to mind all that you have read or learned concerning it, when reading the biographies of holy souls.

What say you now to so desirable a boon? Awaken a desire of its possession, and employ it for overcoming the repugnances of a blinded self-love? Take a strong resolution to think of it frequently, in order to renew these pious resolutions daily. Offer yourself to the divine Heart, implore its grace, and pause and examine yourself every consecutive day on the resolutions inspired by this meditation.

Spiritual Reading.—Rodriguez. Part II. Treatise 1. Chap. 8 and 9.

ASPIRATION.

Dilectus meus mihi, et ego illi. O Jesus, the supreme and only good of my soul! Let me live solely for thee, and grant that thou also be wholly mine.

VISIT.

Recall to mind some of the preceding considerations, and entreat Jesus to give you courage to make trial of the truth of the glorious hopes, which this meditation will have awakened.

PRACTICE.

Observe silence with a most particular attention, and carefully avoid meddling in any way with affairs that do not concern you.

6

EIGHTH DAY.

TO HONOR THE LIFE OF GLORY OF THE SACRED HEART IN THE HOLY EUCHARIST.

Meditation.

First Prelude.—Imagine you see in the opened bosom of Jesus Christ his divine Heart blazing with flames of love, like a fiery furnace, in which elect hearts are liquidated like wax, and purified like fine gold.

Second Prelude.—Offer your heart to these divine ardors with perfect resignation, presenting yourself before that divine Saviour as quite ready and fully disposed to acquiesce in whatever he wishes to do with you.

FIRST POINT.

The glory of the divine Heart is displayed in that *power of love*, which it infuses into souls in this sacrament, and which renders them capable, notwithstanding their natural weakness, of conquering and overthrowing their most terrible enemies. Recall to your memory the numerous beautiful victories gained by a host of admirable Virgins whose memoirs you have frequently perused. *They* were feeble women like yourselves; the dangers, troubles, repugnances, indecisions and temptations in which they were many times found, are a certain proof of this. It was in this sacrament of love (principally) that such prodigious changes were effected. Think what horror seized you when perusing those heroic traits of charity, obedience, mortification and self-hatred! Can you contemplate without being lost in admiration, that mute courage, that meekness, that joy in the midst of long, cruel and unworthy persecutions, during painful maladies—or fearful and continual temptation? Now, how did such feeble creatures attain to the loss of all sentiment of self-compassion, all repugnance for the most painful acts, all sensibility of soul to the most delightful and most innocent inclinations of our nature? Ah! they found their strength in the blessed sacrament; and that power was a *power of love*.

This then, is properly speaking, the *glory* of the *Sacred Heart*, whose ardent love enabled them to surmount such obstacles. If you love Jesus Christ you now comprehend how you should glorify him. What idea takes possession of you when you experience a greater desire of corresponding to his love? Hold as illusions all that will not prove, or will not produce in you the contempt of self, the renouncement of your will, and a blind and loving submission to the divine will. The entire ruin of your self-love is the perfect triumph to which that divine Heart aspires, by means of all the graces that he lavishes upon you in the sacrament of love. Therefore take the resolution of presenting to Jesus Christ, at each visit that you pay to the blessed sacrament, and especially on your days of communion, some *deed of victory gained over yourself*. You cannot find a more appropriate means of corresponding with his love towards you, since this is the *special* interest of the GLORY of his Sacred Heart in the sacrament.

SECOND POINT.

The glory which properly appertains to the Sacred Heart in the sacrament, manifests itself by the *strength of its love*, whereby it raises souls to a height which draws them near to divinity itself. The marvellous victory which love gains over souls, and on which you meditated in the first point, operates in them a change, or rather, transforms them totally. They no longer live but in Jesus Christ, or, as says St. Paul, Jesus Christ lives in them; so that even before being delivered from the infirmities of this mortal life, they lead a life wholly divine. Observe their exterior deportment; what angelic modesty; what unchangeable affability; what amiable meekness, regularity, prudence and sanctity their every action breathes? Could you enter their minds, you would fancy yourself in a kingdom of light, but of that invisible light with which Paradise is resplendent.— The just views, the sublime knowledge which they possess of God and of his mysteries, surpass all expression. Could you penetrate their hearts, what amazement you would experience in beholding the purity, strength, peace, and sanctity of their affections! Their souls have become thrones of divine grace and love, which reign in them supremely. A Gertrude, a Catherine of Sienna, a Theresa, and numerous other souls, enriched with the interior treasures of Jesus Christ, could make known to you how great is the glory of God, the lover of our souls, who elevates them from their native degradation to so perfect a state.

Recreate and nourish your souls with the contemplation of these admirable objects. But not to be discouraged, nor despair of yourself, remember that in the house of God your Father, there are many mansions—which means, that if, through humility, you ought to aspire to such sublime gifts, you are nevertheless obligated by your state, to request some of them for yourself. Renounce without regret, whatever there may be extraordinary in these endow-

ments; but aspire to the gifts of great self-abnega-
tion, constant regularity, sovereign contempt of the
spirit of the world, unbounded patience, and profound recollection. You have a genuine title to
these presents, and the divine Heart will never refuse
them to you, if you desire them with sincerity.—
These gifts will also produce a change in you, which
will exalt you infinitely above your present misery,
and at the same time will *glorify* in your elevation,
the STRENGTH OF THE LOVE OF JESUS CHRIST.—
How long will you remain in this grovelling state,
attached heart and mind to this vile, miserable and
obscure world? Ah! in how many poor handmaids
of the Lord—as are so many souls who dwell amid
the profane world—is our Lord laboring by his love
to establish his glory? And shall he find nought
but dishonor in *your* heart, *the heart* of a *Spouse?*
Courage, then, take a firm resolution, and prepare
yourself; so that on the approaching festival of his
divine Heart, your communion of that day may prove
to you the principle of a new felicity, and may contribute to the glory of Jesus Christ.

Spiritual Reading.—Rodriguez. Part II. Treatise I. Chap. 19 and 20.

ASPIRATION.

I live no more, but Jesus lives in me!

VISIT.

O God, have patience with me, and I will endeavor
to repair thy injured glory.

PRACTICE.

Yield to the frequent inspiration you have experienced to make a certain required sacrifice, and
thus begin the glory of Jesus in your heart.

NINTH DAY.

HONOR THE LIFE OF CONSUMMATION OF JESUS CHRIST IN THE
BLESSED SACRAMENT.

Meditation.

First Prelude.—Contemplate our Lord in the Eucharist, as a lamb laid on the altar of sacrifice; from his Heart, as from a brasier, emanate flames by which he is consumed as a victim.

Second Prelude.—Entreat him to bestow on you a special grace for comprehending the price of his sacrifice, and the degree of courage you need for immolating yourself unreservedly to his love.

FIRST POINT.

In the noblest of the ancient sacrifices, namely, the Holocaust, the victim was totally consumed.— Jesus Christ was not contented with one means only, of sacrificing himself for your sake, but he was victimized in every manner possible to him. Fastened to the ignominious cross through devotedness to us, what was there left for him to bestow, either in goods, honor, or his very life. Having reviewed step by step all that Jesus Christ lavished upon you, make the following reflection. During that cruel agony in which the rage of his executioners spared him not, so thorough was their work of outrage, that his Sacred Heart alone remained intact. That Heart intended to have its share in the sacrifice, and it may be said that the crowning deed of the sacrifice was enacted *in* that divine Heart. It was voluntarily rent and opened—your oblation should resemble his. Compute the sacrifices that you have made—how many of them were hardly commenced—how many more that were lost in sterile and inefficacious desires.

Now, having offered him so little, you do not belong
to him in any greater degree than before, for, in this
case, *the end alone being considered*, whosoever gives
not *all* gives *nothing!* Consider well the reason, if
we do not give the heart to God we give him nought,
because he esteems the heart the most, and prefers it
to all things united, and *we do not yield him the
heart*, unless we immolate it to him entirely and
without any reserve. Hence, the *consummation*,
such as Jesus exacts it from you in your sacrifice,
consists in an entire and sincere resignation of your
whole being, with the unchangeable resolution of
allowing him to guide you according to his own good
will and pleasure. In this state of consummation,
you are obligated to consider yourself as in no-wise
under your own control, but believe that in the trials
as well as in the consolations which he sends you,
God only disposes of what belongs to him alone.

Once more, contemplate with what infinite generosity Jesus Christ gave and consummated himself
for you. Had he any need of belonging to you, to
conduce to his happiness? On the contrary, where
could *you* find happiness on earth except in being all
to him. Interrogate yourself by a *short* but serious
examination, for your conscience will unhesitatingly
reply. What is the particular that has principally
been wanting among so many others, which the Lord
wills you should sacrifice? Ah! commonly there is
one thing which our self-love reserves and hence
renders our sacrifices defective. Apply to this important point the different lights and sentiments with
which God may inspire you. O Sacred Heart, divinely prodigal of thyself, let thy grace enable me to
imitate thy example!

Jesus Christ never subtracted nor diminished aught of the universality of his sacrifice in your behalf. Very far from this, as many times as he renews his sacrifice in the mass, so frequently he reiterates and consummates his gift. What constancy, and what perpetuity of the most perfect love! Now recall to mind the sacrifices that you have so often presented to Jesus Christ. Alas! of nearly all, scarce a trace or vestige remains in your heart. Remember those strong resolutions of leading a recollected, regular, and patient life—those intended sacrifices of your affections, repugnances, self-love and human respect—with all those brilliant commencements of applications, diligence and exactitude in mental prayer and spiritual affairs? Whither are they fled? By whom were they ravished from you? Ah! may you not justly reproach yourself with infidelity and inconstancy, and give way to excessive confusion and profound regret. But shall this confusion and sorrow again prove useless? What would have become of this lost world, had Jesus Christ, as his impious and insensate enemies challenged him, descended from the cross or had that loving Heart closed its sacred wound, precious source of meekness, courage, and love for his faithful souls! Of what an attractive object, and powerful stimulus your timid and uncertain hopes would now be deprived.

Approach therefore, this blessed fountain of life, in the transport of a holy despair. Without thy aid, O omnipotent Heart of my Spouse, whom I have so often deceived, what resource would rest to me in my extreme misery? Now, excite your sorrow, and at the same time animate and kindle within you an ardent desire of being eternally faithful to him; and

from the depths of your desolate heart, cry out:
Yes, O my God, I must absolutely obtain on this day
the grace of constant perseverance in my good resolutions. You can do nothing more acceptable to
that divine Heart, than to present yourself to him,
inflamed with such a desire. Let this reflection
arouse your confidence, by *desiring ardently*, you
will certainly *obtain*. Here, invoke the aid of the
merciful Mother of that thrice merciful Heart; and
conclude this meditation by an offering which includes and renews all those which you have made
previous to this day.

Spiritual Reading.—Rodriguez. I Part. VIII
Treatise. Chap. 3 and 4.

ASPIRATION.

(Beware of any distrust, as a highly dangerous
temptation,) and say:

"In thee, O God, do I put my trust, let me never
be confounded."

VISIT.

Reflect on the price of your redemption, and renew the resolutions and petitions of the morning
meditation.

PRACTICE.

Fidelity and diligence in all your spiritual duties.

PREPARATION FOR THE FEAST OF THE SACRED HEART OF JESUS.

The object for which our Lord taught this "*devotion to his Sacred Heart*," was, to inflame the hearts
of all the faithful with love to him, and to engage
all such as are devout to him, to repair by their most

perfect acts of love, and by the most tender and respectful homage, the injuries which he receives, particularly in the most blessed sacrament, from numerous souls who persist in their ingratitude. He intends also, that whatever you do to honor his sacred Heart on this festival, should be animated with the same sentiments.

On the eve of the feast, if practicable, devote a half-hour in a special visit to the altar, and dispose your heart to becoming sentiments, by the following meditation.

FOR THE VIGIL OF THE FEAST.

ON THE INESTIMABLE MERITS OF THE MOST HOLY HEART OF JESUS.

Meditation.

First Prelude.—Imagine you perceive the sacred Heart of Jesus, in the manner it appeared to M. M. Alacoque, surrounded by flames, encircled by a crown of thorns, and surmounted by a cross.

Second Prelude.—Supplicate your divine Spouse to condescend to enlighten you, and make you capable of honoring him with the sentiments of respect and love that he has a right to expect.

FIRST POINT.

The divinity to which the sacred Heart of Jesus is united in the Incarnation.

The divine nature is not only personally united to the soul of Jesus Christ, but also to his adorable body. So that, by this personal union, his Heart is found united to the divinity of the eternal word of the Father, and was thus, as it will be eternally, a divine Heart, and the Heart of God. God, is therefore, the principle which animates that Heart, and its life is not only human but also divine. But all the honors we, as well as all the faithful offer to it, relate to its divinity. His adorable Heart merits by an equal title, all the religious worship and adorations that the Church prescribes, towards the adorable body of the Man-God. When, therefore, O devout soul, you prostrate before the sacred image of the Heart of your divine Spouse, reflect to what a sublime object you are addressing your veneration, and habituate yourself to animating your acts of devotion, with sentiments of the reverence which become the divinity of so great a Spouse.

How vast, how rich, how divine the quantity and quality of the treasures that emanate from that Heart of the Man-God. O Heart, pure with the purity of God; holy, with the holiness of God; charitable, with the charitableness of God; strong with the omnipotence of God. Heart, meek, liberal, faithful, generous with the meekness, liberality, fidelity and generosity of God himself—Heart, therefore adorable and amiable, as God is adorable and amiable, on this day perhaps, I for the first time begin to be acquainted with thee. Ah! my Saviour and my Spouse, grant that my heart may be found worthy of being offered to thine. Yes, religious soul, God requires this of you. The Heart of your Spouse was created so noble, pure, holy, faithful and strong, in order to become the perfect model on which yours should be corrected and formed.

Compare that wretched heart with all the all-excellent Heart of Jesus Christ; what an immeasurable difference! But whence comes this frightful defor-

mity of heart. Alas! the response is easy, *every*
human heart is defective, and for this reason, you
should propose the most holy Heart of Jesus as your
model. And what is wanting in thee, O divine
Heart, of all which forms my greatest necessities?
O living temple of the divinity, my heart is obscured
with shadows, whilst in thee resides the fulness of
wisdom; my heart is weak, but in thine dwells the
all-powerful; my heart is timid, afflicted, oppressed,
and in a desperate and mortal craving to be relieved
and satisfied; and in thee alone, and by conformity
to thee am I bound to seek, and am resolved to seek
in the future, my real happiness.

SECOND POINT.

The love of which the Sacred Heart ever has been
and ever will be the throne.

The heart is extremely active: and Jesus Christ's
is in this respect similar to ours. O unspeakable
wonder! not only is his Heart animated with an ardent
love towards his divine Father, but also towards us.
O religious yet infervent soul, enter upon this consideration, impatient to acquire thoroughly the secret
history of love in that divine Heart. That divine
Heart commenced loving you when commencing to
live, and for your sake it immediately adopted all
those emotions that constitute the occupation and
toil of the Heart that loves. Present yourself in
spirit at the manger, enter into the Heart of that
infant-God; in that little Heart love is already great,
and it may be said of him, that he "marched forth
like a giant in the beginning of his career," that is,
in the career of love. Oh! how many painful,
fatiguing, and forced steps, during the whole course
of his life! Consider the movements of our own

hearts when seized with a violent attraction. Subtract from this extremely active passion all that is morally imperfect in us: all that remains the Heart of the divine Spouse experienced for you really and sensibly. Love is denominated a fire, because it communicates a genuine and sensible heat to the heart; and when deeply affected with this passion, the human heart becomes heated so violently, that we have read of Saints who were compelled to use cold water and even ice to temper its ardors. It was in such a condition that the Heart of Jesus Christ lived for you during so many years. To all the agitations of a soul that loves, the heart more than any other organ, responds by its own movements. A strong desire causes it to palpitate with violence—coldness and absence wither its tenderness, ingratitude wounds it like a dagger, compassion and pity bind it up, loss dejects it and throws it into a mortal languor.

And you, ever present to the thought of that most loving Redeemer, who not only witnesses your inconstancy but foresaw it, *you*, excite in that tender and susceptible Heart all the various torments of love. Ah! had you been at least *sometimes* as holy as he desired! could I but exhibit to you, not the anguish, but the delight that tender Heart experienced in undergoing the labor and fatigue which his love led him to undertake for you! Could I but express to you how, while loving you, it dilated, how it palpitated with joy, how it was consumed with the most lively and delicious transports!

Yet, this Heart endowed with such an exquisite sensibility, is not less infinitely and imperturbably happy; but its sensibility towards pure, faithful and loving souls, far from being lost turns to its glory. You may yet be to him an object, exciting those divine and delectable movements, that divine and gentle fire with which it is burning for you in the midst of its GLORY. Is not this feeble sketch of the tenderness of the divine Heart towards you, the faithful picture of what you owe to that Heart, hitherto misunderstood and neglected? And that Heart in recompense for so many merits, expects of you a worship of admiration, praise, thanksgiving, and chiefly of desire, with a constant and unchangeable resolution to constitute his love the never-varying occupation of your heart.

The sorrows of the Heart of Jesus.

"No," says the devout Thomas a Kempis, "No, without grief we do not dwell in love;" but the whole life of the Heart of Jesus Christ was a cross and martyrdom." We will, however, restrict this consideration to the share that that divine Heart experienced in the latest sufferings of the PASSION. Remember, therefore, O religious, the sentiments of horror and of compassion that you have more than once experienced when meditating on the impious and cruel affronts and outrages, endured by the adorable body of Jesus, and be assured that all these pains concentrated were but the least portion of his anguish: the most atrocious, was *the secret martyrdom of his Heart.* He began to undergo this martyrdom at his entrance into the garden of Olives, and he only terminated it in his dying sighs upon the Cross. The heart, which is the source of love, is likewise, the source of sorrow; so that no trouble or ill, occasions us sensible suffering, but *when,* and in as much as the *heart* participates in it: but never hope to comprehend all that the Heart of Jesus suf-

fered in his Passion. You know quite well what
portion and in what way it partook of them, by fear,
wearisomeness, sadness in the expectation of the
torments prepared for him, in the privation of all
consolation and of all assistance, and by the hatred
of the sins and ingratitude of men; but bear in
mind, that all the ills that he really experienced in
his body, only caused him as it were consecutive suffering, *but his Heart endured them all at once.*

Reflect again, that however great was the sensibility of the body physically, the physical and moral
sensibility of his Heart was incomparably greater
and more exquisite; and whatsoever were the sufferings and torments which he endured, the Heart more
than any other member of the body, experienced all
its activity; that in fine, the cruelty of his executioners, in all their barbarity, was but a refinement
upon human cruelty, but that in the Passion of his
Heart, the most cruel, the most ferocious, and at the
same time, the *dearest* of his executioners, was his
own eternal love. Who, therefore, can imagine its
anguish, its throbs, its languor, its oppression, its
weakness, spasms, mortal heat and deadly coldness?
Ah! I have no power here to express my emotions;
and what I feel is still inferior to what I believe!
Jesus Christ intended to bestow on us a visible sign
of the secret martyrdom of his Heart; he performed
a miracle, and that miracle was the prodigious sweat
of blood which flowed from his whole body. O my
Jesus! O Heart burning with love, and satiated with
opprobriums and suffering, how shall I compute my
debt towards you? Is it not love for love, sufferings
for sufferings? But, feeble and delicate as I am,
how can I cancel this debt, unless thou, O Jesus,
deign to impart to me a share in thy courage? Ah!

grant me love, grant me a great love. Let love control me: love will teach me to suffer and will aid me to suffer in imitation of thy sacred Heart.

———

For the Day of the Feast.

The feast of the Heart of Jesus, is also the feast of his love. His intention in establishing it, was to obtain that our hearts be touched and awakened to a correspondence with his love. Hasten, therefore, when commencing this day, to offer your heart and all the good actions you will perform, to the amiable Heart of your Spouse, and renew the offering several times during the day. It should be passed in silence and holy recollection, and employed in loving and honoring Jesus Christ, and uniting yourself to his sufferings. Offer your communion, in reparation for all the communions you and all christians have made in coldness, or in unworthy dispositions.

But beware, chiefly, on this day, of a very common error, viz: of falling into disgust and lukewarmness, because after a few good works, you do not experience sensible devotion. Should you act thus, you risk gaining nothing—act candidly and cheerfully —without omitting all that you would do, were you filled with devout fervor.

———

For the Feast of the Sacred Heart.

First Prelude.—Imagine you see the Heart of Jesus cruelly pierced, surrounded by flames, environed by a crown of sharp thorns, and surmounted by a cross. Hear our Lord explaining to you these mysterious symbols which express his love, and what he suffered from the ingratitude of men.

Second Prelude.—Entreat him to disclose to you, and give you grace to sympathize in these two equally incomprehensible excesses, of love in him and ingratitude in us: so that you may adopt a strong resolution of satisfying as much as you are able, for what is due to that Heart, so loving and so little loved.

FIRST POINT.

The sentiments which animate the divine Heart of Jesus towards men, are those of the deepest and most sincere love. The love of Jesus Christ in the sacrament, is like our sun at the hour of noon—in its highest point of light and heat. In this sacrament *Jesus Christ loves us*—and this pronounces the whole, and gives a response to every question that we can ask of him. Why comes he in it? Because he *loves* us. How is he in it? Like a God that *loves* us. What does he demand in it? What *love* requires. Why is he so prodigiously multiplied therein? Why does he remain in it so long? Why does he thus conceal himself? Because *he loves—yes, because he loves!* On the cross, love reigned with justice, nay more, it was subservient to justice. Here love reigns alone, to it all else is subject. Wisdom, power, providence, immensity, all contribute, all are in requisition to satisfy love. O blinded man!—Behold what your Saviour is for you in this sacrament.

And do you not daily experience it? Sinful souls, look how he receives you: his complaints, reprimands, reproaches, and even his terrors, all spring from love.

Lukewarm and imperfect souls, did he ever banish
you from his presence? Does he not on the contrary, offer you remedies, consolations and encouragement? To you, pure and fervent souls, it chiefly
appertains to render testimony to the world concerning the Heart of Jesus in this sacrament. What
condescension, benevolence, and forgetfulness of his
majesty! What complacency—interior colloquies,
and caresses! What a torrent of delights!

Pause here, religious soul, and apply all these reflections to yourself. Take the place which was formerly yours, or that becomes you at the present day,
among *sinners*, the *imperfect*, or *the fervent*. The
sentiments which these reflections should awaken,
will be principally sentiments of admiration, of
praise, of thanksgiving. Ah! mayhap, you have
never during the whole course of your life, thanked
shat divine Heart as you ought, for such an excess
of love.

SECOND POINT.

What sentiments do the greater portion of mankind entertain towards Jesus Christ in the sacrament
of the altar? See how many there are who do not
even know that for love of them, God is reduced to
such a lowly condition. Yet, Jesus Christ in the
Eucharist has no other occupation but love for them
all. Among these some are voluntarily blind,
although they are invited to seek and become acquainted with his loving condescension. *This*, is
truly a monstrous contempt of his love; and yet it is
not the most cruel offence that the greater portion of
christians offer to the love of that divine Heart.
These ungrateful persons *profess to believe* the unspeakable love of their God in the sacrament; but
how do they *correspond with it?*

Number in imagination, devout soul, the neglects, the irreverences, the failures in respect and the insults which christians oblige him to suffer in this august sacrament; again consider the number, even the quality of the persons who add to these injuries. At the view of so many outrages, conceive a holy indignation and after that, review your *own conduct.* Yourself, I ask, how have *you treated that divine Lover?* Review your years that have fled—it may be that your ingratitude has kept pace with your age! How dreadful, if the purity, the devotion, the fervor of your first communions have diminished more and more! Alas! overwhelmed with confusion, cast yourself in spirit before the throne of his love, implore an increase of light in order that you may recognise and detest your deeds, and an abundance of grace for forming the most generous resolutions.

THIRD POINT.

What are the sentiments, which are excited in that divine Heart, by such black ingratitude on the part of men?

To succeed in comprehending it, think first what these sentiments might be in accordance with simple *justice.* You know how the ingratitude of the Hebrews was punished who despised God's residence among them in the Temple. He overthrew their Temple, caused it to be razed to its foundations, and protested that he would abandon their nation forever. The Christians would merit similar treatment, having been more highly favored than were the Jews, but the love of the divine Heart infinitely surpasses our deepest ingratitude. What patience on his part, what charity, what unalterable peace! He is at this present time the Lamb full of meekness and mute beneath the knife of him who abuses and immolates him.

Sometimes he has secretly complained to some privileged souls, but these very complaints are proofs of excessive love. He one day said to the venerable M. M. Alacoque, when complaining of the ingratitude of men: "This ingratitude is more painful to me than were all the torments of my Passion. I am so sensible to it, that would men but love me with a love equal to that I entertain for them, I would consider all that I have hitherto done for them as nothing, and I would do, were it possible to me, still greater things. But I am only met with coldness and repugnance, in return for my eagerness to load them with benefits." Do these loving complaints of God make any impression on you? "But what is most painful to me," added our divine Saviour, "is that I am thus treated by hearts formally consecrated to me."

Jesus Christ addresses you, religious soul, who art cold, unfaithful, insensible to such outrages. Ah! be filled with tender gratitude for so much love, a heartfelt sorrow for such innumerable acts of ingratitude, and a supreme desire for repairing, and atoning for your offences, by acts of homage and of love.— These three sentiments should be the characteristics of a heart really devout towards the adorable Heart of Jesus.

Take the resolution of offering yourself to him. Ask of God the grace of making this offering in a worthy manner, and thus dispose yourself to an entire oblation and sacrifice of your whole being.

———

Conclude your thanksgiving after the holy communion, by an act of consecration of your heart to

Jesus Christ, and after, by an act of Atonement, for our ingratitude and for those of all mankind.

During the day, make as many aspirations of love as possible—but let them be short and heartfelt.

Read anew, and with attention, the meditation of the eve.

Act of Consecration

TO THE

SACRED HEART OF JESUS.

Divine Jesus, thou didst promise that when thou wert "*lifted up, thou wouldst draw all hearts to thee;*" and on the cross, at the moment of the consummation of thy last sacrifice, thou didst *begin* to accomplish that consoling promise the effects of which, thy holy Spouse the Church, has experienced in every succeeding age: but thou didst reserve its especial and full accomplishment to the *present time*, drawing souls to thee by the manifestation of thy Sacred Heart, the symbol and throne of thy love, the centre of every perfection, the bond which unites all hearts, and the object best calculated to captivate and inflame them with the sacred fire of charity, which thou didst bring from heaven!

Thou knowest, O God of love, that our sole desire is, to glorify thy adorable Heart, to love and induce others to love that Heart which has been so liberal to men, and which is so little loved in return; that Heart which was exhausted and consumed to testify its tenderness, and which, for such excessive love, and so numerous favors, receives but ingratitude, indifference and contempt.

Thy charity, O amiable Saviour, urges us to offer thee love for love; and with this intent, *we* humbly prostrate at thy feet, devote and consecrate ourselves to thee as spouses and victims, with all who are united to us in the worship and charity of thy divine Heart, which we are firmly resolved to honor by every means consistent with the end of our Institute and the spirit of our Constitutions and Rules.

We take the same engagement towards the Immaculate Heart of the blessed Virgin Mary, thy most holy Mother and also ours, and we conjure her with sentiments of filial piety to bear before thy throne the offering and solemn consecration of our persons, and all that we possess.

Sacred Heart of Jesus, our God, our Saviour, and Lord, deign to shed thy influence over us, and all the members of this little society, which is consecrated to thee in a special manner to thy glory, under the auspices, and through the mediation of the most amiable Heart of Mary. Divine Heart, ever burning with love, inflame us with thy heavenly fire; and grant that being united to thee and to one another by the links of tender charity, we may merit, by a constant and unanimous zeal in honoring thee, and imitating thy virtues, to be eternally consummated with thee in thy never-ending unity. Amen.

Act of Atonement
TO THE
SACRED HEART OF JESUS.

O sacred Heart of my adorable Saviour! how great is the extent of that love which makes thee compassionate our miseries! O my God! what goodness on thy part, to become our victim in the adorable Eucharist? and yet, what dost thou find in the hearts of the greater portion of mankind, but opposition to thy will, and ingratitude for thy benefits? Was it not sufficient, O Jesus, for thee once to endure that cruel agony in the garden of Olives, overwhelmed by the weight of our iniquities? Must thou yet be daily exposed to the outrages of so many sinners, who would renew thy mortal agony? What were then, and what are now, the sentiments of thy Heart? and how is it possible there are hearts incapable of being softened by thy love? Humbled and prostrate before thee, O my Redeemer, permit me to make atonement to thy sacred Majesty, for all the injuries which thy children cease not offering thee, and for all the bitterness with which they drench thy Heart. O that I could shed tears of blood in all those places where thou hast been outraged, and by humiliation, repair the criminal abuse of thy graces! Would that I could dispose of the hearts of all men, that I might offer them to thee in sacrifice, and by this homage console thee for the guilty insensibility of those who refuse to know thee, or who knowing thee, do not love thee! I will, at least, O Lord, offer thee my own heart; immolate, consume it as thy victim; but first purify it. Grant that I continue to love but thee, that I may have no motion or life but for thee; that I may consecrate my heart irrevocably to *thine;* and that I may find therein my shelter at all times, my peace at the hour of death, and my beatitude for all eternity. Amen.

Prayer for the Agonizing.

O merciful Jesus, thou whose Heart is inflamed with the most ardent love for souls, I entreat thee by the agony of thy most holy Heart, and by the sufferings of thy immaculate Mother, purify in thy blood, all sinners who are now in their last agony, and such as are destined on this day to breathe their last sigh.

Agonizing Heart of Jesus, have mercy on the dying.

100 days' indulgence, each recitation.

Prayer

TO THE

VENERABLE MGT. MARY ALACOQUE.

Great adorer of the sacred Heart of Jesus, blessed Mary Margaret, thou who didst so love and who wast so ardently loved in return—thou who hast so great influence over this adorable Heart, protect those whom he has chosen to be his Spouses, and exert thy powerful intercession in obtaining the favor we petition, to the greater glory of the sacred Hearts of Jesus and Mary. May we after having imitated thee in bearing the crosses and sufferings of this life, with unalterable love and patience, enjoy the happiness of contemplating the Heart of Jesus, overflowing with love during all eternity. Amen.

PRAYERS FOR NOVENAS.

It is a pious custom to recite the Hymn before each prayer.

Hymn.

Veni, Creator Spiritus,
Mentes tuorum visita,
Imple superna gratia.
Quæ tu creasti pectora.

Qui diceris paracletus,
Donum Dei altissimi,
Fons vivus, ignis, charitas,
Et spiritalis unctio.

Tu septiformis munere,
Dextræ Dei tu digitus,
Tu rite promissum Patris,
Sermone ditans guttura.

Accende lumen sensibus,
Infunde amorem cordibus,
Infirma nostri corporis,
Virtute firmans perpeti.

Hostem repellas longius,
Pacemque dones protinus,
Ductore sic te prævio,
Vitemus omne noxium.

Per te sciamus da Patrem,
Noscamus atque Filium;
Te utriusque Spiritum
Credamus omni tempore.

Deo Patri sit gloria,
Et Filio, qui a mortuis,
Surrexit, ac Paraclito,
In seculorum secula. *Amen.*

℣. Emittte spiritum tuum, et creabuntur.

℟. Et renovabis faciem terræ.

OREMUS.

Deus, qui corda fidelium Sancti Spiritus illustratione docuisti, da nobis in eodem Spiritu recta sapere, et de ejus semper consolatione gaudere. Per Christum Dominum nostrum. Amen.

For the Assumption B. V. M.

Sovereign Ruler of heaven and earth, who didst subvert the laws of nature, in becoming the Son of the ever blessed Virgin Mary, we adore thy infinite power, wisdom and bounty; we return thee thanks for having preserved the soul of Mary from original and actual sin, for having enriched her with thy gifts, and preserved her virginal body from the corruption of the tomb. Forever blessed be the moment in which thou wert pleased to re-unite her most pure body to her happy soul, and receive them into immortal glory.

O compassionate Mother, be our advocate with the adorable Trinity. Behold from thy throne our combats, obtain for us the conquest of our enemies, grace to avoid sin, hearts detached from earthly affections, and the possession of a blessed eternity. Amen.

For the Heart of Mary.

O Lord of infinite clemency, who for the salvation of sinners and help of the afflicted, hast given to the blessed Virgin Mary a heart similar to that of her divine Son, and hast made of it a source of meekness and mercy, grant we beseech thee that those who honor this immaculate Heart, may, through its merits and her intercession, become according to the Heart of Jesus.

Immaculate Heart of Mary, heart ever gentle and compassionate, be our consolation in the trials of life, and our secure refuge in the hour of death. Amen.

For the Seben Dolors.

O, the most desolate of all Mothers! what a terrible sword of sorrow penetrated thy soul! All the blows that Jesus received fell upon thee, each of his wounds rent thy soul: but especially his last adieu revived all thy sorrows. What but supernatural strength sustained thy soul when thou didst witness his expiring sigh? O Mother of love and of sorrow, grant that I may love and suffer in imitation of thy sacred example. Queen of Martyrs let me share thy martyrdom. Love gave thee the cross, may the cross give me holy love; and if to love it be necessary for me to suffer and die, obtain for me the grace of loving all that comes from God, even though it be sufferings and *death*. Amen.

For St. Ignatius.

O God, who by the ministry of St. Ignatius, hast given to the Church militant a new aid for spreading abroad the glory of thy holy Name, grant that assisted by his protection and example, after having combatted on earth, we may merit to be crowned immortally in heaven. Through our Lord Jesus Christ. Amen.

For St. F. Xavier.

O God, who by the preaching and miracles of St. Francis Xavier, drew to the true faith the nations of the East, and mercifully ranked them among the children of thy Church, be propitious to us, and grant us the grace of imitating perfectly the virtues of him whose glorious merits we honor, through our Lord Jesus Christ. Amen. Three *Pater* and *Ave*.

St. Aloysius.

FOR SIX SUNDAYS.

O Lord, assist our weakness, cast upon us a look of condescension and mercy in favor of thy blessed Confessor, our holy patron, Louis de Gonzague, who preserved purity in the midst of the world, practiced austerity though surrounded with allurements to pleasure, and humility in the bosom of earthly pomp and magnificence, so that in imitation of him we may pass through the perils which surround us, without receiving any injury; we humbly hope for this favor through thy divine assistance and his gracious intercession. Six *Pater*, *Ave*, and *Gloria*.

St. Stanislas.

O God, who among the wonders of thy grace, granted to St. Stanislas, from an early age the grace of an accomplished sanctity, grant we beseech thee, the grace of redeeming the time past, by continually practicing good works, and thus attain eternal rest, through our Lord Jesus Christ. Amen.

—

Nine Tuesdays' Devotion

ST. ANTONY OF PADUA.

This Novena consists, (according to that Saint's own direction,) in Confessing, and receiving Holy Communion on nine consecutive Tuesdays, and reciting before his picture some approved vocal prayer, or devoting a short time to meditation in a Chapel dedicated to his honor. It is also recommended to read portions of his life during the Novena, and to perform other acts of piety consistent with those prescribed for it. The following prayers are customary:

Responsory of St. Antony of Padua.

Ascribed to St. Buonaventura.

Si quæris miracula: mors, error, calamitas,
    Dæmon, lepra fungiunt: ægri surgunt sani,
Cedunt mare, vincula. Membra, resque perditas
    Petunt et accipiunt juvenes et cani.
Pereunt pericula, cessat et necessitas.
    Narrent hi qui sentiunt, dicant Paduani.
Cedunt mare, vincula. Membra, resque perditas
    Petunt et accipiunt juvenes et cani.

℣. Ora pro nobis, Sancte Antoni,
℞. Ut digni efficiamur promissionibus Christe.

Ecclesiam tuam, Deus, beati Antonii Confessoris tui solemnitas votiva lætificet; ut spiritualibus semper muniatur auxiliis, et gaudiis perfrui mereatur æternis. Per Dominum nostrum, Jesum Christum, filium tuum, qui tecum vivit et regnat, in unitate Spiritus Sancti Deus, per omnia sæcula sæculorum. Amen.

Translation.

If miracles are worked, let the Paduans declare the wonders they have witnessed! Calamity, leprosy, error, death and Satan, flee when they implore St. Antony's intercession. The youthful and the aged petition the restoration of disabled limbs, and the recovery of lost objects, and their prayer is heard; the sea becomes powerless, chains no longer bind, while danger vanishes and necessities cease, at the invocation of that all-prevalent name! Therefore

V̌. Pray for us, St. Antony.

R. That we may be made worthy of the promises of Christ.

LET US PRAY.

O God, may the votive celebration of thy confessor, blessed St. Antony, gladden thy Church, and fortify her with spiritual aid, enable her to deserve the possession of eternal joys, through Jesus Christ our Lord, who liveth and reigneth in the unity of the Holy Ghost, one God, world without end. Amen.

HYMN.

O gloriosa Virginum,
Sublimis inter sidera:
Qui te creavit, parvulum
Lactente nutris ubere.

Quod Heva tristris abstulit,
Tu reddis almo germine:
Intrent ut astra flebiles,
Cœli recludis cardines.

Tu Regis alti janua,
Et aula lucis fulgida:
Vitam datam per Virginem
Gentes redemptæ plaudite.

Jesu, tibi sit gloria,
Qui natus es de Virgine,
Cum Patre et almo Spiritu,
In sempertina sæcula. AMEN.*

Translation.

O Queen of all the Virgin choir!
   Enthroned above the starry sky!
Who with pure milk from thy own breast
   Thy own Creator didst supply.

What man had lost in hapless Eve,
   Thy sacred womb to man restores;
Thou to the wretched here beneath,
   Hast open'd Heaven's eternal doors.

Hail, O refulgent Hall of light!
   Hail, gate sublime of Heaven's high King!
Through Thee redeem'd to endless life,
   Thy praise let all the nations sing.

---

* This hymn was St. Antony's favorite prayer, and he sung it just before expiring.

O Jesus! born of Virgin bright,
　　Immortal glory be to Thee;
Praise to the Father infinite,
　　And Holy Ghost eternally.

———

A prayer to obtain light concerning a vocation to a state of life, or to discover God's will on any other important enterprise.

Prayer.

O Lord, Omnipotent King, all events are subject to thy power, and no one can with impunity resist thy holy will. My sincere desire is, to know what thou askest of me, that I may cheerfully and generously submit to it. But none can enter into thy designs, nor comprehend what is "*thy will*," unless thou dost impart to them thy wisdom, and send thy Holy Spirit to rectify their views, and teach them what will prove most agreeable to thee. I come to thee, therefore, O my Father and my God, and though I am but dust in thy presence, I humbly ask thee, "*what wilt thou have me to do?*" "Show me the way in which I should walk, for I have lifted up my soul to thee. Thou art my light and my salvation: thee alone do I wish to hear, for thou art the way, and the truth and the life." Suffer me not to wander from thy will, by pursuing my own thoughts and conducting myself, nor to deceive myself by adopting my inclinations or the will of creatures for thine. Help me to accomplish thy will at *present*, so that I may merit the knowledge of what thou wilt ask of me in *future*. Give me strength to surmount all the obstacles that nature, the world or Satan, may oppose to the execution of that adorable and most amiable will. Let me not be in the number of those servants who were severely punished, because "*they knew thy will and did it not,*" but aid me to follow the example of my divine Master, who was obedient to thee, even to death on the cross, so that on my bed of death, I may confidently say with my Jesus: "Father, all is consummated, into thy hands I commend my spirit!" Amen.

Act of Consecration to the Blessed Virgin.

(For the Assumption.)

August Mary, mother of Jesus, perpetual and immaculate virgin, sovereign of angels and men, the purest, holiest, and nearest to perfection of all creatures, mother of grace and mercy, inexhaustible source of beneficence, meekness and love, except thy divine Son, the most accomplished model of every virtue, behold us humbly prostrate at thy feet to render thee our homage, to lay before thee our petitions, and to give and consecrate ourselves to thee with the most sincere protestations of unreserved devotedness.

O powerful Queen of heaven and earth, who art also our mother, but the kindest, tenderest and most compassionate of all mothers, we thank thee with heart-felt gratitude for the innumerable benefits that we have received from the divine Heart of Jesus, by the intercession of thy maternal Heart, which has so deeply sympathized with our trials and wretchedness; from that Heart which loved and still loves men with passion and transport, with ineffable and ecstatic tenderness! We unite our devotion to that of all those pure souls whose most delightful occupation is honoring, loving, praising and serving thee, according to the desires of the divine Heart of Jesus, of whose thine is a perfect portrait. We implore thee by thy ardent charity, to receive us this day and forever into the number of thy disciples, servants and cherished children—may we never degenerate from these glorious qualities, but by complete submission to every expression of thy will, by a truly filial piety towards thee, and above all, by the faithful imitation of thy virtues, prove to the world that we have sincerely adopted thee for our queen, mother and model.

O amiable Mary, this is our desire—and relying on thy powerful protection, we dare promise that after Jesus, thou shalt be, not only the object of our confidence, but thy example shall form the rule of our daily conduct. Deign, therefore, O best of mothers, to shield us in danger, support and strengthen us in temptation, console us in trials, assist us in our necessities, protect us during life, encourage us as our hope in the hour of death, and be our advocate, mediatrix and security with the Supreme Judge, in that dread instant which must decide our eternal destiny, our bliss, and our crown!

To the greater glory of God the Father, whose daughter thou art, of the Holy Ghost, of whom thou art the immaculate spouse, and of God the Son, of whom thou art the ever blessed mother! Amen.

MEDITATIONS AND DEVOUT PRACTICES

PREPARATORY TO THE

Festibal of the Sacred Heart of Mary.

(Or, for each First Saturday of the Month.)

———

TRANSLATED FROM THE
ITALIAN OF GUISEPPE M. MANFREDINI, S. J.

———

SS. C. J. M.

FIRST DAY.

Grant, O my God, that during meditation, all my thoughts, and all the intentions of my heart and soul, may tend entirely to thy greater honor and glory.

First Prelude.—Imagine you see our holy Mother in the act of offering her heart unreservedly to God—and hear the eternal Father saying to her: Beloved Daughter, thou art my delight!

Second Prelude.—Ask of God, to grant us through the merits of the Heart of Mary, grace to imitate as nearly as possible, the sublime purity of Mary, and thus become his delight and that of his beloved Mother.

1. *The Heart of Mary is the model of purity.*

A Heart that has never contracted any blemish, deformity or fault, must be replete with *purity;* and hence, may be considered a model of that virtue. The holy Heart of Mary is the only heart merely human, that never was sullied with any defilement. Mary was immaculate in her Conception—and free from even the most minute actual fault during her whole life; and as she possessed the purest of all Hearts, except the Sacred Heart of Jesus, she is the most perfect model among creatures, of the angelical virtue of holy purity. Devout soul, have you not hitherto entertained an erroneous idea concerning sanctity?—True holiness consists in preserving the heart pure and unsullied from every kind of sin. A heart in which sin dwells, is an object of horror to the pure and holy sight of God, for the defiled heart is *deformed!* Do not imagine, that grievous sin alone, tarnishes the brilliancy of the soul, and destroys the loveliness of the heart; deliberate venial sin *deforms it also;* and although it does not render it an object of hatred and of execration to God, as does mortal sin, still it causes it to be far less pleasing to him.

Do not sloth in the service of God, wilful negli-gence in the duties of your state, with acts of impa-tience and dissipation in your religious exercises, sully your heart! Ah! the blessed Virgin did not so conduct herself! She desired to belong wholly to God, and therefore, endeavored to render her heart conformable to the heart of God. By a continual study of the divine perfections, she strove to retrace his image in her soul. She not only detested grave faults, but even those falsely styled insignificant, and such was her diligent attention, such the vigilance of her solicitude, that with the abundance of grace that she had received from God, she preserved herself ever exempt from the slightest imperfection. I know well, that we cannot think of attaining so exalted a height, but I am also certain, that with the help of grace, which will not be wanting to us, we can aim at a much higher degree of perfection than we do at present. I know that many stains, contracted through negligence, might have been avoided. I am confi-dent that we could pay more serious attention to the fulfilment of our duties, and be more watchful over our own senses. Let us study earnestly the heart of Mary, and endeavor to copy in ours, the lineaments of that perfect model of purity. True, she was con-firmed in grace—this was a powerful aid: but her correspondence was full and free, and her great sanctity arose from that liberal and generous corre-spondence. Begin, religious or christian soul, now to coperate faithfully with grace—the virtue which

has increased so little of late, will become perfection
and sanctity. In the meantime, be convinced that
your living in so many defects, and even sins, is not
because the tender mercy of God is wanting to you,
but because you are deficient towards that mercy;
resolve therefore, to become faithful to all its divine
inspirations.

2. *The Heart of Mary is the mirror of Purity.*

The quality of a mirror is, to represent to the life
any object placed before it. When any one is placed
opposite it, he is represented such as he really is.
The Heart of Mary is the most spotless of mirrors.
Speculum sine macula. (Wis. 7.) Entreat our
blessed Mother to present this mirror to us, that we
may discover all that is imperfect, deformed and revolting in our hearts, not only in the sight of God,
but in our own eyes. Observe, O religious soul, in
the Heart of Mary, recollection, union with God and
every affection of her soul turned towards her Creator: in yours, dissipation, effusion of the powers of
the mind on exterior affairs, and attachment to a
variety of creatures. In the Heart of Mary purity
of intention in every deed; her sole aim, the good
pleasure of God; in your heart a *general* intention
perhaps of doing God's will, destroyed sometimes by
private ends, and generally by your inordinate self-
love. In the Heart of Mary an ever onward progress from one degree of perfection to a higher; in
yours, it may be a gradual decline from sin to sin.
How deplorable is your state when examined by such
a test! Your heart is excessively poor in spirituality,
loving its own ease and convenience, sensitive to the
slightest injury, in short, a compound of defects and
miseries—and yet, *God hates sin!* In view of such
wretchedness, humble yourself, but beware of dis-

couragement. If you *will*, you can easily rise from this unhappy condition, the blessed Virgin will intercede for you, and receive you with true confidence into her tender, maternal Heart.

In particular, Mary is the mirror of purity of body, for her Heart was so pure that *no Angel*, whatever be his transcendent excellence, can be compared with her in even the most remote degree. The virginal innocence of Mary excelled in whiteness the snow or the purest lily, and not only was its brilliancy never tarnished but it was never dimmed by the faintest shade. It is piously believed that the Immaculate Mother was the first that ever dedicated her virginity to God by a vow, and that vow she observed with a holy jealousy, so much so that she would prefer resigning the dignity of the Divine Maternity to the renunciation of her favorite virtue. O precious purity! it is impossible not to delight in this excellent virtue, which assimilates man to the Angels of Paradise. But alas! how easy to be eternally lost, if we are not vigilant in shielding it. In what a variety of ways does the infernal enemy assail us, and our own concupiscence allure us. Devout soul, affections sometimes have a holy beginning, but terminate in unbecoming sensibility and tenderness. An object simply awakens curiosity, the fancy however remaining strongly impressed, an emotion is excited in the heart, and when least suspected the temptation will gain a victory. What degree of affection do you cultivate towards *this* virtue of the Heart of Mary? You admire and extol it in the Saints, why do you not take the means of promoting it in yourself. Assiduous mortification. frequent meditation, with fervent prayer to the pure Heart of Mary, are the most efficacious means of maintaining purity.

Homage to the Heart of Mary.

PRACTICE.

Spend a quarter of an hour in reflecting on this virtue, before a picture or statue of the blessed Virgin, supplicate her to form your heart to purity, so that it may become the delight of God, and a subject for her complacency.

ASPIRATION.

Hail, most pure Heart of Mary.

SECOND DAY.

Preparatory Prayer.—As usual.

First Prelude.—Imagine that you see the beloved Mary, ever virgin, offering herself with her whole heart, to God in the temple of Jerusalem, and hear the eternal Father saying: O my beloved, my Dove!

Second Prelude.—Ask of God, the grace (through the intercession of Mary,) to comprehend the value of mortification, and strength to practice it.

FIRST POINT.

The Heart of Mary is mortified in its affections, despising the riches of this world.

How wretched, how degraded is a heart that bestows its affections on the goods of this fleeting world. Tell me, said St. Augustine, what thou lovest, and I will tell thee what thou art! Dost thou cling to things of earth, thou art earthly. The holy Heart of Mary having found pleasure in God, never condescended to bestow even the least of its affections upon terrestrial things. God was to her the source of every blessing, and in Him she sought satisfaction and sweet content. Religious soul, it appears that you have not sufficient control over your affections, to prevent them from clinging to this miserable world, and to its worthless possessions. Ah! how long will you live in illusion. Is not self-love the originator of an idea you entertain of necessity? That matter of convenience which you seek with such earnest solicitude, that toy that you preserve so carefully, nay, anxiously, though not in correspondence with your profession, the books and different objects, which not unfrequently, superiors concede to you, not because they are requisite, but because your virtue is weak, give evident signs that your heart is still attached to perishable things; for whatever is superfluous is simply of earth, vile grovelling earth!—What wonder, therefore, if your soul is so coldly affected towards heavenly things, if your heart still sends out its liveliest aspirations towards the earth—for in proportion as your affections become detached from earth, your soul will become assimilated in its emotions, to those which are cherished in heaven.

But what do we discover in you, but excessive resentment in the privation of necessaries, murmurs, lamentation and annoyance of the whole house, because you cannot find wherewith to satisfy your delicacy. The Heart of Mary was the same in its nature and dispositions as yours; as that sacred Heart detaching itself from all other love, became united to God, so will yours also attain that blessed state, as soon as it is dispossessed of all foreign attractions. Remember the promise you have made to follow Jesus in poverty—and why did you contract this obligation, unless that you might be free to give yourself wholly to God, without the weight of earth drawing you to its own baseness. And yet, what disorder! perchance you renounced a handsome patrimony, or extensive possessions on entering religion, and now you are incapable of withdrawing your affection from mean, petty objects. Excite yourself to shame and sorrow in the presence of Mary, and resolve to amend. Give her a token of your love, by restoring anything you may have that is not in common, or which you may have appropriated to your own use.

SECOND POINT.

The Heart of Mary was mortified in its affections towards her kindred.

Inordinate love for relatives is displeasing to God. Therefore, when the divine Redeemer said: *he that hateth not father and mother,* (*Luke* xiv., 16.) he meant the same as when he said: *Whoso loveth father and mother more than me is not worthy of being my disciple.* The mortification of Mary in such affections, is manifested in the alacrity with which she devoted herself to God, at the tender age of three years. Religious soul, you have forsaken father, mother and relatives, and have retired into religion; but why that excessive solicitude which you still preserve for them—why dwell corporeally in religion and mentally in your family? What thoughts are those that wander into your own home, sometimes attended with a sentiment of disgust at having left it? It was God, who in infinite mercy, commanded you as he did Abraham of old, to leave the hearth of your fathers: *egredere—de domo patris tui.* (*Gen.* xii, 1.) and perchance you regret having obeyed? God gave you the generosity necessary for resisting the tears of disconsolate parents, for withdrawing from numerous attachments, and perchance you are displeased with that act of heroism, and you would once more unite the severed links of those worldly chains? The Heart of Mary on the contrary, far from lessening its generosity, experienced an immense increase, the facility which she enjoyed of uniting her heart to God in his temple, induced her to offer him uninterrupted thanksgiving, for the grace of her consecration. Ah! neither want of reflection, nor your tender and inexperienced years, nor even ignorance of the world, caused you to resolve to withdraw from all that was dear to nature, and its legitimate affections—it was the powerful, soul-subduing grace of your God. Your actual tepidity therefore, is the cause of those unworldly thoughts! Return to your former mortified life, renew your early generosity, and you find once more, your primitive content. Love your kindred, but *in* God, and *for the love* of God; change your *natural* affection for them into a *spiritual* one: pray for them assiduously, and whenever you can prove useful to them by good counsel or pious conversations, allow no opportunity to escape. Strengthen your resolution by prayer, renew the early fervor of your blessed vocation, by recalling that divinely inspired impulse, which prompted you to give your heart totally to God, correspond to it with fidelity, and your mortification and self conquest, will cause you to be once more dear and acceptable to your God.

THIRD POINT.

The Heart of Mary is mortified in love to itself.

When we speak of *self-love*, we do not understand that *well ordered affection* with which every one should consider himself: but we mean that inordinate attachment which we show to the body, satisfying *it*, by sacrificing the soul to it. In this sense our divine Saviour said: *He who does not hate himself cannot be my disciple.* (*loc. cit.*) This hatred that is due to ourselves, consists in a real mortification of self, in all circumstances which are really offensive to God, or may lead to his offence. Let us return to this beautiful virtue in the Heart of Mary, to decide that this perfectly mortified heart entertained no inordinate self-love, it will be sufficient to consider her private life in the Temple. Her implicit obedience to whomsoever held the place of God to her, was a real and continual abnegation of self-will. Her earnest and zealous attention to labor, in the functions assigned her, were a veritable self-mortification. Her angelic modesty, her scrupulous custody of the tongue, promptitude in repairing to the public service of God, and her careful avoidance of idleness; all teach us how we *can*, and how we *ought*, to mortify ourselves, and render our hearts less dissimilar to Mary's. Devout soul, what say you to this illustrious example? Is your obedience that of the *intellect* as well as of the *will?* perchance it rests only in *execution?* Do you never seek excuses for eluding commands, make observations and find a thousand difficulties? Ah! can you suppose that you merit the title of religious, without practicing obedience? How do you observe modesty of the eyes? has not neglect of this practice occasioned you numerous falls? let the past cause you to be more prudent. How do you watch over your tongue—idle words even, are defects, but how often have you offended against charity? To detract the neighbor, is wounding God in "the apple of his eye." In this manner run over during your meditation the other virtues, and discover to what a state you are reduced through want of mortification, and humble yourself in the presence of God. Then turn to the Heart of blessed Mary, the model for mortified hearts, and entreat her to conform your heart to hers. The delight of the religious should be mortification, because by its practice she is assimilated to her Spouse, *Jesus*, and to his holy Mother, and thus merits the highest favors bestowed upon elect souls.

PRACTICE—TO HONOR MARY IMMACULATE.

During the day, make three acts of interior mortification of your will, and three exterior of the senses.

ASPIRATION.

Draw me after thee, holy Mother.

THIRD DAY.

Preparatory Prayer.—As usual.

First Prelude.—Imagine that you see Holy Mary in the act of presenting her heart to God, while responding to the Angel, *Ecce ancilla Domini.* At the same time the eternal Father is pleased with her.

Second Prelude.—Ask of God grace, through the most humble Heart of Mary, to discover clearly our absolute nothingness, and to adopt sentiments that are becoming to an humble heart.

FIRST POINT.

The Heart of Mary is humble, through the effect of knowledge.

Learn of me, said our divine Lord, that I am meek and humble of heart. (Matt. xi, 28.) To become humble of heart, we must comprehend our own

nothingness, and attribute to its true source whatever may seem to be valuable in us. The blessed
Virgin, the most exalted among mere creatures, is
the most humble hearted among them, for she knows
intimately, and sees clearly, that if the plenitude of
grace, like a superabundant benediction, distinguishes her above all women, it is a gift of the infinite liberality of God. She understands how to
separate the precious from the vile: and we know
well, that there is nothing of degradation in Mary,
her origin was holy, and every instant of her life
was holy, yet, she acknowledges that what she has
proceeds from the grace of God, and with the deepest
humility attributes all to Him and nothing to herself.
Religious soul, take a view of your own heart, and
examine what you *really are!* We are nothing in
our existence, nothing in the work of its continued
preservation, for we received our being from God,
and it is preserved only by his concurrent operation.
Consider now, your natural endowments, on account
of which you sometimes despise others. What have
you that is your own? Do your talents, quick and
brilliant genius, foresight, discernment, natural prudence, etc., appertain to you? Are you the author
of your health, strength, and the admirable propor-
tions of your body. Did you bestow upon yourself
a noble, or at least, respectable birth, with a becoming deportment and accomplished manners? Ah!
for mercy's sake, divide the precious from the vile;
know yourself. Nothingness and sinfulness are your
portion, and the good that you possess proceeds from
God. Then why seek motives for self-arrogance,
glorify yourself, and use the gift to insult the Giver?
If there be anything in you that is extraordinary, it
is a token of God's extraordinary love towards you:

therefore, you owe him an extraordinary correspondence. But alas! you have amazing pretensions, and still worse, you display extraordinary ingratitude towards God.

All this arises from the want of self-knowledge. You do not know yourself, and therefore, you are arrogant in your speech. You do not know yourself, and hence your own praises are frequently in your lips. You do not know yourself, and for this reason, in the intimity of your heart, you despise others.— For this same cause you are exasperated at every trifling word, which you fancy indicates little esteem for you. Ah! when, O most humble Heart of Mary, will a ray of your heavenly light penetrate *my* mind, and teach me to know, and consequently esteem myself justly?

SECOND POINT.

The Heart of Mary is humble in sentiment.

If we have the humility that springs from knowledge, we shall also possess that which arises from sentiment—because the belief that we are vile, results from the conviction we entertain of our nothingness. Humility of sentiment was principally displayed in the Heart of Mary, in the mystery of the Annunciation. Mary is quite alarmed at the magnificent declaration of the angel, for she did not believe that she merited it: *et cogitabat qualis esset ista salutatio.* (*Luke* i, 29.) When assured that she would preserve her purity by becoming a Mother, as the work was to be performed by the divine Spirit, and by the virtue of the Most High, the response given by Mary shows distinctly her humility of thought. "Behold," said she, "the handmaid of the Lord, be it done unto me according to thy word."— (Luke 38.) So also at the praises, which St. Elizabeth uttered, by inspiration of the Holy Ghost, blessed Mary responded according to the lowly opinion of her Heart, that the *Lord* had done great things in her, and on that account, she was filled with gratitude, and magnified him alone, from whom proceeded all the blessings she enjoyed. Such humility penetrating the heavens, moved the Heart of God, and (says St. Bernard,) though her virginity was pleasing to Almighty God, it was through her humility that she conceived the Eternal Word. Try, religious soul, to comprehend humility of sentiment —it is difficult for you to entertain a low opinion of yourself, simply because you are unwilling to acquire self-knowledge. Examine thoroughly the recesses of your heart, and recall the first point of the meditation, convince your mind of that truth, and you will perceive the idea you should conceive of yourself— for to accomplish great things in us, God wishes this lowly opinion of ourselves. Whenever, says St. Lawrence Justinian, the Lord wishes to create divine things, he has need of nothingness only. It is because you are destitute of humility, that God denies you his more distinguished favors, his choice graces. Indeed, it would be impossible to expect remarkable gifts from God, if, on account of these, you increase in haughtiness, and believe that your virtue proves you a favorite of heaven. Let *him*, says St. Ignatius of Loyola, who wishes to increase greatly in holiness, descend lower and lower in proportion to the ardor of his desires. The moth which consumes all the virtues, is pride, that pride that arises from the idea that we harbor of our consequence. Now, let us undeceive ourselves—and learn from the most lowly Heart of Mary, to be truly modest and humble in sentiment.

THIRD POINT.

The Heart of Mary is humble in will.

A knowledge of our insignificance, a lowly estimate of ourselves, should naturally incline us to
cherish whatever can contribute to our abjection.
This is at once the most necessary and the most difficult point of practical humility, to accept humiliations cordially and even to desire them.   Mary, the
humble of Heart, gives a sublime example of
humility in the will.   That holy Mother could have
easily removed from the mind of her spouse, St.
Joseph, all the apprehension and distress which
afflicted it, by simply avowing to him her divine
maternity; but this did not comport with her humility
and *she was silent.*   She resigned herself to the
protection of God, rather than reveal that secret
mystery, because it would have augmented in St.
Joseph the veneration and love that he already felt
for her.   Such virtue is incomprehensible to self-love!
We, O religious soul, are not only incapable of concealing the gifts of God beneath the mantle of
humility, but we cannot endure a little reprehension,
or a penance for a defect of which we do not believe
ourselves guilty, nay! even for a fault that we have
actually committed we seek an excuse, or endeavor
to shield ourselves from a reproof or a penance.
Humility pleases you, you even desire to be humble:
but are you aware of the nature of *that* humility?
It is a humility which terminates in pride.   You are
willing to speak of yourself as miserable before God;
incapable of any good action, nay, unworthy of the
divine presence: but wo; to any one who believes
your declaration, wo to him who would speak of you
in the same style, disparaging or comtemning your

views or conduct. And yet you wish us to give you credit for the *virtue* of humility when you thus discourse of yourself. False, deceitful personification of humility, whose crown is arrogance! It is indeed well not to talk of yourself, but, at least willingly admit a little word that expresses far less than your own declarations concerning yourself. Observe the Heart of Mary—when that Immaculate Mother speaks, see in what manner she does it, and how reserved she is concerning the favors of heaven. She is denominated Mother of God, and *she* styles *herself* his *handmaid*: she ranks *Queen* of Angels and of Saints, and she is obedient to St. Joseph, a *mere man!* She is styled *elect* and *blessed*, but she refers the whole to the divine omnipotence that has deigned "*to do great things in her*," solely by an effect of his infinite goodness and mercy. Study this sacred Heart, in order to learn humility in speech and action. Yet do not take a *general* resolution to become humble: but, resolve to do something *positive*, descend to some determinate circumstances that suit your particular case, and directly put your hand to the work. Reproach yourself, that in the school of humility, in "*religion*," you are so haughty; and adopt a speedy remedy to its consequent evils. O, Heart of Mary, most humble, how shall I be sufficiently overcome with shame and confusion in your sight.

PRACTICE.

Beware of uttering any phrase that may redound to your credit, or praise of yourself.

ASPIRATION.

Hail, most humble Heart of Mary!

FOURTH DAY.

Preparatory Prayer.—As usual.

First Prelude.—Imagine you see the blessed Virgin offering her Heart to God, and hear him styling her, *"beloved daughter," "enclosed garden," "sealed fountain!"*

Second Prelude.—Ask of God, by the merits of the Heart of Mary, to make known to us the value of being hidden in him.

FIRST POINT.

The Heart of Mary is hidden from the view of men.

A life hidden from the eyes of creatures appears to be harsh, irksome, and quite unfitted to a reasonable creature. But this idea originates in our inordinate self-love, which is continually on the lookout for self-gratification. The divine Redeemer, infinitely wise, judged it well to spend thirty years in an insignificant employment, in the obscurity of a workshop, and thus concealed from what we commonly call the world, or gaze of mankind. And what effect has intercourse with the world upon us, but to render us worse than we are? What *can* men do for us, but make us more defective, and oblige us to repeat with the Author of the Imitation: *"when I associated with creatures I returned less a man."* The blessed Virgin adopting this maxim of true wisdom, sought nothing more eagerly than to be unknown, and completely hidden, and this disposition of her sacred Heart becomes us. While yet a child she retired into the Temple, and in silence and forgotten by all, she lived only for her God, embellishing her Heart with ever amiable and enduring virtues, which rendered her an object of complacency to the adorable Trinity. By divine inspiration she gave herself as a spouse to St. Joseph, but she studied how to live unknowing and unknown in the bosom of her little family. However, she did not think it requisite to her peace and union with God, to decline the performance of deeds of fraternal charity. Consider her in the mountains of Judea, visiting her kinswoman Elizabeth, and serving her during a long month. Neither did she disown her allegiance to an earthly power, and hence, although pregnant with the Divine Infant, she turned her obedient steps with her reputed spouse Joseph, to Bethlehem, in order to pay the tribute due to Cæsar. Yet, in this seeming public transaction, no one is so hidden from the world. This is a striking example for you, O religious, on whom solitude and silence often hang heavily. You have separated yourself from the world; then why wish to enter anew into that world and learn its proceedings and conform yourself perchance to its spirit, which you are bound to hold in detestation. The reason is evident, you have lost that relish that attracted you to intimate communion with God, and now you are seeking consolation in creatures. But, pray, what *real* good has the world, that is cursed by our Lord, to bestow on you? During those moments in which you diffuse yourself outwardly, you may perhaps feel a little counterfeit alleviation: but soon you will return to solitude with an increased heaviness of heart—you will have spent your energies in the deceitful flame, which dazzled you, and you will not find God, to whom you would gladly turn in your heart's anguish. Remember the early years of your holy retreat, when the solitary cell, with its crucifix and devout silence formed your delight, and when with frequent and ardent aspirations you united your soul to God? Had you not been faithful in the beginning, God would not have allowed you to hear his divine voice. But now the passions that were once subjected have budded anew, and you find your heart in an almost fatal desolation. O hidden life, delicious relief to the care-worn, wearied heart, why not recall it to console you once more? An act of real mortification would suffice, deprive yourself of that seeming pleasure that you taste when holding communion with creatures, and you will find true peace and delight in God. Consider how many religious there are, who are contented in perpetual silence, and in unbroken retirement, they have sought and found the "*pearl of price*," because for however little they have removed from earth and its allurements, they have approached nearer to God, who has recompensed them with comfort and heaven-born peace, and a hundred-fold greater than the world could have ever bestowed. For this it is not necessary to withdraw from the duties incumbent on offices of charity in order to seek a mere corporal repose; the peace that you might then possibly enjoy, would not emanate from God, and would consequently be illusive. God never contradicts himself—true charity is his gift, and did you really possess it you would cheerfully forego the soothing delight you experience in prayer and contemplation, to occupy yourself in deeds of fraternal charity. These may be fatiguing, difficult, and even repulsive, yet if they are acts of charity, it suffices. Cast a glance on the blessed Virgin, toiling over the mountainous acclivities of Judea; consider her in her comforting mission in the house of St. Elizabeth, and let her example excite you to sacrifice even the most lawful of pleasures, for God's greater glory, in the practice of charity. Now consider, how dissimilar you are to the Heart of Mary in the manner of giving and withholding in those offices in which you ought to exercise charity. You take pleasure in the exercise of charity when you experience no positive inconvenience from it, but if there be any thing aggravating or injurious to be suffered, alas! how many excuses are invented, how many pretexts originated, nay, even it may be sharp or forbidding replies uttered, and interior or exterior resentment felt or exhibited. Ah! the hidden life is not one of idleness and inertness, but on the contrary an ever active, busy life, because continually occupied with God, and for the love of God, with the promoting of good in the souls of others. Endeavor to appreciate this truth—perhaps hitherto not realized, and then resolve.

SECOND POINT.

The Heart of Mary was hidden to itself.

To be hidden from self, implies that the soul considers itself unworthy of esteem, perceiving in itself no intrinsic merit, nor any claim to receive honors from others. This is the height of perfection, and may be reduced to this—the love and relish of being totally unknown. Alas! when shall we reach this degree of humility. Let us come to the sweet and gentle Heart of Mary, humble in sentiment as we have already meditated, and learn from her how to practice total concealment. We know that she gave no explanation to the Magi, who adored her divine Infant, nor to Simeon, who prophecied to her a sword of sorrow; we learn, however, from the Evangelist St. Luke, that she preserved all these things in her Heart, dwelling upon and meditating them, in order to extract sentiments in accordance with humility.

(Luke ii, 19.) This concealment from self is exhibited still more clearly in her expression in the Canticle, *Magnificat; respexit humilitatem ancillæ suæ*, the true signification of which is, her intimate consciousness of her own comparative littleness, lowliness and baseness, interdicting herself from mentioning, or even thinking on the lofty gifts of God, who had "done great things in her."

Religious soul, by the light of this ray, glittering from the Heart of this holiest of virgins, allow me to penetrate into the recesses and abysses of your interior views—to the bottom of your heart. Ah! how ambitious, how base, how degrading are your sentiments. You believe yourself to be something what you are not, you are even swelled with sentiments of self-esteem, and a persuasion of your excellence. You are in admiration of what you fancy you have done for the welfare of the Church, the practice of piety, and the promotion of God's greater glory, and secretly, you believe yourself to be of consequence, because the Lord makes use of *you*, the weakest, the homeliest of instruments, for the accomplishment of his designs.

Let us examine your mode of conversing, for "out of the abundance of the heart the mouth speaketh." Your words are exteriorly humble, but pride prompts them—because you are yourself most frequently their subject—and you recount what you have done, and sometimes with exaggeration. Again, although you return thanks to God for the good you appear to have effected, yet you feel an interior complacency in having succeeded, and in the honor and esteem that arose from it. On the other hand, it may be that you indulge a secret opinion, that you are not employed in accordance with your talents or capacity and requirements, you think that in certain occupations you excel others, even though they are placed in authority over you! Have you not frequently believed yourself slighted, put down, and neglected purposely?— Ah! this is far from being concealed from our own good opinion, it is to be desirous of being known and appraised according to our own inflated self-esteem. *Ama nescire, et pro nihilo reputare.* Love to be ignored and forgotten, or reputed fit for nothing, says the author of the Imitation, and he means not only by others but by yourself.

In fact, what is the interior spirit that forms the soul of all the beautiful and acceptable actions we perform for God—that spirit which is absolutely necessary to the attainment of PERFECTION? It is a spirit that leads us to perform things with a just estimate of ourselves; a spirit which prompts us to consider nothing contemptible that is accomplished in the house of God, for it is done to serve the great Master; a spirit which convinces the soul that earthly pomp and grandeur, and all human glory, are but vapor and dissolving mist, and to crave the reputation and honor that proceed from them, is folly in the extreme.

Ah! my God, how remote are we from such perfection! but yet we can attain to it with thy will. Let us cast our prayerful eyes upon the humble Heart of Mary, and implore its intercession with faith and fervor.

PRACTICE.

Write effectual resolutions concerning the practice of humility. Establish a formal rule, by which you may derive practical fruit from this meditation, and aim at a higher degree of perfection.

Ave Cor Mariæ, quanto pro Deo vilius, tanto Deo carius.

Hail, most holy Heart of Mary, that became more acceptable to God, in proportion as it was more humble.

FIFTH DAY.

Preparatory Prayer.—As usual.

First Prelude.—Imagine you see blessed Mary when fleeing into Egypt—amid the weariness of the journey and the melancholy thought of future trials, she presses the Holy Infant more closely to her Heart, and offers herself anew to follow him at the least expression of his will.

Second Prelude.—Let us ask God, through the intercession of the Heart of Mary, to grant us the grace of knowing the value of practicing meekness, and embellishing our hearts with this virtue.

FIRST POINT.

The Heart of Mary is meek during spiritual afflictions.

Consider, the Heart of Mary was during her whole life a subject of contradiction, and suffered a continual martyrdom. From the instant that Mary was saluted Mother of God, until her latest breath, her Heart was a prey to a thousand afflictions. And yet not even a secret lamentation escaped her venerable lips—indeed it may be observed of her, as it is of the Divine Redeemer by his prophet, she remained silent under the knife that was to victimize her.

Religious, or Christian, take a cursory view of the different passages of the biography of Mary. As Mother of the Incarnate Word, behold her afflicted by the anguish of her reputed Spouse. When her precious Babe is born, she is so destitute of this world's wealth, that she has neither house nor roof wherewith to cover her tender Infant. Go with her to the Temple, and unpretending as she had ever been, she is declared to be a sign of contradiction, and is thus publicly held up to invidious scorn. She was not allowed to caress and enjoy her little Jesus in peace, for she was obliged to flee into Egypt, in order to avoid the fury of the jealous Herod. When having returned to her native land, true, her Divine Infant increased in years, but then she lost him in the TEMPLE! At every period of her earthly pilgrimage, you will find her bending silently and meekly beneath the weight of keen, heartfelt affliction. And when we reflect that as her Divine Son grew in years, and in manliness of stature, she saw him ripening for a horrid, unjust and blasphemous execution, may we not exclaim: O afflicted Heart of Mary, at what hour of your existence were you ever exempt from grief? Christian, or even religious, what a subject of self-reproach is here presented you in the silence and resignation of Mary You indeed know the *word* meekness, and its loveliness, its heroism attract you, and when you pause before a picture or an image of either the Heart of Jesus, or the Heart of Mary, you seem to be persuaded by the lesson that they inwardly repeat to you, resolve to undertake resolutely a profound and diligent study of those sacred Hearts, and by fidelity in self-conquest to adorn your heart with this amiable virtue. Examine your own poor heart, is it not in continual commotion, incessant contest? Whence arise the frequent acts of impatience, the sudden anger, the impetuous disdain which you exhibit? You seem unable to endure a trifling affliction, the puncture of a thorn or a little pressure of the cross! your condition is indeed pitiful! Be persuaded there is no peace except in the actual practice of meekness and pious resignation, nay, consider that very often your trouble is but the creation of a heated fancy, or if it really exist, you increase its burden by your regrets and efforts to shake it off. How many times have your sighs and tears been called forth, because you were incapable of succeeding in some enterprise, and you were thence lowered in the estimation that you fancied to be your due, how often because you could not triumph in a point of honor. Ah! then there arose melancholy, tediousness, murmurings, etc., succeeded by agitation of the soul, and a general disturbance in the affections of the will. Let us not aspire to great acts, and difficult occasions of suffering, as long as trifles distinctly demonstrate that our virtue is still feeble, and only beginning to develope.

Let not this graphic picture of our miseries excite us to discouragement, but let us implore God to grant us speedy assistance, through the intercession of the meek, resigned, and tranquil Heart of Mary.

SECOND POINT.

The Heart of Mary is meek amid contradictions that proceed from men.

The virtue of meekness should not only reside in the heart, but disclose its presence by words and outward acts. It should be displayed chiefly during contradictions. It is easy to be calm and amiable, when all goes forward prosperously, and we meet with no opposition. Neither does the exercise of this virtue appear very difficult to us, when we dwell upon it in the silence of meditation, but we find that thinking and performing are widely different. The blessed Virgin discovered the plenitude of meekness existing in her Heart, by the calm with which she endured contradiction, for no sorrow ever disturbed her peace. The execution of the command to fly into Egypt to escape the blood-thirsty Herod was very difficult, but she obeyed it promptly without thinking of the many means there were of escaping him, without undergoing such extreme inconvenience. She did not ask where she would lodge, she did not object that the people were idolatrous and the sworn enemies of the Hebrew name, or enquire what means of subsistence she might find in a foreign land. She thought only of complying with the order, and its bitterness changed not the intentions of that gentle and docile Heart. Christian, a trifling requisition disturbs your peace, and you break out in resentful remarks unbecoming your holy profession, and in lamentations destructive to the perfection of obedience. Enough, that your designs have been interfered with or frustrated, to create an interior combat, with harshness of language and vexation in your actions. And do you presume to style yourself meek? Let obedience impose a duty hard to self-love, or requiring a sacrifice, and we shall quickly discover the degree of benignity with which your heart is furnished. Answer yourself, is your execution of orders prompt, like Mary's? is it careful? cheerful, hidden? Ah! me, the steps you have taken in the path of virtue are few and limited. Yet do not lose courage, contradictions will never be wanting to you, therefore begin to resist and conquer yourself, and you will soon be able with the help of the Heart of Mary to acquire the lovely virtue of benignity.

The Heart of Mary is meek in trials that proceed directly from God.

It is most necessary to live by faith in this world. All that *we* call grievous comes from the merciful hand of God, who either willed it or permitted it for our good. There are therefore, tribulations, which proceed immediately from him; I mean to say, that he strikes with his *own* hand, and not by means of *another.* These are the interior anguish that arises from aridity, spiritual desolation and abandonment. Holy Mary was severely tried in these species of trouble, on the occasion of the loss of the child Jesus in the Temple. Examine this dolor attentively, and judge of the depth of her sorrow by the intensity of her love for the most amiable and most endearing of sons. Think of the seemingly cold reply he gave her, in the moment of her exultation at finding him again. How trying also was the reply that Jesus gave to Mary at the wedding in Cana of Galilee.— " *Woman,* what is that to me."—(JOHN ii, 4.) Ah! how mild must a heart become, that practices meekness under such trials.

Religious, or Christian, what kind of emotions are excited in your soul, when God gives you an occasion of progressing in benignity? You correspond in a feeble manner, or not at all, *then* you become less recollected, and in fine, you abandon prayer.— Fervor in frequenting the sacraments abates, and ere long you cease going or go rarely and coldly. In this state you seek consolation in creatures, and while shrinking from what God does to awaken or renew your fervor, you perhaps abandon him. Alas! insensate and ungrateful soul, is it wonderful, if after long years spent in a religious house, or in the character of a devotee, you find your passions as strong as in the beginning of your profession of piety, and that your falls are not seldom. No wonder that regular observance has become intolerable to you, and that your days are rolling by in deplorable tepidity, and great spiritual poverty. Miserable soul! you might easily become a saint, and you provoke God to "*vomit you from his mouth.*" Shall these things continue? Ah, turn once more with a lively faith to your spouse Jesus, implore of him pardon for your life passed amid imperfections and sins, and through the mediation of the benignant Heart of Mary, I promise that you will obtain full remission. Implore Jesus to send you crosses, afflictions and trials, that will conduct you sincerely to his Heart, and grace to practice while enduring them, that meekness which you have meditated as belonging to the Heart of Mary. Remember, the nearer your heart approaches in similitude to the Heart of Mary, the more acceptable will it be to God.

PRACTICE.

Endeavor to animate all your daily actions with rectitude of intention, and act with such affections as you ought to entertain when in the immediate presence of God.

ASPIRATION.

Ave Cor mitissimum.
Hail, benign Heart of Mary.

SIXTH DAY.

Preparatory Prayer.—As usual.

First Prelude.—Imagine you see the Heart of the
blessed Virgin, like a resplendent sun, which gradu-
lly increases in brightness, and the eternal Father
aying to it, Arise, O my beloved, advance and reign!

Second Prelude.—Ask of God, through the merits
f the Heart of Mary, stability in the choice you
ave made, of passing your life in the divine service.

FIRST POINT.

*The Heart of Mary is unmoved amid the highest
onors.*

Honors are the most insidious enemies of sanctity,
nd therefore, an extra degree of virtue is requisite
or remaining firm in the practice of good, while
urrounded with them. We have a dreadful example
n Lucifer, who, when precipitated from the highest
eaven, drew with him an immense multitude of
piritual beings, destroyed by the pride in which they
ndulged, amid their exalted glories. We have an-
ther example in our first parents, who joined in
ransgressing the formal prohibition of God. Giddy
ith the honor of having subject to them, the wild
easts of the forest, the winged inhabitants of air,
nd the countless creatures that dwell in the deep
ea, they forgot the author of their royal sway, their
reat benefactor, and miserably prevaricating, they
verwhelmed themselves and us, in one immense bur-
len of bitter and countless evils. We may observe
hat *in general*, man when enjoying positions of hon-
r, loses his good sense and sound judgment. Not
o was it with Holy Mary, her heart remained firm
n the practice of justice, amid the most exalted
onors. In pronouncing Mary most honored, we
nean that in her divine maternity, she touched the
imit of divinity. In becoming Mother of God, she
vas immediately raised to a sovereignty in heaven

and on earth. Her ministers are the most sublime angels of the empyreal heaven; her subjects the noblest and greatest men on earth. Would you know how she lived when surrounded by such honors, recall what you have just meditated concerning her mansuetude of Heart.

Devout soul, how do you behave in relation to the gifts with which God has endowed you?—do they lead you to crave honors? Alas! you are ambitious for your ruin! In proportion as you seek distinctions, you are unworthy of them. And in fact, what good sense is there in striving for honors, if these are to prove the most ponderous weapon that can be exercised by the industrious hand of our enemy, in the destruction of sanctity. Be not deluded by the idea, that a brilliant reputation is the most delightful thing in the world—it is mere frivolity, pure emptiness! What will it avail you if men speak favorably of you, and what can they take from you in speaking ill of you—will you be in the former case, more pleasing, or in the latter, less pleasing to Almighty God? And were you even to live quite unknown in the world, would you thereby lose a place in heaven? How many souls, favored with the most perfect gifts of holiness, have passed their lives ignored by the world, as much as though they had no being. It is self-love that bids us covet earthly reputation. O futile, degrading desire! Rejoice, solely because your names are written in heaven, said the blessed Saviour to his Apostles. In *that* blessed abode we *ought* to seek to be known. Perchance you are a seeker of posts of honor in religion—if so, believe me, you are proud, or foolish in coveting what is not becoming to you. To consider the rank or grade that you may hold in religion, is pure vanity, it cannot confer virtue on you, but supposes it to exist in you, and does not increase your merit in the least. Hence, it is useless to wish it. But reflect well into how many false steps such ambitious desires have led souls, into how many imperfections of various kinds, and even into sins. The poor soul that aspires to honors, or has obtained them, loses its stability in righteousness, and not being capable of attaining perfection in obscurity, becomes hateful to God, and risks consequently, her eternal peace and salvation.

SECOND POINT.

The Heart of Mary is unmoved amid ignominies.

There are many souls, that are turned away from God by real or dreaded ignominy. In the gospel, we read of a youth who feared the disgrace attendant on poverty. He was perfect in the most exact observance of the divine law, but when the Redeemer gave him the precious counsel to go and sell all he had and give his possessions to the poor, (Matt. 19. 21.) the pious young man became sad, and could not summon the courage. The ignominy that the divine Saviour endured in his passion, and which was to become the portion also of all his faithful followers caused many a one to lay down the cross which he had taken while all seemed prosperous. What happened in that early day, happens also now; christian, religious, well you know it is so. A word of irony has power to induce you to leave off a useful practice of piety, which held your soul united to Jesus Christ. Human respect, is sufficient to make you slacken the onward march you were treading in the footsteps of your crucified Lord! Nay, more! the dread of a criticism from such an *one*, which will cause you a trifling dishonor, has force sufficient to

cause you to desist from the resolutions you had
adopted for leading a holy life, the result of a light
that penetrated your mind during a certain spiritual
exercise, or in the precious solitude of a holy retreat.
Is this true virtue?

Consider Holy Mary, she did not draw back from
avowing herself to be the Mother of the Crucified—
nay, she even desired the disgrace that fell upon her
Son to devolve upon her, hence she never retired a
step in the painful journey. Her Heart was established in justice, and therefore unmoved amid the
ignominies of Jesus. Your sanctity depends upon
circumstances and events, and not being fixed, is
overthrown at the least disgrace that you encounter
in God's service. What sentiments of confusion
this should produce! In the very school of Jesus
Christ, with so many means of sanctity, with so many
examples of saintly souls to remain so weak! You
do not love your Spouse Jesus, because you have an
inordinate dread of dishonor and opprobrium, and to
love him in truth you must like and embrace these
in order to be assimilated to him. And whence
think you, did so many innocent Virgins, so many
ingenious youth, so many weak souls, draw strength
and courage to meet the worst of ignominies and the
most atrocious of dishonors rather than forsake Jesus,
and the holy life they were leading, if not from the
ardent love that they entertained for Jesus Christ,
born, living and dying in reproach. However they
possessed the same nature as we, were subject to the
same miseries, had hearts of similar temperament,
why then does there exist such a marked difference
between them and us? When perusing the life, or
listening to the narrative of the deeds of some illustrious hero of the Church, you see him in fancy

bound with chains in the presence of a tyrant, unshaken in his faith amid galling torments, rejoicing in opprobrium and in human threats, you are excited to a holy envy, and you imagine that in such circumstances you too would be animated with such marvellous confidence. But in reality you cannot bear a correction charitably given you, and for just reasons—nay more, you cannot tolerate in peace of soul a neglect from one who governs you. It appears to you too difficult to endure contempt and forgetfulness. Examine minutely every fibre of your heart, alas! how much wretchedness will you find in its recesses. Ah! me, what numerous resolutions it will be necessary to adopt! Consider that inasmuch as you have abandoned leading a holy life, you have forsaken your God, humble yourself and determine to do better.

Holy Heart of Mary, unshaken amid the honors attached to your dignity, never forsaking God even when enduring the extreme of ignominy, established in sanctity and justice, take pity on my instability.

PRACTICE.

Visit the blessed sacrament, and ask of Jesus grace, through the mediation of the Heart of Mary, to know your predominant defect, and the means that you should adopt for correcting it.

ASPIRATION.

Ave Cor Maria, speculum justitiæ!
Hail, Heart of Mary, spotless mirror of justice!

SEVENTH DAY.

Preparatory Prayer.—As usual.

First Prelude.—Imagine you see the Heart of Mary, transpierced with a sword, while she is assist ing at the death-scene of her Son, on Calvary!

Second Prelude.—Let us ask of the Lord, through the merits of the wounded Heart of Mary, to remove from our hearts, whatever is an occasion of death to Jesus, or of grief to Mary.

FIRST POINT.

The Heart of Mary is pierced by the anguish of Jesus.

It is sufficient to consider that the Heart of Mary is a mother's heart, to enable us to understand what must have been its poignant grief, at the agony of her divine, her only Son. A heart that loves, can- not fail to sympathise deeply with the sorrows of the object beloved. Now, the Heart of Mary loved the Heart of Jesus more deeply and tenderly, than any other creature's heart can love, and hence, it was more sensibly afflicted by the trials and agony of her Son's Passion. Religious, while meditating with at- tention on the interior sorrows of the loving Heart of Jesus, your heart melted with pity, and perhaps you even shed tears of sympathizing compassion.— But, was a sterile compassion the sole fruit of your meditations? Are you continually fixed in your habits of imperfection, the result of an obstinate will, and a heedless ingratitude? Reflect, that Jesus foresaw that you would sin; this augmented his suf- fering, and if your guilt cannot now cause him to mourn, because he is impassable and glorious in hea- ven, yet forget not that it has already been a cause of suffering, and consequently, was also a motive of grief and trouble to the Heart of Mary, whose wounds were aggravated in the same ratio as were the sorrows of Jesus. Consider the Heart of Mary, therefore, wounded through your fault, and console her in her trials as far as you are able. You can alleviate its pangs by pitying it, by leading a more regular and consistent life, by affectionately imploring God to have mercy on poor sinners, by propagating the devotion of her Heart—and when occasions offer, by bringing back to the Gospel fold some strayed member, or leading some soul to aspire to a higher degree of sanctity. In order to convert sinners, it is not necessary to resort to pulpit eloquence, to the explanation of dogmas in a sermonising manner, or to fulminate harsh views concerning vice. How many souls have been converted by a christian maxim, kindly offered in the proper time and place, with some salutary and well-adapted reflection accompanying it. Facts prove, that persons who have remained obdurate, under the most efficacious and unanswerable arguments of our holy religion, have been touched, softened, and moved by the simple sayings of a friend. Why then, O devout soul, do you lose time in fancying the grand occasions that may arrive, while great and easy means are at present in your power. Those imaginary, pompous discourses, and logical positions and inferences, serve only to gratify your intellect, and engross your time and attention so *fully*, as to make you leave the little means, of kind words and attentions, and of well-adapted remarks, by which you might sanctify yourself and others, and hence, console the most afflicted Heart of Mary.

SECOND POINT.

The Heart of Mary is afflicted by the sorrows of her Son.

If the love of Mary penetrated the Heart of Jesus, and retraced in it her griefs and troubles, how much

more must the view of the sufferings and dolors of
Jesus have martyrized her holy Heart. The sharp
and cruel thorns that crowned the bleeding brow of
the Saviour, encircled also the tender Heart of Mary:
the spear that lacerated the flesh of Jesus, stabbed
the Heart of that faithful Mother. Jesus suspended
by nails to the cross, an object of terror and of dread,
is the cruel sword that passed through the Heart of
Mary, prophecied by Simeon: *tuam ipsius animam
pertransibit gladius.* (*Luke. II.* 35.) O blessed
Heart, infatuated with love, what sorrow and tender
pity you excite in my soul. You saw your Son dying
amid agonies of interior anguish, and exterior endurance, and at the same time you perceived, that all
that Passion would prevail but little for the salvation
of those for whom it was borne. But her sorrow
was increased not alone by the consideration of the
wasted blood of her Son: but by the knowledge that
the greater part of those reprobates would be forced
to accuse and condemn themselves of wilfully merit-
ing a second hell. Religious soul, if you have a
heart, can you not sympathize in the afflictions of the
transfixed Heart of Mary: but perhaps you yourself
have thrust that atrocious spear, *you*, have dilacerated
that sorrowful Heart. Recall your life past, consider
maturely your present life, and you will perhaps discover that the reflection above suggested is just.
You therefore need to repair your evil deeds. Ah!
if by any scandal you have taken a soul from Jesus,
contemplate the weeping Mother's heart—if you have
led any soul to eternal loss, ah, me! how have you
wrung that loving Heart, hasten to restore that soul
to God by the mediation of that sorrowful and inter-
ceding Heart. The *easy* method I have taught you
in the first point of the meditation. Now reflect,

nd convince yourself, on what you ought to do.
Iow frequently to obtain any object desired you em-
loy the most delicate artifice and refined tact, why
annot you do for the glory of the Heart of Mary,
·hat you would do through caprice, or, to attain a
1ere human end.

If you have supported irregularities in religion,
r have taken part in intrigues, or have given dis-
dification by negligence in your profession, set to
·ork at once, and resolve that your future conduct
hall be exact and holy; renounce your former re-
1issness and negligence, and in proportion to your
ad example, make reparation by giving the highest
dification.

THIRD POINT.

*The Heart of Mary is afflicted by the words of
er divine Son.*

Besides the view of a beloved object in affliction,
he words the cherished one utters, are an occasion
f pain to the sorrow-stricken heart. I will not in-
ite you to join me in following Mary when she went
orth to meet Jesus, while bearing his cross to Cal-
ary—for no one has ascribed any words to Jesus or
) Mary, on that heart-rending occasion—perhaps
·esus whispered "*Mother*," and it may be that Mary
ighed, "*My Son!*" but with what an account of
orrow those probable words were pronounced, who
1ay depict? Let us reflect on the words uttered by
ur Redeemer on the cross, as recounted by the
acred penman. The charity of the Saviour in im-
loring pardon for his executioners, inflicted a wound
t once amorous and cruel in the Heart of Mary,
morous, for it displayed the moral sublimity of the
entiments of her beloved Son, *cruel,* for this saying

demonstrated that he was near breathing his expiring
sigh. This grief was confirmed and strengthened
by the promise he made the penitent thief—"*this
day shalt thou be with me in Paradise.*" But, ah!
how keen her sorrow when they took Jesus from her,
giving *her* as mother to *another* man, and *him* as son
to her. When Jesus believed himself forsaken by
God himself—and called upon his holy name—when
he begged a refreshment for his parched and burning lips, and she was unable to offer him consolation,
either interior or exterior, who can measure the sensibility and depth of the wo that pervaded every
fibre of her loving, tender and affectionate Heart.—
"It is finished"—said the dying Saviour, and recommended his spirit to his Father—*yet, Mary did
not die of grief!* for he sustained her, who would
have her displayed to future ages as, the *Queen of
Martyrs!* Religious, what thoughts occupy you
when reading this little meditation? Ah! they are
thoughts of pity, love and sympathy,—and you are
right—for, where find a heart that would coldly bear
such injuries, offered to any mother standing beside
a dying son—and much more, of *such a Mother*, beside *such a Son!* But let your tears be tears of
sincere repentance, these will relieve and refresh her
crushed and burdened heart—resolve to be fervent—
and from time to time, think of the sufferings and
farewell words of Jesus, and convinced that you have
in them a heavy share, learn the occasions you have
given to the Heart of Mary, of renewed sorrow and
affliction.

PRACTICE.

Recite seven times, the Hail Mary, in honor of
Mary's seven dolors, with your arms outspread in the
form of a cross.

Ave Cor Mariæ, doloris gladio transfixum.
Hail, O wounded Heart of Mary!

EIGHTH DAY.

Preparatory Prayer.—As usual.

First Prelude.—Imagine you see the blessed Virgin after the death of her divine Son, offering her Heart to the eternal Father, and expressing her readiness to give her *life*, if it will contribute to his honor.

Second Prelude.—Ask of our Lord, through the intercession of Mary, a generous will.

FIRST POINT.

The Heart of Mary was victorious on Mount Calvary.

"The Mother was *standing* at the foot of the cross," says the Gospel. And in this saying the victorious Heart of Mary is depicted. It does not contradict the generosity of Mary in her personal afflictions! but it declares that she was capable of *standing* on such an occasion! Jesus, also, in the summit of his affliction, was supreme, victorious over it. Now the same degree of love that excited the grief of Mary, inspired her with force to triumph over every consideration of what the world calls honor or reputation. She is not ashamed to own herself the Mother of Jesus, when he is suspended on the gibbet between two thieves! The revolting rebellious looks of the multitude were turned upon *her;* to *her*, were directed the contumelious words, on *her*, were reflected all the insults and affronts that

8

were lavished upon Jesus. Her Heart nobly contemned, and soared victoriously above the whole. She overcame even that strongest of emotions, maternal tenderness, assisting, motionless beside that infamous bed (the cross) at the expiring breath of her divine Son. She conquered herself by conforming her will to the will of the eternal Father, wishing with him the death of the Incarnate Word, *and,* in that depth of disgrace, in that acme of grief, in that total abandonment in which the Father had decreed it. O noble, O victorious Heart of Mary! *Here,* devout christian, or religious, is the beau-ideal of heroism Imagine *yourself* before the barbarous tyrants of earth, would you be able to disdain every human eye, when they would assail the honor of God? Do you know even *now,* how to resist the wit of every giddy critic, when there is question of leading a more regular and perfect life? Can you directly overcome inordinate attachments, and is it your delight to belong wholly to God, and conform without reserve to every, the least sign of God's will? If so you will be in proportion a great and victorious soul. But be not deceived, it was love for Jesus that infused this sublime degree of virtue into the Heart of Mary, if you are destitute of *this,* you will *never* overcome. I suggest this thought frequently, because I desire you to be intimately convinced of it. The excessive repugnance you feel to overcoming yourself on trifling occasions, indicates that your love for Jesus is feeble; contemplate "*the mother,*" motionless at the foot of the cross, and from that model, ask fortitude, proportionate to the difficulty you feel in self-conquest. Ah! a constant victory over self, over the world, the flesh and the demon, would be crowned with such a complete dominion over all the passions, as to resist the attacks of the most formidable enemies. And *then*, you would find yourself numbered among the holy people of God, to whom is promised the fullness of PEACE. And whence do so many souls derive their serenity of mind, their constant joyousness and calm content, whence that imperturbable hilarity amid every misfortune, if not from their generous victories? Why cannot *we* do, what so many *others* do? We shall enjoy the blessings of eternity in kind and degree in proportion as we have vanquished ourselves. Be convinced, you will triumph, if you possess a truly generous heart.

SECOND POINT.

The Heart of Mary is victorious at the Tomb of Jesus.

They struck the body of the divine Redeemer, they pierced his side with a cruel spear, and thus drew from the Heart of Jesus the last remaining drops of his blood. Jesus was insensible to this blow, it was spent and felt in the Heart of Mary! But not one resentful word escaped her revered lips, at the sight of this inhuman act, on the contrary, she offered those last drops of blood to the eternal Father, for the salvation of that brutal soldier.— When the sacred corpse was taken down from the cross, her arms embraced her lifeless Jesus. Alas! what a contrast between this embrace and the caresses with which she pressed him to her bosom in infancy. Nevertheless, with the same generosity and fortitude, she now offers him to the eternal Father for the salvation of men. And *you*, who meditate this, have you the courage to hear it? She *herself*, contributed to all the pious offices of the burial. She assisted the devout disciples in wrapping the sacred Head in a napkin, and enveloping the lifeless body in its winding-sheet, and as they laid the precious remains in the sepulchre, her gentle hand composed all in order. This alone, is abundant proof of the magnanimity of Mary in self-conquest. But now, let us remain near that cherished tomb which contains the languid body—let us study the holy Heart of Mary, and discern its inmost affections. Though grief is at its height, it does not prevail, generosity and fortitude prevail, and victory is hers. All is consummated by him who cried *consummatum est.* And now my God, what more dost thou ask from me. I have sacrificed to thee my divine Son, for the salvation of mankind, nought remains to me but life, which is thy gift, but if thou wilt, *here, in presence of the clay-cold body of thy son and mine, I give it thee!* Generous, courageous Heart! Ah! communicate to *my poor heart* a small portion, even of your admirable generosity and sublime fortitude. You see, O Mary, how weak and incapable it is! Alas! where are the sacrifices that I have offered to my God, and yet he has not required much from me. The solemn sacrifice of self, that he has often required of me in mercy, has been given nominally only, for it has been diminished by rapine in the holocaust. I consecrated to God my purity of heart —but then—O God, have pity on me. I gave all things to God, professing to detach my heart from all created objects—but alas! do I not continually seek and find means for gratifying my delicacy. I made a formal oblation to God of my self-will, to be always renewed at the least signal for obedience—but do I not ever act according to my own views and intentions. Ah! generous Heart of Mary, grant my mpoverished heart a share in your courage, fortitude and generosity.

The Heart of Mary is victorious in the loss of her Son Jesus after his death.

Death and the sepulchre will deprive Mary of the presence and society of her dear Jesus; but they will disclose another triumph of the generous Heart of that most desolate of mothers. No—we are not to fancy swoonings and sinking, and convulsive sobs in Mary, when she was required to yield to the removal and burial of her Son. These, are evidences of ordinary sorrow. These, are tokens becoming a heart that suffers itself to be overcome by passion, not of a heart that subdues and overcomes itself.— The night that succeeded the death of Jesus was passed by the Heart of Mary in acts of generous resignation, of candid offering, of total abandonment to the holy and solemn decrees of heaven—indeed, she was thus occupied until near the dawn of the third morning after the death of the Saviour. Fixed in grief, she was also firm in sacrifice. Religious, or christian reader, let us beware of thinking that when Jesus conceals himself, and leaves us a prey to our fears, allowing us to be assailed by temptation and mental agitation, he has forgotten us; if we serve him diligently—he desires to try our fidelity! You perceive how courageous Mary is when deprived of Jesus; imitate her. On the contrary, *you* lose charity, eave off your practices of devotion, and are idle in the hour of prayer; perhaps you are incapable of exciting a single good thought. You should humble yourself before God, but never be discouraged.— Banish sadness and uneasiness. If you can do no more, you can say: "Thy will, O God, be done."

Fiat voluntas tua. Cry loudly to God in the intimity of your heart: "Jesus, be to me a Jesus." *O Jesu, esto mihi Jesu.* This is the voice of firmness and generosity, by this you will give glory to God, you will hasten the amorous coming of your Saviour, and imitate the victorious Heart of Mary.

PRACTICE.

To-day, sacrifice what is most pleasing to you, in God's honor, and for Mary's love.

ASPIRATION.

Ave Cor Mariæ admirabile.
Hail, O admirable Heart of Mary.

NINTH DAY.

Preparatory Prayer.—As usual.

First Prelude.—Imagine you see the Heart of Mary darting the most ardent flames of charity, and bathed in delight while enjoying the presence of her beloved Jesus, who is risen from the dead.

Second Prelude.—Let us supplicate a participation in its spiritual consolations.

FIRST POINT.

The Heart of Mary is radiant with the glory of the risen Saviour.

As the Heart of Mary was transfixed by the exquisite anguish of Jesus: so is it brilliant with the reflected glory of Jesus resuscitated. To suffer with Jesus is to merit to be crowned with him. The Heart of Mary was remaining absorbed with her generous sacrifice, after her Son's death and sepulture, when suddenly, behold! Jesus! living, and surrounded by the Patriarchs, Prophets and other just souls freed from Limbo, already enjoying the fruits of his sufferings, and presenting himself to Mary! O consoling spectacle! Ah, who shall declare the joy of Mary! Behold her no longer pallid and wan with interior sufferings, but beautiful in her Virgin Majesty. She looks for the wounds that lately disfigured the body of the divine Liberator, they send forth a light not of earth. In his hands, feet and side are only the scars of those cruel wounds, which like so many charitable tongues intercede for and speak to the hearts that adore them. Behold him, impassible, immortal, and glorious, and therefore the Heart of Mary beams with light and life and unutterable joy. See, O faithful soul, to what contentment lead the sacrifices that are made *for* and *with* Jesus. The moment will come, rest assured, the moment will come when the Lord will also visit our weary souls. And oh! that visit will compensate for all that we have undergone, in such a manner, that we shall be constrained to exclaim blessed mortifications, fortunate sacrifices, blessed humiliations, which have procured us so much good.

However, you sigh for the sweets of Paradise, but you are not willing to sip the bitter and nauseating draughts by which they are to be attained. You are in illusion. In proportion to the part we have shared in the chalice of Jesus, in such proportion will he recompense us. Jesus elevates the Heart of Mary to a paradise of delight by his tender visit: but why? because that Heart had suffered more than all others for love of him, had made more liberal sacrifices for him than any, gaining victories over itself, the love of honor, human respect, etc. O did you but comprehend that the select favors of the Heart of Jesus are to be obtained but by a life of sacrifice, you would not be so slow in immolating yourself to him. You have perhaps professed to belong to God during many years, and yet have not begun to taste "how sweet the Lord is," it is because you have not yet learned to overcome yourself. Make the trial, and you will quickly learn the truth of this assertion.

SECOND POINT.

The Heart of Mary is triumphant through the victories of the risen Saviour.

Not only did the resurrection of her Son fill the Heart of Mary with ecstatic delight, and crown her with a halo of glory: but his triumphs found an echo in her Heart in as perfect a manner as did his ignominies. His triumphs are, victory over hell, destruction of sin, the opening of the gate of heaven, the reconciliation of God and man, the establishment of his kingdom, the foundation of the Church, and his solemn ascension into heaven. What a number of motives for joy to the Heart of Mary.

She conquered, by rejoicing at his triumphant prosperity. No, she did *not* murmur when he left her, to ascend to heaven, because she believed his promise that he would remain with her in the sacrament of his love. How often and with what unutterable fervor did she receive her Jesus in holy communion. Imagine with what charity she pressed him to her Heart, and what were her words with him in those blessed moments. Religious, daughter of Mary, you can very easily imitate what the blessed Virgin here teaches you. Direct your daily meditation in every portion of the ecclesiastical year to this blessed Mystery. Imagine yourself really present with Jesus, and praise him in his triumphs, *then*

you will feel in *your* heart that ineffable joy which
filled the Heart of Mary. But remember, that in
that sacrament Jesus is actually present to you as he
was to Mary. He is in the neighboring Church, in
the house, in fine always with you: and reiterates to
you: *ecce Ejo vobiscum sum.* (*Matt. c. ult.,*) thus
inviting you, calling on you continually and drawing
you to him with the voice of charity. In the counsels that he suggests to your heart, he proves himself
the most loving of Fathers. In the affability with
which he treats you, he proves himself the most
affectionate of Brothers, and in the communication
of his benefits and treasures, ah! who shall define
the extent of his friendship. In this sacrament he
is your pastor and nourishes you with his own flesh,
he loves you, *he is your all.* And yet, devout soul,
in what manner do you approach this divine banquet?
perhaps with coldness and indifference, it may be
with disgust? can such ingratitude be possible?
Beats there a heart within you? and if so, is it a
human heart? We are deeply impressed with the
favors that we receive from men, and we are so
anxious that they should know that we are conscious
of our obligations, that we protest to them a thousand
times, and in the formulas prescribed by the nicest
sensibility, and for so infinite a blessing from the
Heart of Jesus, we are cold, silent and insensible!
Alas! my own ungrateful heart. I could tear thee
from my breast, thou art unworthy to be styled the
Spouse of God. O Jesus, give me a new heart.
And, O Mary, grant me a ray, a scintillation of thy
charity, that I may become truly the friend of Jesus.

THIRD POINT.

*The Heart of Mary is glorious in her exalted re-
compense.*

The glory of the *Heart* of Mary commenced in the triumphant resurrection of Jesus, but remained to be completely perfected in the Assumption of Mary—when, after death it would be taken with her body into heaven. And what portion had her Heart in her exaltation?—the lovely share of the *purest affections.* Think what were its emotions, when her soul, roused from its customary beatings, met the blessed Virgin, escorted by angels and saints advancing into heaven, grateful to God for divesting her of the pallor of death, and releasing her of the funereal silence of the tomb. What its emotions, when her divine Son introduced her into his kingdom, presented her at the throne of the Omnipotent, and gave her a seat nearest him, at the same time crowning her Queen of Angels and of Saints. Love, blended with thanksgiving, jubilation, overflowing gratitude, content and unmingled satisfaction were the affections which filled that holy Heart. O blessed, beatified and glorified Heart of Mary, how rejoiced I am at the thought of thy splendor.

Religious, or faithful child of Mary, there is also an immortal kingdom prepared for you, to which Jesus, the spouse of the soul invites you: there is also a throne placed for you, and *near to Jesus,* with a diadem of unending life and empire in the heavens. Arouse your faith, amid the trying scenes of this transitory life; lift your eyes to heaven, and say: *there,* my consolations will be eternal, *there* earthly evils will end, and in proportion to the extent of my sufferings, will be my participation in the glory of that "better land." These thoughts will enable you to bear up, when the spirit is ready to faint with the weight, or with the complication of difficulties, and render you strong to profit by them, and increase in sanctity.   Paradise is unbounded, and every portion of it is blessed, and for all eternity.   *There*, the soul shall experience the contentment of every desire, its inordinate wishes will cease, its every appetite will be perfected, and it will possess God himself, who is the fountain of all good.   To that inheritance will your body be called, as the faithful companion of your soul in its penances, prayers, vigils and mortifications.   *Then*, it will be endowed with all the qualities of the resuscitated body of our Lord.   O sweetest, gentlest of Hearts—Heart of glorious Mary, amid the ocean of delights in which you dwell, forget not a soul that far away in exile, pants to attain the bliss of heaven.   Behold it moreover, not only distant, but surrounded by enemies—and take compassion on it in its combats.

PRACTICE.

Consider during a quarter of an hour, what obstacle would have most influence in retarding your entrance into heaven, at the moment of death.   Try to remedy it without delay.

ASPIRATION.

Ave Cor Mariæ gloriosum.
Hail! glorious Heart of Mary.

For the Feast
OF THE
HOLY HEART OF MARY.

The festival of the Heart of Mary may be styled the festival of Mary's love for man.   Love, will therefore, be the subject of this day's meditation.—

It is a theme of obligation, from which we are not willing to dispense you. The day should be occupied in studying the loving Heart of our venerable Mother, and in corresponding with its pure affections. I shall, however, be contented, if your earliest thoughts be thoughts of love for Mary—after, give some time to the meditation assigned you, and approach the holy Eucharist with great fervor, and during the day repeat from time to time, an ejaculatory prayer to Mary's blessed Heart.

Meditation.

Preparatory Prayer.—As usual.

First Prelude.—Imagine you see the blessed Virgin kindly turning to you, and showing her Heart amidst ardent flames. At the same time, saying to you: Behold my Heart, give me thine in return.

Second Prelude.—Excite your heart to strong emotions, and then answer to her what your heart suggests, for an offering so precious.

MARY HAS A LOVING MOTHER'S HEART.

From our earliest years we have heard how the blessed Virgin was given to St. John the evangelist, as his mother, by the dying Saviour. St. John, there (on Mt. Calvary,) represented all the faithful, and from that moment our dear mother Mary regarded him as a son, newly purchased by her heavy grief. Now, that holy Mary has been deputed to be our mother—it is not enough that she bestows on us occasional blessings, it is necessary for her to entertain love for us; and not only a guarding and sustaining love, but one that has all the dispositions and qualities of maternal affection. Yes, to please Jesus, and indeed to obey him, she must ask for that interest in us to be infused into her Heart by her Son, and at the same time we should receive the impress of filial love for her. This sentiment is alive in all of us, even though we are sinners. It is one of unusual tenderness, combined with a confidence widely different from that, that we feel towards other saints. It is not a servile affection and devotedness, but a reverence and regard wholly *filial*. O happy emotion, of how many consolations is it the messenger to him who is fortunate as to consider it well. Mary is indicated to us as our mother, this proves that we are her sons, and points out our relations.

Constancy and longanimity are the characteristics of Mary's love for us. She never forgets us, although we have often forgotten her. She shows the most tender solicitude in our affairs, although we do not have recourse to her. She compassionates us in our miseries, and in our excesses she interposes between us and God, appeases his anger kindled against us, suspends his chastisements, and reconciles us to him. Recall in detail all the favors of your past life: the blessings showered upon you from heaven came through the hands of Mary. If you did not die in your sins, Mary's intercession preserved you from it. Were you conqueror in the moment of temptation, Mary obtained for you the strength. If you escaped any imminent danger, you owe it to Mary's propitious care. Your passions were overcome by an appeal to her, and a certain obstacle which appeared invincible in the way of your salvation was subdued by Mary's aid. You must see, that you are a living proof of St. Bernard's assertion, that we receive all good, temporal and spiritual, by means of Mary. O, dear and holy Mother, continue to manifest to me the affectionate testimonies of your motherly assiduity:

but grant me also grace to correspond sincerely by a filial love.

From the above facts we may conclude that the Heart of Mary is for you the mother of grace. Now this love is quite different from a common mother's, and moreover of a species never communicated to any human heart. The love that dwells in that holy sanctuary, redounds upon us, and creates a sensible influence in her Heart, such as the changes, impulses and other usual and perceptible effects of maternal anxiety, and this profound interest became the source of deep affliction to her. The greatest grief for a mother's heart is to see her son treated as unnatural and neglected, contemned and forgotten. This grief the Heart of Mary suffered in the highest degree. O, what black ingratitude, what deep injuries, what crying injustice her Son endured? Yet, she never slighted our well-being even in thought. She foresaw when she consented to become our Mother our base ingratitude, the very many offences we would commit against her, so that from that instant her martyrdom began. O what share have you taken in the martyrdom of her Heart. Is it trifling to live in neglect of Mary? recall to mind the injuries and even insults you have offered her, and then consider how she has treated you. What resentment did she exhibit? What sighs did she utter? what revenge did she take? Ah! she ever acted towards you with the most perfect charity, and was unceasingly occupied in her pious and prevalent intercession with our Lord, in order to obtain for you grace and pardon.

Besides, when accepting us as her sons she foresaw the eternal loss of innumerable christians, although they had been ransomed by the precious blood of Jesus Christ. Ah! poor Heart! what must have been its distress at their condemnation. As the Heart of Jesus, when contemplating the waste of his blood and sufferings in the garden of Olives, fell into a mortal agony; so, Mary's Heart underwent the bitterest anguish on seeing that both the labors of her Son and her motherly care and solicitude were to prove fruitless. Mary was also plunged in a sea of sorrow, on perceiving that so many souls would remain obstinate and die in final impenitence. Let this grief prove to us the dispositions of that amiable, tender and solicitous Heart.

O, did the Heart of Mary find a correspondent love in ours, what good would it leave unobtained for us? How many choice graces and distinguished favors would it procure from our ever willing Lord! To what a high degree of sanctity would she conduct us, to what a resplendent diadem for the weary soul, in the immortal repose of heaven! Hear again the summary of the dispositions of the Heart of Mary, love—sincere, persuasive, and maternal—and give her love for love.

PRACTICE.

Make an unreserved offering of yourself, (chiefly of your *heart*,) to the tender Heart of the blessed Virgin—and let it be a generous and perennial offering.

ASPIRATION.

I give thee my heart, mother of my beneficent Saviour, Mother of divine LOVE!

1st Day.—The Heart of Mary is pure.
2d Day.—The Heart of Mary is mortified.
3d Day.—The Heart of Mary is humble.
4th Day.—The Heart of Mary is hidden.
5th Day.—The Heart of Mary is meek.
6th Day.—The Heart of Mary is holy.
7th Day.—The Heart of Mary is afflicted.
8th Day.—The Heart of Mary is victorious.
9th Day.—The Heart of Mary is glorious.
For the Festival.
Mary's is a loving, maternal Heart.

CONSIDERATIONS

FOR THE

Principal Festibals of the Blessed Virgin.

Translated from the French of Rev. F. Hueguet.

SS. C. J. M.

Purification of Mary.

DOCILITY TO GOD'S WILL.

The moment of the purification having arrived, Mary, in conformity with the law, goes to present Jesus in the temple, and her chaste spouse presents himself with her. She consents therefore, to appear as other mother's did, in the eyes of the world; she conceals the secret of her miraculous virginity.— What humility! let us imitate her example, by hiding under an ordinary exterior, the graces with which God may have favored us, and never hesitate to submit to things from which we may have the right to be exempted.

Heavenly favors are *great*, but the humility which conceals them is far *greater*. Did we receive seraphic favors, we should always act so as to be considered common souls. We must, without doubt, become holy; we are under obligation to edify our neighbor by our discourses and daily conduct; but we shall never be truly pious, except in proportion as we shall endeavor to bury in our hearts, so to speak, the gifts of heaven, and avoid distinguishing ourselves exteriorly from others.

It is not rare to find devout persons who generously sacrifice to God their riches, their pleasures, their liberty, and even their life. But there are very few who, attaining the highest effort of christian generosity, consent to expose themselves voluntarily to contempt, disgrace, particularly when there is no positive obligation to submit to it, and they can find arguments for avoiding it.

Mary does not reason in order to find a pretext for dispensing herself from the law of purification; however, powerful motives, which would not have failed to prove sufficient to us, seemed to impose exemption on her as a rigorous duty. For, although motives drawn from her own glory, suffering detraction, were incapable of moving her, how could she be indifferent to the glory of her Son? In confounding herself with other mothers, by her submission to a humiliating ceremony, did she not appear to confound him with the other children of Israel? And could she publicly conceal the honor of her divine maternity, without depriving her Son of the glory of his eternal origin, and preparing remotely, proofs to the incredulity and blasphemies of his enemies.

But Mary had learned during her retreat in Nazareth that the eye of grace is simple; that too much reason, when there is question of the ways of God, is an excess of light which dazzles and leads astray; that the life of faith always leaves some obscurities and difficulties, in order not to subtract from the just soul the merit of its docility; and that there is an eye of scandal which must be torn out and cast aside, for fear of looking too far forward in the way in which grace invites us. She submits with simplicity, and adores in the order of God, the eternal designs of a step which apparently offers to reason nothing but inevitable inconveniences.

This mode of conduct finds very few imitators, even among such as live in the habitual practice of virtue. In promoting God's greater glory, we almost always seek pretexts for dispensing ourselves from his holy law. Hence, we would, say we, retrench many things which God's holy law requires of us; but we fear to render piety odious, by singularities that would excite the ridicule of the world. We should be less susceptible of an injury, or suffer a calumny without complaint, but the glory of God and the interest of piety are enlisted in it or will be compromised. Thus religion itself frequently serves as an asylum or support to our self-love; as though God's glory could be uniquely found in the success of some splendid work of zeal, in the confusion of an enemy to virtue; whilst God is often more truly glorified by the patience of a just person under persecution, or the silence of a faithful soul when calumniated. These secret and painful acts of faith include something greater and more worthy of its glory, than the most pompous honors rendered to virtue. By exercising the just with opprobriums, the Lord knows how to promote his own glory.

By being faithful to minor observances, sometimes persons pass for narrow minded; and it is noble to rise above the thoughts, observations, and contempt of men and a kind of persecution on their part.

Whatever bears the impress of the will of God, and his good pleasure, is great, however insignificant it may seem to be intrinsically. Hence, as soon as we are assured by an interior voice, that God desires some thing of us, his infinite greatness cannot allow us to consider as trifling and indifferent, what forms the object of his desire. To refuse God, deliberately and with reflection, anything whatsoever, under pretext that it is small, is failing in delicacy of love, is rejecting familiarity and intimate union with God; it is robbing him of his glory, for in this he finds his glory, that the creature never regard as little, whatever pleases or displeases God, and be always disposed to sacrifice every thing to the least evidence of God's holy will.

If there were little things in the law, the practicing them through a motive of love would render them great. Ordinarily, men esteem lightly the small services that are rendered them, both because they are not useful to them, and because they do not see the bottom of the heart, nor the desire, less or great, that persons have of rendering them service.

But God, who has need of nothing, and who knows the degree of good will entertained for him, judges far otherwise. We please in proportion to our desires. In this preparation of heart, we have the merit of a thousand good actions, that we do not perform.

The perfection of virtue does not consist in the sublimity of our obligations, but in the lively faith that may accompany the commonest works. Often, we fancy ourselves advancing, simply because we are employed in higher functions, in lectures of higher spirituality, or in methods of higher perfection.— But if you carry into these sublime ways the defects of the weak and the imperfect, you are like the Apostles contemplating the Lord's glory on Mt. Tabor; you retain in them a relish for the things of flesh and blood, and still think of building on earth a tabernacle and abiding city.

Mary, in quality of an indigent person, offered two doves, as the law prescribed. God considers not the hand but the heart. The rich, who presented him more munificent offerings, were not so agreeable to him, because their interior dispositions were less perfect. What matters it to God the amount we give him, if it be not offered in love, and when love bestows, it is of little consequence to him, whether we give him much or little. Love can reserve nothing when God demands, it gives all, or is ready to give it according as it may be required. Mary, destitute of all temporal goods, understood this truth,

and never regretted having but little to give to God.
But the portion she offered, was presented with such
ineffable love, that no one will ever give as much as
she. Our sacrifices all derive their value from the
love that prompts us to make them. The Apostles
only left their little barks and fishing nets. Yet
kings and queens, that have forsaken thrones, have
given less than they, because they renounced with a
lower degree of generosity and love. Men regard
the exterior sacrifice, God looks at the heart; and
the *"heart"* whether we be rich or poor, depends
solely upon ourselves.

SENTIMENTS.

O, Immaculate Virgin, blessed among all women,
and yet consenting to be regarded as the last among
them, grant that after thy example, I may conceal
the favors of God from the eyes of men. In offering thy divine Son Jesus to his Father, thou didst rejoice the angelic choirs; present my poor heart to God,
so that all its sentiments may be agreeable to him, and
that it may participate in thy glory in heaven.

ASPIRATION AND PRACTICE.

O Holy Mary, make thyself known and loved!

Honor Mary particularly on Saturday, which is
dedicated to her, hear mass, or give some alms that
day in her honor.

Pray for souls faithful to their obligation—recite
the *Remember*, etc.

The Annunciation.

RESIGNATION TO THE WILL OF GOD.

The oracles of the prophets are about to be accomplished; the earth is going to open and bring forth the just one! The God of Jacob casts a favorable eye on his people, he is about to efface the opprobrium of Israel, and re-light the extinct flambeau of David. Ready to quit the splendors of the saints which radiate in brilliancy around his eternal origin, he meditates a second birth among men. He purposes being born of a mortal mother, and to this end, he must select among all his creatures, the one who bears the closest resemblance with the God who created her.

Guided by his own unerring wisdom, he will seek in obscurity an humble and simple virgin, who knows not the world, and of whom the world is wholly ignorant; who withdraws from the sight of men, and attracts the attention of God; who is nothing on earth but whom heaven prefers above all that the world esteems; a virgin in fine, who is of no rank among her people, to whom her nation offers but insults and contempt, and that Juda almost blushes to number among her daughters. Behold the one whom he invites to accept the first position in the universe, and whom he intends acknowledging as his Mother.

What then does the Most High perceive in Mary, that determines him to give her the preference in so glorious a choice? He perceives all that he loves: innocence, modesty, the most eminent piety, the most precious fruits of the abundant graces of which he is the author, and above all *humility*, a virtue hitherto unknown on earth. These God sees in Mary; and to discover these the eye of God was re-

quisite, so completely had the modesty of that solitary
virgin closely veiled whatsoever could distinguish
her.   Let us study this mystery in which Mary offers
to the angels the spectacle of the deepest humility
joined to the fullness of merit.

The Archangel Gabriel was sent by God himself
to Mary; for, says St. Gregory, it was meet that the
greatest of all events should be announced by the
highest of the celestial hierarchy.   That angel,
says St. Ambrose, found her alone.   In quitting the
temple, that august Virgin left there her heart.
Having returned to the world, she was not less a
solitary; labor and prayer divided her every moment;
retreat concealed and preserved all her virtues.   An
angel was necessary to gain access to her; and again
the sight of even an angel was capable of alarming
her!   The profession she had made of never, as a
virgin, holding private conversation but with her
God; her exact and severe regularity, the bashful-
ness and modesty that were more than natural to her,
all, awakened a fear she was not ashamed to exhibit,
because to be thus troubled is the genuine characteristic of a virgin faithful to God.   But if the presence
of the angel disconcerts her, the discourse he
addresses her alarms her no less.   The Angel hum-
bles himself before her, and respectfully salutes her:
*Hail, full of grace, the Lord is with thee; thou art
blessed among all women.*   Mary does not recognise
this eulogium as belonging to her; she is ignorant
of the treasures of grace that she possesses.   She
knows as little of the mysteries of her own heart, as
she does of the mysteries of divine Providence.   The
only reply she gives to the offered praises is anxiety.
Turbata est.   Alway occupied, both with God's
greatness and her own littleness, she cannot hear

without embarrassment, language so different from the ideas that her humility gives her of herself. That prudent Virgin, says St. Bernard, was aware that the angel of Satan sometimes transforms himself into an angel of light; and because she was infinitely humble, she never thought that the Angel of God would speak so graciously to her. Ignorant of what reply she ought to make, she maintains silence, until she has examined, with sage precaution, who it is that speaks to her: *Cogitabat qualis esset ista salutatio.* Pious souls, imitate the prudence of the ever blessed Virgin, never act without knowledge, seek instruction on the doubts which arise in your mind, and endeavor not to perform any important action, without ascertaining whether you can do it conscientiously. How different are Mary's sentiments from ours! Praise never troubles us: we hear it tranquilly and accept it as our due. What excites our emotion is, that we are deprived of the portion of praise we imagine we deserve.

How agreeable to God, were these thoughts which agitated Mary concerning a salutation that she could not be persuaded referred to her. If he caused her to be saluted in such terms it was because he knew that she was incapable of attributing any thing of it to herself. The strongest temptation to vain-glory to which the soul can be exposed, is undoubtedly the reception of praises from God, who is truth itself. They must be received, believed to be just; and yet we must not take complacency in them, and must refer all the honor to Almighty God. What virtue less solid than Mary's would not have given way? but the triumph of her humility is, that it increases, notwithstanding this aliment so apparently capable of weakening it.

Mary, only is able to describe the emotions of her soul, at the announcement of a fact so little expected. Of all the sentiments that occupied her great soul, one alone escapes, to serve as an authentic testimony to her extreme love for purity. *Quomodo fiet istud.*

Mary, says St. Bernard, blushed at receiving the blessing as a woman, because she only wished that of a virgin. Seized with a sudden fear on hearing this voice, she recalls the engagements she has taken with the Lord. Thou knowest, O my God, her heart exclaimed, that I have passed my infancy in the secret of thy sanctuary; innocence was the companion of my earliest proceedings; virginity appeared to me an offering worthy of thee; I vowed it, thou didst receive my sacrifice—could it be possible that my purity was not agreeable to thee? *"Fear not,"* said the Angel, *"thou shalt have a son, and he shall be called Jesus; he shall be great, and shall be called the Son of the Most High."* I, the mother of my God, exclaimed Mary; it was sufficient glory for me to be his handmaid. I love, adore, and should be undoubtedly, too happy to carry him in my arms, to watch over his slumbers, to wipe his sacred tears, to mingle my lamentations with his, to dare to call him my son, and hear him call me mother; but the Lord knoweth that I have sworn to him in his sanctuary, and I prefer pleasing him to commanding him. Ah! could the designs of God over his servant, be executed without prejudice to a virtue which I hold so dear, I leave to the women of Juda, those benedictions that form the object of their ardent desires, and I renounce the divine maternity, rather than cease to be a virgin! To dissipate these fears, the angel was obliged to re-assure her. Fear not, Mary; you will become a mother, but remain a virgin. That son whom I announce to you, shall be the Son of God himself, and far from that divine operation sullying the splendor of thy virginity, it shall become infinitely more pure, by the residence of God with thee.

In submitting to the declaration of the angel, Mary instructs us never to reason on the will of God, when it is clearly known to us; to apprehend no danger when he calls upon us to expose our dearest interest, and to believe confidently, that he will take better care of them than we can.   Oh! how pure, how worthy of God, is resignation like that of Mary.

How admirable also is Mary, when through attachment to the most perfect of the virtues, she consents to sacrifice the glory that is offered to her!   Virginity, what is thy value! thou alone canst make a Mother of God, but thou art estimated more highly than that sublime dignity!   Let us avow with St. Jerome, that, in the Mother of our God, there is, we may say, a species of greatness, even more elevated than the divine maternity; it is that love which in virtue esteems nought but virtue itself; which, remote from seeking virtue for its glory, shuns the glory for the perfection of the virtue.   Let us admit, that in placing herself as it were, above the divine maternity, by the humble opposition which she exhibits, Mary acquires a grandeur that the divine maternity never could have bestowed upon her.   In effect, the honor offered her, is only the effect of the liberality and munificence of the Lord; but the virtues that she practices are at once the gifts of God and the glory of Mary.

Pious souls! in order to conform to the will and pleasure of God, value more during your whole life, the smallest act of virtue, than all celestial gifts, because it is not these gifts, but the virtues, the exercise of which opposes our miserable nature, which glorify God and sanctify our souls. The gifts of God, that of prayer for instance, are not granted to us for themselves, but to facilitate the practice of what is most perfect in the evangelical code, renouncement, resignation and death to self. Every grace from God, that is not productive of such effects, however great we may suppose it, will only serve for our condemnation.

SENTIMENTS.

To know God's will is the sweetest fruit of faith —to love it and follow it is the only real happiness. Oh, Mary! thou who art the most perfect of all pious souls, gain for me grace to follow thee faithfully, and to imitate thy resignation to God, and thy faith in his providence. Break the bonds which hold me captive to my imperfections and miseries. Obtain for me, Virgin most clement, and powerful Queen of Heaven, to die to myself, and to live only to God, and according to his eternal and ever amiable designs.— Grant that I may love God for God; that I may serve him for the sole motive of glorifying him and pleasing him, by accomplishing his adorable will faithfully, even to death.

ASPIRATION AND PRACTICE.

O Mary, look kindly on me and draw me to God.
O Mary, I love thee, and trust in thee.
Recite the Rosary devoutly.
In time of trouble, exterior or interior, invoke the sweet name of Mary.
Pray for haughty and discouraged persons. *Remember*, etc.

Mary, Sorrowing Mother.

(The Compassion.)

UTILITY OF THE CROSS.

Mary was remotely prepared for the ignominious and dolorous Passion of her Son. He who had so often predicted it to his disciples, did not leave his mother in ignorance of it. Besides, the destiny of Mary was too intimately connected with that of Jesus Christ, for her not to have the most extensive acquaintance with what was to happen to him. Besides, the holy Scriptures had lifted the veil for her; and Jesus, suffering and crucified, was ever present to her thoughts. All that forms the consolation of other mothers, was changed for her into a sort of torment. If Jesus stretched out his innocent hands towards her, she fancied that she already saw them loaded with chains, or pierced with the nails that were destined to fasten them to the infamous gibbet. If he smiled sweetly on her, or fixed on her a look of tenderness, soliciting her caresses, she represented to her mind, his languishing and dying eyes, his countenance covered with blood, and his sacred body torn and bruised. It was a torment of each succeeding moment, ever renewing, and that none but love like hers could ever support, She saw the moment of sacrifice daily approaching, and we can imagine what impression that frightful, ever-present spectacle must have made on her maternal heart. The certain expectation and foresight of an inevitable evil, is often a ruder cross to bear than the ill itself.

God, who designed not to spare the Mother more than the Son, would not allow her to be ignorant of any of the principal circumstances of his passion; they were so many blows that he had resolved she should receive. Besides, in quality of Mother could she fail to be eager in learning all the details of the evil treatment that was to be offered to her Son?

Mary was therefore instructed concerning the treason of Judas and the violent seizure of Jesus; she knew, from John who was witness, of it, all that happened during the night in the house of Annas and Caiphas; she saw him really in the pretorium of Pilate and in the palace of Herod; she was present when the people preferred Barabbas to Jesus, when he was displayed, his body all bruised and torn with scourges, his head encircled with the crown of thorns, and his shoulders covered with an old purple mantle, bearing in his hand a reed for his sceptre. She followed him, when he was carrying his cross, to the summit of Calvary, and sinking under that weight with weakness and exhaustion at almost every step: she was present when in divesting him of his tunic, they renewed all his wounds, when they stretched him on the cross, pierced him with cruel nails, raised him up with horrible shaking, and when the chief persons among the people and the multitude outraged him with the most cutting and sarcastic derision. What a spectacle for such a Mother and for such a Son. What must have been the excess of her sorrow! how deep and yet how submissive! how firm was she and how tranquil! Her noble Heart was *not* overwhelmed; an extraordinary grace sustained her, so that she might suffer more keenly. In fine, when Mary obtained leave, she approached the cross; she remained by it *standing*, which proves her strength and courage quite divine. We do not read that Mary appeared in Jerusalem, when her Son was received there with so much honor by the people; but she feared not to show herself publicly on Calvary, not drawing back for shame of being recognized as the Mother of the condemned, who was about to submit to a punishment reputed infamous by the Jewish nation. What sentiments then occupied her heart? not one that was not heroic and supernatural. Stronger and more generous than the Mother of the Machabees, she offered to God the full and entire sacrifice of her cherished Son; she united herself to the justice of the heavenly Father who was immolating that great victim to his own glory; she immolated with him that new Isaac, become the pledge for the sins of mankind; she offered with a great heart his death for the salvation of each one of us, and to that offering she joined that of her own immense grief, so that she actually co-operated in the work of our redemption. The sacrifice of the Mother was not separated from the Son's; it would have cost her less to have given her own life; and for this reason she is justly styled the Queen of Martyrs.

What sublime lessons does Mary here give us? and how well is she, in this circumstance, the perfect model of pious souls whom God subjects to the extremest trials! Their pains are excessive, but can they be compared with hers? Let them not complain then; but, for their support let them cast their eyes upon that Mother of sorrow, and let them invoke her, in order to obtain by her intercession, force to imitate her firmness, constancy and generosity. After *Jesus on the cross*, the most desirable and beautiful book for them to read is *Mary at the foot of the cross.*

O how few there are, even among pious persons, who follow Jesus, as did Mary, to the very foot of the cross. They excuse themselves on vain pretexts, they tremble, they draw back with cowardice as soon

as they must appear destitute and loaded with opprobriums with the Man of Sorrows. O my God, you
are loved for the consolation you give; but we desire
not to follow you as did blessed Mary, to the death
of the cross. All shun you, and flee away, all forsake you, despise and deny you. And yet crosses
are "daily bread;" the soul has need each day of a
certain measure of sufferings for detaching itself,
just as the body requires a certain quantity of
aliments for its conservation.

There are many souls who make a profession of
piety, and yet they find great difficulty in being convinced of the goodness which God exhibits in loading
with crosses the souls that he loves. Why, say they,
does he take pleasure in causing us to suffer? Could
he not render us good without afflicting us? Yes,
undoubtedly God could, for to him nothing is impossible. He holds in his omnipotent hands the
hearts of all men, and turns them as he will, but
God who *could* save us without the cross, would not
do it; just as he preferred leaving men to advance
by degrees through all the embarrassments and
miseries of infancy and childhood, rather than endow
them at once with the strength and faculties of
mature age. In all this, he is master; we must
silently adore his profound wisdom without comprehending it. What we see clearly is, that we cannot
become good but inasmuch as we become humble,
disinterested, detached from ourselves so as to refer
all to God, without any anxiety for ourselves.

Nothing happens in the world, sin excepted, that
God does not wish. He does all, he regulates all,
and gives to each one what he has. *He* has numbered the hairs of our heads, the leaves of every
tree, the grains of sand on the sea-shore, and the

drops of water that compose the abyss of ocean.—
When forming the universe, his wisdom scanned and
weighed even the minutest atom. He every instant
produces and renews the breath of life that animates
us; he has numbered our days, and holds in his potent hands the keys of the tomb to open or to close it.

The cross is never fruitless, when it is received in
a spirit of sacrifice. We should accept it, adoring
the hand of God who charges us with it, in order
to sanctify us. Happy is he who is ready for all
things like Mary; who neves says: "it is too much,"
who relies not on himself, but on the Omnipotent;
who wishes no consolation but inasmuch as God himself deigns to bestow it, and who is fed and nourished with *his* pure will.

There are in crosses so many tokens of mercy, and
such a plentiful harvest of graces for faithful souls,
that if nature is afflicted by them, grace ought to
rejoice in them. The purest pleasures arise from
submission and unreserved sacrifice. To *that*, God
pushes a soul, in order to detach it from all that is
not himself. What remains to be done but to embrace the cross which he presents, and allow ourselves to be nailed to it and crucified? Let us therefore, be glad, when our heavenly Father tries us here
below, by divers interior and exterior temptations,
rendering us contradictory within and afflicted without. Let us rejoice, for by such sorrows, our faith
more precious than fine gold, is purified.

Let us rejoice, also, at experiencing the nothingness and deceit of all that is not God; for it is by
that crucifying experience that we are torn away
from ourselves and all worldly desires. What! shall
we be discouraged, when the hand of God hastens to
accomplish its work! We daily wish and pray that

he would do this; and as soon as he begins to do it
we become troubled; our cowardliness and our impatience arrest the hand of God. Piety without
crosses is a barren piety, and has no solid foundation.

O dear Lord, thy saints were great masters in this
science of perfect sacrifice! Drink the cup of tribulation, says St. Ambrose; drink it, so that the sentiments of suffering may penetrate the bottom of the
heart. Attach yourself strongly to the cross, said
St. Augustine, be not so imprudent as to remove one
nail which binds you to it. I cannot resist the desire
I feel of suffering, exclaimed the seraphic St. Teresa,
give me, O Jesus, sufferings or give me death.—
Lord, said St. John of the Cross, I wish no other recompense than thee; I would only suffer and be despised for love of thee.

SENTIMENTS.

O Mary, mother of love and of suffering, grant
that I may love and suffer in accordance with thy
great example; Queen of Martyrs, give me a share
in thy martyrdom! Love gave thee the cross, grant
that the cross may give me love; and if to *love*, suffering and death are necessary, obtain for me this
grace, that I may love all that is sent from the hand
of God, even trials and death Holy Mother, engrave deeply in my heart the wounds of Jesus crucified. (*Indul. 300 days.*)

ASPIRATION AND PRACTICES.

O Mary, the most afflicted of Mothers, give me a
share in thy sufferings.

Recite the Chaplet of Seven Dolors—to which
great indulgences are attached.

Celebrate devoutly, the festival of our Lady of
Sorrows. *Remember*, etc.

The Visitation.

CHARACTERISTICS OF CHARITY.—RULES FOR VISITS AND CONVERSATIONS.

Elizabeth did not in the least expect the visit of Mary, whom she did not suppose acquainted with her secret; and Mary firmly resolving to guard hers which she had not even revealed to Joseph, did not come to seek the congratulations of Elizabeth. But the Lord, for the execution of his designs, and for the consolation of both, made known to the mother of the Precursor that her youthful relative was the mother of the Messiah. The blessed Virgin had no sooner entered the house of Zachary, than she hastened to salute her cousin and testify the share she took in her happiness.

At the voice of Mary, Elizabeth was suddenly filled with the Holy Ghost. Her unborn infant joyfully rendered his first homage to him whose ways he was destined to prepare. A kind of combat of humility and charity arose between the two relatives: each one striving to humble herself the more profoundly, and to celebrate with greater magnificence the mercies of the Lord. This is not a visit of pure ceremony. The first interview is not passed in fine words, reciprocal eulogiums mutually exchanged with refined tact; vain civility, which hearts truly friendly cheerfully spare each other. All those obliging expressions which ordinarily occur, were in this instance turned into thanksgiving to God. Elizabeth in surprise exclaims, touched by a lively emotion of gratitude: *Whence this favor, that the Mother of my Lord should come to me?* The subject of her gratitude, says St. Ambrose, is her conviction that the grace that she receives is not bestowed on account of any personal merit on her part but is a pure effect of the mercy of the Lord. Thou art happy, O Mary, *because thou hast been faithful, and hast believed.* Let us believe, and we shall be like Mary blest. Let us place all our delight in faith; let us not be insensible to that beatitude proposed to us by Jesus Christ himself.

Remark also, for your instruction that one of the best dispositions which prepared Elizabeth for such abundant graces, was that deep and prolonged retreat of six months, during which she withdrew from the world and intercourse with creatures as the Gospel expressly declares: *Occultabat se mensibus sex.* Had she been absent from home, when the Son of God, borne by his blessed Mother came to pay her this visit, perhaps she would have been deprived of all his graces; but she received them in abundance, because God found her in solitude. God delights to find souls in retirement; he conducts them there when he desires to favor them with his divine caresses, and speak to them heart to heart, for the noise and busy hum of the world are not suitable to conversation with him. Alas! need we be astonished if we are deprived of his real visits? O were the soul always recollected, attentive, and candid with God, did she give him a cordial reception, remaining peaceable and in profound respect before him, like Magdalen at his sacred feet when he deigned to visit her, how many choice benedictions would she receive. If she contracted, with time, a holy habit of being forgetful of all else and solely attentive to him, Jesus would enter. If he finds our hearts detached, alone, that is desiring merely his divine presence; alone occupied with no other love but his; alone in fine, without any will but his good pleasure, he will enter.

Jesus uses Mary to convey his most precious favors to John and Elizabeth, in order to teach us that henceforward it will be through the agency of his holy Mother that he will communicate all his graces. The sanctification of St. John the Baptist was the first fruit of the Incarnation of the Word. The voice of Mary served as its instrument, and was the sensible sign of the operation of invisible grace. It is a great incentive to confidence in Mary, to find her intercession in the first application which was made of the merits of Jesus Christ after his Incarnation, and particularly in the sanctification of the holiest among the sons of women. Let us then confidently recur to Mary in our wants, and in our moments of trouble and anxiety.

Mary remained about three months in the house of Elizabeth, and then returned to her own home. Charity ought not to be transient; Mary remained three months with Elizabeth. Whoever is the bearer of grace should not hasten onward, but leave it time sufficient to complete its operations.

Who can describe the respectful attentions and the cares full of tenderness that Elizabeth exhibited to her young relation, whose age gave Elizabeth the right to consider her as her daughter, and whose supreme dignity raised her much above all, even the most perfect of creatures. Mary, on her side, showed no less consideration, nor less assiduity for a virtuous kinswoman whom she regarded as her Mother, and in whom she admired the gifts of God. On either side the attentions were reciprocal, thus rendering their intercourse equally holy and consoling. Wherever, the spirit of God reigns, there also is found sincerity, union of heart, the sweets of social intercourse and domestic peace. How holy and delightful

9

must the conversations of Mary and Elizabeth have been, for they spoke from the abundance of their hearts, and having them filled with God, all their conversations were concerning God and the bliss of heaven. How ravishing, O God of goodness, never to converse with each other but of thee and thy attributes! Adieu, vain and worldly conversations; let us think of God, and speak of God, nothing can be more fascinating to a soul that loves him.

The eagerness of Mary in going to visit her cousin, and her friendly abiding with her, teaches us that, in order to fulfill certain obligations that relationship and propriety exact, we must comprehend how to sacrifice when required, retirement, silence, meditation, and other exercises of piety, and show no difficulty in displaying our efforts and attentions without. Had the piety of Mary been regulated, how many apparent reasons had she for omitting that visit, and remaining shut up with God, in the solitude of Nazareth! Grace does not permit us to neglect what we owe to our neighbor, even through simple good-breeding; and the renunciation of this species of duty, under a pretext of devotion, is an abuse or caprice. Let us comfort ourselves like Mary, in these indispensable occasions, and our piety will not suffer diminution, only let us guard against dissipation, and the inclination of displaying ourselves exteriorly.— Mary forgets herself to be occupied wholly with her cousin; but she does not forget God, and in the outward distractions inseparable from such a journey, she never even for a moment, loses the holy presence of God; all her discourses were of God or related to him. By her attentions and charity towards her cousin, her modesty, affability and heavenly air, by all her virtues which she had occasion to practice, she edified the family of Elizabeth, and the persons who came to visit her in that simple abode.

Mary furnishes us, in this circumstance, four excellent rules for our relations with the neighbor.— 1. Let us not seek the occasion of seeing the neighbor, but wait till God presents them. Be retired, like Mary, through choice; but when it is necessary, or grace seems to demand it, let us be communicative like her. 2. Let us, as far as depends on us, associate only with pious persons, who can be useful to us. We need not regret the time we spend with them, so long as good reasons oblige us to it; and let us only show ourselves to others, to whom we render duties of civility, when we perceive that neither they nor we profit by it. 3. Let us dread dissipation in the intercourse with creatures, not visiting them simply to remove wearisomeness, nor in search of human consolations. Interior recollection can never subsist with such visits. When we possess God in our hearts, we can cheerfully consent to leave conversation with men, and only lend ourselves to it when charity demands it. 4. Finally, in pursuance of Mary's example, let us never prolong our visits beyond the necessary time, though they may have charity for their object. If we follow these rules of prudence and discretion, we need not fear occasionally to quit our retirement to converse with the neighbor. Let the wicked hide themselves, if they wish, the world will lose nothing by not seeing them, but the good become useful by at times presenting themselves. Besides, the world ought to know, that a life devoted to piety is neither sad nor severe, but simple, sweet and easy to practice; that far from being an obstacle to the social relations, it facilitates them, ameliorates, purifies and sanctifies them. The great

design of God, in the visit of Mary, was the sanctification of the Precursor. You may pay or receive a
visit that seems to be one of pure ceremony; perhaps God wishes to use it for the spiritual welfare of
the person who comes to see you. A word, spoken
as it were accidentally, will open the heart of one
who is speaking to you, and will produce fruits of
grace. How many conversions have resulted from
such conversations, in which at first, nothing serious
was proposed. How many souls have thus entered
the path of perfection. St. Francis of Sales did
more good by his conversation, than by his sermons
and controversies!

Cultivate then, pious souls, the social duties of
kinsfolk and relatives, be friends, christian women,
like Mary and Elizabeth; let your conversations be
full of God, let your friendship be an exercise of
piety. Jesus will be in your midst, and you will feel
his presence.

SENTIMENTS.

O my God, sanctify my visits, take from them curiosity, inutility, passion, anxiety and dissimulation;
let cordiality, simplicity, and good example reign in
them. Mary, my mother and patroness, let thy example enlighten me, and thy goodness aid me in correcting the human and too natural views, that have
hitherto influenced me.

ASPIRATION AND PRACTICE.

O Mary, happy is he who serves thee and confides
in thee.

In conversation, delight to speak of the prerogatives and love of Mary.

Pray for devout souls, who are employed in exterior works of mercy.

The glorious titles that the Church bestows on Mary, when calling her the Mother of grace and mercy, should especially excite us to implore her *protection*, for by these words she proves to us, that if there are souls elect, and favored with special graces, they are indebted for it to the protection of the blessed Virgin, who procured it for them.

St. Bernard, who has ever been considered one of the most faithful and most illustrious defenders of Mary, was fully persuaded of her great zeal for our perfection, and of her immense power with Jesus, when he declared that God granted no grace except by the intervention of Mary; that all pious emotions and holy inspirations come to us through her mediation; that the fervor, force and courage that we feel for practicing any virtue, for combatting vices and for overcoming temptations, are communicated to us through her intercession; and that in fine, according to the present disposition of Providence, all the gifts that we receive from his mercy, pass through the hands of his holy and potent Mother, who is the steward, treasurer and dispenser of them, to distribute them to whomsoever it may please him, when it pleases him, and in proportion as it pleases him.

Be faithful, says St. Liguori, in honoring and loving that good mother; take care to induce others to love her; and believe me, if you persevere until death, in this sincere devotion towards Mary, your salvation is secured.

But we cannot too often repeat in favor of those, who live piously in Jesus Christ, that of all the persons who place themselves under the protection of the blessed Virgin, those who lead an interior life, enjoy more particularly, that glorious privilege, because being the most cherished of the sheep-fold of the sovereign pastor, the most beautiful and attractive flowers of the garden of the church, and the most considerable of his portion in this world, that mother of mercy interests herself more zealously in their perfection, employs her power with God with greater constancy, so as to obtain for them stronger and more plentiful graces.

If the clemency of Mary, says a pious author, extends itself so generously towards all such as have repaid her benefits with base ingratitude; if she implores so earnestly the return of the wanderer, grace for those who are on the point of being stricken by the divine justice, what will she not do for pious and grateful souls, who aspire to pleasing Jesus Christ, and who have no other desire than of pleasing him and loving him? Ah! she is ever considering them with a vigilant maternal eye; she is moved to pity by their feeblest cry; her heart always disposed to console them, is overcome with grief at their dangers, miseries and trials. That tender mother asks for those beloved souls, the good will, to which perseverance is attached. If they fall through weakness she stretches out her gentle hand to their assistance; if they stray she brings them back to the path of rectitude; if they yield to discouragement, trouble and alarms, she excites their courage, re-assures them, and causes calm and serenity to succeed to the tempest.

Will you, pious souls, possess a true and solid devotion to the blessed Virgin? Apply principally to the study of her life; use great care in copying the interior of Mary, expressing feature by feature, and exerting yourselves to attain the perfection of each particular trait. The more closely you pursue this study, the more reason you will have to hope and believe that you are of the number of the predestined, and of the most acceptable servants of Mary. It *must* be possible for us to imitate Mary, for the Gospel has proposed to us the imitation of Jesus Christ, a model infinitely more accomplished, and our predestination is wholly founded on our conformity with the Heart of Jesus Christ. God, therefore demands that we approach the perfection of Jesus and Mary, in proportion to the measure of grace that he bestows on us. Give as she did, in proportion to what you have received. Devote yourself to her, persist in that devotedness, correspond to grace and avoid the smallest infidelity. Cultivate a strong and firm will in doing good: humble yourself for the faults that you may commit, and repair them by an act of love to God.

The blessed Simon Stock, often asked the blessed Virgin to teach him, in what way he could honor her. One day while he was meditating before her statue, she appeared to him bearing in her hands a scapular, which she gave him, adding that it was the means with which she desired he should promote her honor, and a badge of distinction for her real servants. She promised him that this holy habit should be a sign of salvation; so that, whoever should be so happy as to wear it until death, *should never suffer the flames of hell.* The Sovereign Pontiffs who gave bulls of Indulgences, in favor of this devotion, having confirmed these consoling words, a great number of persons of both sexes and of every condition, hastened to be clothed with the scapular. God has authorized this devotion by great miracles.

SENTIMENTS.

O Mary, full of kindness, take pity on me thy child, and never suffer me to abandon thy service; keep me under thy protection and preserve me in thy love. If I fall, raise me; if I wander, bring me back; if I combat, defend me; if I am weak, fortify me; if I suffer shipwreck, save me; if I am sick, heal me; receive my soul into thy hands, and present it to thy Son, in the splendor of the saints.

ASPIRATION AND PRACTICE.

O Mary, my refuge, pray to Jesus for me!

Receive Holy Communion on the Festivals of Mary.

Wear with respect and piety, the scapular of Mount Carmel, regarding it as the honorable livery of the Queen of Heaven.

Our Lady of the Angels.

"*Mary hath chosen the better part, which shall not be taken from her.*" (*Gospel.*)

Mary first chose to be nothing for herself. She never considered her own interest, not even spiritual ones; she never desired that God should distinguish her from other women in any respect; and although she was indeed eminently distinguished from the moment of her Immaculate Conception, she never esteemed herself above others on account of it, and never had a vain conceit or sentiment of vain-glory in reference to it. Her heart was never divided; her intentions were ever pure, all her actions tended solely to God. Whatever be our efforts, we shall never on these two points attain the perfection of

Mary; but we are bound to tend to it, and we can approach it more and more closely. Let therefore our great object be to be nothing to ourselves and wholly to God. Let us not be satisfied with willing in general, and lulling ourselves in those beautiful desires, as do many who being dead to themselves live to God only in speculation; but let us go to the practice, renouncing ourselves wherever we perceive any self-seeking; let us turn all to God, even the most indifferent things. In this respect we shall always have something to reform, some new degree of perfection to acquire. Dying to self and living to God is the affair of a life-time.

Mary chose to unite contemplation to action, in such manner that one can never interfere with the other. It is the highest perfection to join the two together, so that they may mutually assist each other and labor in concert to the glory of Jesus Christ. Mary fulfilled perfectly all the duties of the contemplative life, no one ever tasted so perfectly the sweetness of the Lord. She was inebriated with the abundance of the riches of the house of God, who gave her to drink in long draughts of the torrents of delight. Her meditation had more of the contemplation of the blessed and of the light of glory than of the obscurity of faith. Heaven was her home, in which she had enclosed all her thoughts, and her desires. Eternity was her school; for she was entirely separated and disengaged from temporal and perishable things. In fine, divine union was the source of her repose; for God alone was the bond and the treasure of her heart.

This intimate and continual union with God never hindered Mary from fulfilling the duties of the active life. The blessed Virgin never omitted any domestic duty, nor any obligation of charity towards the neighbor. Poor as she was, and having no one to assist her, we may suppose that her labor was almost continual, whilst she dwelt with Joseph. It was much the same when she was with St. John, taking care of the temporal, whilst he was occupied with his apostolical functions. But her work did not suspend her prayer, and never troubled or disturbed her interior peace. Contemplation is naturally opposed to activity, and if we are not careful it tends to idleness, and inspires us with distaste for exterior occupations, even the most indispensable. There are many pious persons in the world, and in the cloister who err on this point. Labor on the contrary, nourishes the activity of the temper, with eagerness, self-love, and inquietude of humor; it dissipates the mind, withers the heart, by degrees withdraws it from holy contemplation, and intrudes into its sacred moments with all its embarrassments and its distractions. It is not easy to preserve the soul from these two defects, and to make a love of labor accord with a relish for prayer. Yet, *it is obligatory* to *pray* and *to work;* and as these two things are ordained by Almighty God, it is evident that we can unite them, and that we must apply to it faithfully during our whole lives.

The children of the blessed Virgin should follow her example, and learn from her how to unite the occupations of Martha and Mary, that is, to pass from contemplation to action, and from action to contemplation; to imitate the angels that ascend and descend on the ladder of Jacob; to soar to God by the exercise of meditation, to descend to the neighbor by the exercise of good works.

It would be forming a very false idea, and even a

dangerous one, concerning the life of the blessed
Virgin at Nazareth, to suppose that the only exercise
of her life was prayer and pious reading. True, she
gave considerable time to prayer, but she proportioned it to the exigencies of her state. The details
of the ordinary life and the interior of the family,
are the characteristics of Mary in her humble retreat. Far from that indolent and slothful piety,
which is the lot of so many rich females, enemies of
wholesome toil, because they do not need it as a means
of living. Mary had no time for such prayers. Let
us then represent to ourselves, the Queen of Angels,
occupied in employments which seem to us rude and
degrading, bent down with the weight of the bur-
dens she carried, sometimes employing her pure
hands in cultivating the earth by the sweat of her
brow; sometimes making the clothes of all her family, according to the custom of the Jewish women;
occasionally she fetched the water for domestic use,
after the example of the wives of the illustrious
patriarchs; and sometimes getting ready a repast
that she was to partake of in the company of her divine Son and her chaste Spouse. How beautiful to
see her thus submitting to these humble fatigues,
mortifying her innocent body in order to excite a
blush in the women of the world, by an example
which so justly confounds their vanity and delicacy.
Hers was not a work of fancy but of necessity—a
kind of labor painful, obscure, humbling and sub-
jecting. How perverted is the view of persons of
the present age, these details of the hidden life of
Mary, appear to them minute and unworthy of the
mother of God! Ah! how differently the Holy
Spirit judged, when he drew the portrait of the
strong woman, and followed her in all the details of

the private and domestic life. These are contemned and supposed to be unworthy of their *position*.— Alas! and Mary, mother of God incarnate, in her humility, took delight in what has become, through a natural effect of pride, a subject of contempt to women in the world, who are led by its maxims.

True piety consists principally, in the accomplishment of the duties of our state; nothing can dispense from this; devotion itself has for object to obtain for us the grace requisite for fulfilling them; hence, it can never be a pretext for neglecting them; on the contrary, true and solid piety gives to prayer the time of which our legitimate occupations permit us to dispose; it also requires that in what is *not* of *obligation* for God's service, we should condescend to the desires, even to the weakness of persons, whom we are bound to indulge, and that for the sake of peace we should sometimes sacrifice our most lawful tastes.

Apply then, after Mary's example, never to separate the occupation of Mary from that of Martha, and to subordinate them, so that one may never interfere with the other. Neglect no duty of your state, not even mere propriety and decorum; but place at the head of all its obligations inseparable union with God, and continual dependence on grace. Speak, pray, and act in peace under the direction of divine grace, *and aspire to seeking God alone.*

EXAMPLE.

St. Francis of Assissium, founder of the order of Friars Minor, burned with an ardent love for Mary. It was under her auspices, in the church of the Portioncule, that he desired to attempt the kind of life which the Holy Spirit pressed him to embrace. He chose the Queen of Angels as the special patroness of his order. Among numerous practices which he selected for honoring Mary, he fasted in her honor, from the eve of St. Peter until the Assumption. St. Francis received during his life, the most remarkable graces in the sanctuary, become so renowned under the title of our "Lady of the Angels."

ASPIRATION AND PRACTICE.

O Mary, Queen of Heaven, shield us.

Recite the little office of the Immaculate Conception.

Often invoke the choirs of Angels, and recite the Rosary in union with them.

The Assumption.

Mary remained a long time on earth after the triumphant ascension of the Saviour Jesus, and the descent of the Holy Spirit. Who could comprehend her merits, and holy extacies during her prolonged pilgrimage in this land of exile? What seraph inflamed with love could worthily explain with what force Mary was attracted to her beloved, and what violence her heart experienced in this separation? If loving Jesus, and being loved by Jesus, are two things which attract the divine benedictions on souls, what abyss must have inundated the soul of Mary? Who can describe the impetuosity of that mutual love, in which concurred all that nature possesses of deepest tenderness, all that grace includes which is most efficacious? Jesus was never weary of loving his Mother; and that holy Mother never thought that she could love that Son sufficiently, and asked no other grace from her Son than that of loving him more. It is impossible for us to measure the holy impatience she felt to be united again to her Son, except by the degree of vehemence which characterized her love. If the great Apostle longed to be delivered from the body in order to seek his Master at the right hand of his Father, what must have been the emotion of maternal love? The young Tobias, by an absence of a year, pierced the heart of his mother with inconsolable grief, how wide the difference between Jesus and Tobias! and what keen regret must not Mary have endured on being so long separated from a Son whom she so devotedly loved. "Alas!" would she say, when she saw some faithful soul leaving the world, as for example St. Stephen, and others, "my Son to what do you henceforward reserve me, and why do you leave me till the last? I saw the holy old man Simon, after having embraced you ask but to quit this life, so delicious is it to enjoy even a moment of your presence; and must I not long to go to you and embrace you on the throne of your glory! Suffer, my *love* only to act; it will soon disunite my soul from this mortal frame, to transport me to you in whom alone I live."

The divine love, that reigned without any obstacle in the heart of Mary, occupied her every thought, augmenting itself daily by its own action, perfecting itself by its desires, and multiplying itself; so that finally, it reached such a degree of perfection that the earth could no longer contain it.

Her love was so ardent, so strong, and so inflamed, it uttered not a sigh that was not capable of breaking all these mortal bonds; it formed not a regret but was sufficiently powerful to dissolve its wonderful harmony; it conceived no desire for heaven, which was not efficacious enough to draw after it the whole undivided soul, nence the activity of ner love was the sole cause of the death of Mary—and therefore the blessed Virgin gave up her soul without pain or violence into the hands of her divine Son. It was not necessary that her love should use extraordinary energy—as the gentlest zephyr detaches from its parent tree the already matured fruit; as a flame rises and mounts to its own element, so was that beatified soul suddenly gathered and transported to heaven. Thus died the excellent, the blessed Mary, her soul was borne to heaven on a cloud of sacred desires.

The happiness of dying like Mary, in the peace and joy of the Lord, is certainly of all the advantages of the pious life, the most precious and the most desirable. How sweet to the faithful soul, to perceive the time of trials closing! How happy to leave, at last, the earth on which we have so long been strangers and captives, to soar into a home of joy, peace and eternal serenity, in which there is no other occupation but the enjoyment of God, undisturbed by the dread of losing him. That soul closes its eyes joyfully upon all creatures, and peacefully returns to God who gave it. It is like the flight of a dove, which freed from captivity, wings rapidly its way and hides itself in sweet solitude; it is the weakened music of a rippling stream that loses itself in a calm and peaceful lake. I could never have believed it is so sweet to die, repeated on his death-bed the pious Suarès, so devoted to Mary, that he would have given all his vast science for the merit of one single *Ave, Maria.*

Saviour Jesus, kindle thy love in our hearts by a holy impatience; and since it arose in the heart of Mary from that intimate union that thou hadst with her, satiate us so completely with thy holy mysteries, be in us by the participation of thy flesh and blood, that, living more in thee than in ourselves, we may only languish to be consummated with thee in the glory that thou hast prepared for us.

That holy and blessed soul attracted after her, her body by an anticipated resurrection. For, although God had designated a common term for the resurrection of all the dead, there are particular reasons which influence him to advance the term in favor of the blessed Virgin. The sun produces fruits only in their proper season; but we sometimes see lands so perfectly well prepared, that they draw down a more prompt and more efficacious influence. There are also forward trees in the garden of the Spouse; and the holy flesh of Mary is a portion too well prepared to wait the usual period for producing fruits of immortality.

After the melancholy hours and bitter trials of exile, the sorrow of Mary is turned into joy, her humiliations into a glorious triumph. But, if according to the testimony of the great Apostle, ravished to the third heaven, the eye of man hath not seen nor his ear heard, nor his understanding comprehended the happiness reserved for the least of the predestined; how can we form any just idea of the recompense prepared for her, who according to the thought of St. Denis, forms a separate hierarchy, the sublimest of all, and the first after God? Mary is next to the adorable Trinity, the most ravishing brightness of the celestial court; she is its delight and joy. She is the STRONG WOMAN clothed with the sun and crowned with the most radiant stars of heaven. Queen of the celestial hosts, Mary is seated at the right hand of the Eternal Word, as the Word is at the right

of the Eternal Father; Jesus Christ is the splendor
of the MOST HIGH; Mary is the softened splendor of
her SON, and is crowned with honor and glory by
the august TRINITY. The Father acknowledges her
for his beloved daughter, the Word for his blessed
Mother, the Holy Spirit for his chaste spouse, and
her immortal diadem glitters with all the gifts of God.
Queen of the Angelic choirs, she commands the hierarchies of heaven, which are paled amidst the splendid
brilliancy of her glory, saying with admiration: *Who
is she that cometh up from the desert, inundated with
delight, and leaning on her beloved?*

Jesus did not recompense MARY, precisely, because
she was his MOTHER: but because she was perfectly
faithful to grace at every instant of her life, and
accepted and suffered courageously all the trials
inseparable from the divine maternity. It is not the
purely gratuitous favors of God that he crowns in
us, but the virtues and merits we have acquired by
his grace. Hence, it is not so much her quality of
Mother of God, as that of chaste, humble and faithful servant of the Lord that procured such a weight
of honor and glory to Mary. Her love of God, her
forgetfulness and contempt of herself, her charity
for others, have had no equal among creatures; for
this reason alone is her bliss unequalled. Therefore,
when admiring what God did that is great for Mary,
let us admire, as much as we can, what Mary did
great for God. Our portion of grace is and always
will be less than hers; but God also expects and
exacts less from us. He is infinitely just, not desiring to reap what he has not sown, but he wills that
what he has sown should produce its fruit; and this
fruit, by our good will, by the immensity of our
desires, far more than by our works, can augment to

infinity: this fruit he will gather into his granary, and it will be the measure of our recompense.

O Mystic Rose, thou hast no thorn, nothing in thee repulses and wounds! For this thou didst attract the pure and jealous spirit of God. He crowned thee with choice gifts and favors, but, transient as are all the loveliest flowers of earth, like them thou wert destined to disappear. One day it was perceived that death had touched thee; for God had commanded his angels to call thee. Thou wert transplanted into the heavenly Eden, where a more genial soil would nourish thee, a more brilliant sun enlighten thee. Heaven sang her hymn of joy; but earth mourns and regrets thee. She has naught so pure, so beautiful, so worthy of the attention of God and of his angels. Those that thou hast left on this stricken earth, extend towards thee their drooping stems, and implore thee for a few drops of that heavenly dew which gently glitters on thee; for one of those rays of light that embellish thee: O gentle Queen, ask for them the favors of heaven: *Regina cœli, ora pro nobis.*

ASPIRATION AND PRACTICE.

O Mary, pray for us at the hour of our death. Daily invoke the assistance of the blessed Virgin at the closing hour of our lives. Say the Rosary with serious attention.

The Nativity. B. V. M.

God, who designed to favor the humility of his servant, left us in ignorance of the place in which the incomparable Virgin receives life. The Evangelists themselves appear willing to cast a veil over the splendor of her origin. If they observe her descent, they conceal it under the genealogy of Joseph. That birth, so much desired by the patriarchs and prophets, which excites the joy and admiration of all the celestial hierarchies, is an obscure and unknown event on earth, which scarcely attracts the attention of a few relatives and friends, very remote themselves from suspecting what treasure is given to the world. Mary is born in indigence and obscurity, and her holy mother, grateful for this miraculous blessing from heaven, says the sole *Hosanna* over her cradle. What would have been the veneration of men towards this admirable infant, had they been able to see, as saw the celestial spirits! But nothing distinguishes her in their sight from the other children of Judea; they confound in the common mass, *her*, whom an invisible and unknown grace had separated; and the only really innocent creature that ever was on earth, she who surpasses in sanctity the seraphim themselves, sees around her cradle only that gentle domestic joy that conceals in the interior its pains and its pleasures: nothing that reveals her future glory. Also, being as modest as holy, far from being afflicted at this obscurity, she will rejoice during her whole life, at the forgetfulness of men, which assists her in being lost in the crowd, according to the spirit of her humility.

O how widely different are the thoughts of God from those of men, and how remote are the dictates of self-love from the reign of Jesus in the pious soul!

The Lord, who destined Mary to serve as a model to every age of the world, and to all the various conditions of human life, caused her to descend from parents of illustrious name and royal blood, but now poor and unknown. Let us beware of losing this great lesson. The condition, simple or elevated, rich or poor, in which we are born, depends not on ourselves; but what depends upon us, is to think of our condition, whatever it may be, as did Mary of hers. Sprung from ancestors whose heads had been adorned with the crown of royalty, the blessed Virgin never took pride in this, and never blushed to share in the labors and privations of the poorest and humblest of her sex; and never did she complain that divine Providence had placed her so low. If we have been born rich, powerful, great, let the example of Mary teach us not to make of these frivolities a vain title for becoming haughty, scarcely considering as human those who are born in a state inferior to ours If we were born in meanness, in poverty, let us learn never to blush at our birth, never to try to forget it ourselves, or induce others to forget it, and never to envy the higher conditions, interiorly lamenting ours as one of humiliation.

If we were truly pious, far from applauding ourselves on a distinguished origin, we should be on our guard against the haughtiness and emptiness of that human advantage. How many dangers to real piety arise from a splendid condition! alas! how numerous shipwrecks does it daily cause! It is excessively difficult, says a master of the spiritual life, to be great according to the world, and to be great before God; to live honored in and by the world, and not adopt and become attached to its maxims. Now, nothing is more diametrically opposed to progress in the ways of God, than that disorder of the affections. Modest, affable and anticipating the needs of others, we should not be so sensitive concerning what we believe to be our due. Those, on the contrary, who occupy the lowest rank in society, instead of being ashamed and afflicted on this account, should glory in it and congratulate themselves for possessing a feature in conformity with those that divine Providence bestowed on Mary. Piously eager for such humiliations as their state exposes them to receive, instead of apprehending and shunning them, they would not adopt so many precautions to dissemble with others, what they really are.

St. Bernardin of Sienna, had adopted, from his earliest childhood, the pious custom of going to salute, every morning, a statue of the blessed Virgin, placed at one of the gates of the city; and there prostrate on both knees, he devoted himself to her service. His zeal and piety were so pleasing to the Mother of God, that she obtained him the grace of a religious vocation, the gift of converting sinners, and the power of working miracles. From his eighth year he was faithful to fast every Saturday, in honor of the blessed Virgin. He was born on the eighth of September, the day of the blessed Virgin's nativity; he selected this day particularly for taking the habit, for celebrating his first mass and preaching his first sermon, wishing by this choice to testify his confidence in Mary, and place his most important undertakings under her special protection. The holy Virgin, sensible to so much love, blessed his ministry and crowned him with favors. St. Bernardin was in effect an apostle, and filled the whole Church with the light of his doctrine and the splendor of his virtue.

SENTIMENTS.

O Mary, shall I tell thee, quite transported with

joy, hope and love, what would be our misery and our poverty, had not the Father of Mercy drawn thee from his treasures to give thee to us? O my delight! my life, I confide in thy holy name; I feel that my heart wishes to love thee, that my mouth wishes to praise thee, my mind to contemplate thee, that my tongue desires to pray to thee, and my soul burns with ardor to belong totally to thee. Receive me; sustain me, defend me, preserve me; I can never perish in thy hands. (*St. Anselm.*)

ASPIRATION AND PRACTICE.

Hail Mary, our life, our sweetness and our hope.

Daily thank the blessed Virgin for the blessings that she has granted us.

Pray for Missionaries who propagate the devotion to the Heart of Mary.

Seben Dolors.

MARY AT THE FOOT OF THE CROSS.

Mary was standing near the cross, and Jesus perceiving his Mother and the disciple whom he loved, said to his Mother: Woman, behold thy son: and then to his disciple, behold thy Mother. And from that moment that disciple took her to his own. The last sorrow of Mary was, to be in a manner rejected by her own Son. At the same time in which she was offering him the strongest mark of her affection rising above all fear so as not to forsake him in his last sigh; at the moment in which Jesus himself was compassionating the affliction of his Mother, and should have given her the liveliest demonstrations of his filial tenderness he addresses her not by the

sweet name of Mother. Ah! Lord, hast thou, in
expiring, no sweeter name to give than that of
Woman! Another shall be her son! a stranger
shall call her by the name of Mother, which thou
dost refuse her! What an exchange is this, exclaims
St. Bernard? They give her John for Jesus, the
servant for the master, the son of Zebedee for the
Son of God. Has she then lost her divine maternity? Alas! was it not sufficient humiliation, enough
of desolation for her, to be witness of your punishment and death, without the last adieu which ought
to have proved her consolation, covering her with
confusion and grief? And it is Jesus on the point
of expiring, who thus treats his Mother! It would
be blasphemous to suspect him of harshness, or even
of indifference. There is consequently a mystery:
let us try to penetrate it, but let us beware of
bringing to this examination the reasonings of human
prudence and human wisdom; let the heart and
faith alone guide us in this admirable subject.

As the sacrifice of Jesus would have been imperfect, if in abandoning himself to his Father, he had
not been apparently abandoned by him; so there
would have been something wanting in the sacrifice
of Mary, if, when consenting to lose her Son, she had
not also been in some sort, renounced by him when
on the cross. It was requisite on each side that all
circumstances should be pushed to extremes, and
that the desolation of the Mother should correspond
to that of her Son. Jesus was in a state of humiliation, and it was necessary that his holy Mother
should be so with him. Jesus has God for his Father,
and Mary has God for her Son. That divine Saviour
lost his Father, and he only calls him his God; Mary
must also lose her Son; he only calls her by the title

woman, and gives her not that most sweet name
mother.   The keenest anguish of Jesus, was without comparison, that abandonment by his Father;
and similarly, the greatest trial of Mary was rejection
on the part of her Son.   Jesus acted thus so as to
give the crowning piece to the virtue of his Mother,
just as a skilful   artist takes pleasure in giving the
last and finishing touches to his most perfect and
most sublime piece of composition.

Afflicted souls, God, who cherishes you as Jesus
cherished Mary, requires of you to make to him the
sacrifice of your dearest interests, and there would be
something wanting in your holocaust, did not God
appear on his side, to reject you.   Because you are
so sensitive to it, you must submit to this trial, for
without it your spiritual death would be incomplete.
You will not advance the interior edifice, but in
proportion to your self-denial; when you have
nothing left, you will put the finishing stroke.   If
God wishes to glorify himself in you, he will treat
you in a manner approaching that in which he
treated his own dear Mother.

When God calls souls to that state of sacrifice
without reserve, he treats them in proportion to the
gifts with which he has favored them.   He is insatiable of death, of losses, of renunciation; he is even
jealous of his own gifts, because the excellence of
his favors secretly nourishes within us a certain self-
confidence.   All must be destroyed, all must be lost,
since we have received all.   O my God how few
souls there are who love thee as Mary, in spirit and
in truth.   Almost all seek themselves in thy gifts,
instead of seeking thee all alone in the cross and in
self-renunciation.   We say that we do not cling to
any thing earthly, and we are frightened at the most

insignificant loss! We wish to possess thee, but we are not willing to lose ourselves so as to be possessed by thee. This is not loving thee, but wishing to be loved by thee, O blessed Redeemer.

However, to consider things under another point of view, Jesus acquitted himself of the duty of a grateful Son, by providing for the temporal interests of his Mother. She was about to remain alone, without a subsistence and he gives her a resource in the person of his cherished disciple, to whom he leaves Mary as by testament, charging him to take care of her, as of his own mother. Poor resource, indeed, but suitable to a woman who had always lived in poverty, and who after the loss of her Son, would have regarded as a torment the enjoyment of the conveniencies of life. Therefore, from that time John took her to his own; he loved her, respected her, provided for her and cared for her as for his mother; he never separated from her. When he quitted Jerusalem, she followed him to Ephesus; and as far as his apostolical labors admitted, he accompanied her until she died. Thus Jesus associated in one same thought and in one same home those whom he had most dearly loved, and who had been invariably faithful to him during his mortal life.

The holy Fathers have remarked that all the children of the Church were here figured by St. John, and that in the person of that apostle, Mary was established the mother of all the faithful. She therefore became our Mother in the most agonizing moment of her life; she gave us birth spiritually at the foot of the cross. She has recovered Jesus Christ, but she has not for that reason withdrawn her affection; she has not forgotten that he substituted us in his place, and that he would cherish us as himself. When showing each one of us to her in spirit, Jesus said to her, *behold thy Son.* I give them to thee; they are the price of my blood which is also thine. They cost you too dear not to belong to you, cherish them as you cherished me. Therefore let us not doubt of the love of Mary towards us, any more than we doubt of the love, respect and obedience of Mary for her Son.

Virgins have here a special right, for St. Jerome declares, that Jesus chose St. John who was a virgin to recommend him to the blessed Virgin, his mother. Jesus does not love all souls with an equal love; he entertains for all a love as Creator and Redeemer; but yet among all, he loves best those who are faithful, and among the faithful the just; and among the just those who are his spouses; and among his spouses, those who are virgins, verifying the words of the wise man : *" he who loves purity of heart shall have the King for his friend."*

The Rev. F. Bernard, that holy priest, so celebrated in Paris during the last age, for his charity and his devotion to Mary, was conducting to the scaffold a man condemned to death. This wretch to all his horrible crimes added blasphemy against God. Although he had already tired the patience of those who had exhorted him, Fr. Bernard, mounted the scaffold with him, and pressed him zealously to repent, and wished to embrace him; the criminal repulsed him and with a violent blow of his foot, threw him to the bottom of the ladder on the pavement. Father Bernard, although wounded, arose immediately, knelt down, and invoked Mary, by reciting aloud the *Remember*, the prayer was no sooner ended, than the impenitent man shed tears of compunction, was sincerely converted, and gave as

much edification by his repentance, as he had excited
horror by his obstinacy.

Comforter of the afflicted, pray for us.

Make the way of the cross in union with Mary.

Gain indulgences for the suffering souls in purgatory.

Pray for souls who relish suffering.

—

The Presentation.

Prevented with the rarest and most precious gifts
of grace from the first instant of her privileged conception, Mary had devoted herself totally to God's
service, and had offered to her Creator the homage of
her gratitude and love, before heaven had yet given
her to the world.   From the tenderest age, she had
consummated her sacrifice, seeking in the sanctuary
an asylum for her virtue, and confiding to the shadow
of the tabernacle the precious deposit of her innocence.   O spectacle worthy of the admiration of the
angels.   Scarcely three years had elapsed since her
birth, and already sensible to the attraction of grace,
she accomplishes the word of God, which addresses
her in the bottom of her heart: cherished daughter
of heaven lend an ear and follow the voice which
calls you; forget thy people and the house of thy
father, and the King will be ravished with the
beauty!

Divine vocation, of which Mary at first compre-
hends the mystery.   The same ray of grace that
made known to her that she is called into retreat,
disclosed to her the place to which she must retire;

it is to the temple of the Lord, that house of God, in which, disengaged from all profane objects, she will constantly walk in the presence of the sovereign Master whom she adores; where quite recollected in that supreme Majesty, she shall see or hear nothing that can divide her heart and distract her mind from the contemplation of eternal truths. To this her desires incline with a reason unimpeded by the weakness of infancy, this is what she finds to be the most desirable state. Faithful to grace, she does not waver, she does not put off the sacrifice; her resolution, once taken, nothing is capable of retarding its execution.

But what! to renounce the world at so tender an age, is it not in some manner dying before living? Besides, should we not try the world, and not flee from it before we are assured of its dangers. The career is long; why not wait? why anticipate the time? all will come right; God will have his turn, and it is not refusing him what is due to him to defer it to a more mature age. Besides, it is well that there should be in the world models of regularity and of virtue: we can be faithful to God and save our souls every where. Vain, futile reasoning of which the world still makes use at the present day, to retain in the world privileged souls whom God calls, as he did Mary into retirement and solitude.

The views and thoughts of the blessed Virgin are wholly different from those of the children of men. She learned in the secret of prayer, that God is equally God in every age and at all times; that it is dividing our life in a manner very injurious to the Master who bestowed it, to pretend to reserve for him only some remains tarnished by indulgence of the passions, and offered after all the natural inclinations have lost their freshness; that the younger we are, the purer and more innocent we are before God, and that spotless victims, innocent hearts are the most pleasing to him; Finally, to decline giving the soul to God in early life is risking the danger of never belonging to him, for that delay tends to remove God so far from us, and us so far from God, that in the end we lose the inclination and energy requisite for returning to him.

Joachim and Anne, faithful to the inspiration of heaven, seconded the attraction of their august daughter; those faithful Israelites were not of those parents prejudiced by worldly errors, who, abusing the ascendancy that nature gives them over their children, constitute themselves the arbiters of their vocation, and often oppose the designs of Providence. In vain, a thousand marks of vocation to a pious life appear in the person of their child, a thousand desires of separation and retreat that grace produces in the soul, make known the designs of God over it, these holy movements of grace are treated as childish levities; they declare it incapable of choosing a state, and then offer that of the world. Under pretext of trying the vocation it is destroyed; they exact a knowledge of the world, and expect that it will prove attractive, reason must ripen to the destruction of innocence; pleasures must be enjoyed to prove the strength of resolution, and the poor soul is placed in circumstances which corrupt it. How different is the conduct of the virtuous parents of Mary! Without doubt they loved more than life itself, that only daughter that heaven had granted them by a miracle, but they also knew well, that they had received her from God as a sacred trust, which they were obliged to restore to him when he required it.

Mary on her part, loved and honored her virtuous parents as the living images of God; but she knew perfectly well that he who was to leave the bosom of his Eternal Father to give himself to us, merited that she should cheerfully leave her father and her mother, in order to devote herself betimes to his service; and after only three years consecrated to their tenderness, she hastened to the temple, devoting the remainder of her days to God. An example very suitable for confounding those souls who, notwithstanding the divine call, remain in the world, retained by the bonds of flesh and blood.

We cannot doubt that the dispositions and sentiments of Mary in her consecration were as perfect as her age and her degree of grace would lead us to presume; and that in so important an action, she received an increase of grace which she faithfully employed for increasing in sanctity. Hence, in the shadow of the sanctuary, concealed from the eyes of men, solely occupied with God and his worship, she daily made eminent progress in the interior life, and without being conscious of it, prepared herself for the exalted dignity to which God had destined her. The designs of God were unknown to her, but she suffered herself to be conducted by his inspirations: she thought only of uniting herself more and more closely to him, without pretending to anything beyond remaining in her lowliness and insignificance, known but to God, and regardless of all beside.

Mary, exempt from concupiscence, which inclines us all to evil, distrusted herself and withdrew from the dangers of the world. And we, feeble creatures, quite filled with miseries and inconstancy, we dread not exposing our frailty to occasions frequently the most dangerous. Let us tremble, for one only thought of presumption may suffice to make a demon of an angel.

Pious soul, if you are obliged to live in the world, live in it as though not living in it, use it as not using it; build for yourself like St. Catherine of Sienna, an interior solitude in the depth of your soul, in which you may freely converse with your Spouse. Live to God betimes, after the example of blessed Mary. We are not born in grace; but we must die in a state of grace, and we shall never thus *die*, unless we thus *live*.

St. Teresa was entirely devoted from her earliest years, to the love of the blessed Virgin. Her tenderness for that holy Mother inspired her with numerous practices for honoring her. She erected in her paternal residence a little oratory in which she placed the image of Mary; there, she paid her frequent visits, offered her flowers and other little presents; always accompanying these offerings with some fervent prayer. At the age of twelve years, Teresa having had the misfortune to lose her pious mother, she felt keenly its greatness, and ran directly to prostrate herself before the statue of the blessed Virgin, in order to implore her to design in future to become her mother, and to accept her as a daughter. This offering was so agreeable to Mary, that she took her at once under her special protection, and directed her in all her enterprises. Thus, Mary loves and protect those who give their hearts to God, as she did, "in the days of her youth."

Virgin most pure pray for us.

Renew the promises made at baptism, on each festival of the Presentation.

Invoke Mary in temptations against purity.

Immaculate Conception.

The design of God to conduct all things to their end by ways worthy of himself, is as admirable in itself as consoling in reference to men. Hence, Mary having been chosen from all eternity in the thought of the Father, to become the *Mother* of the incarnate Word, it cannot be doubted that in creating her, he distinguished her soul by all the privileges, and enriched it with all the graces suited to such a lofty dignity, alone among all the daughters of Adam, as a lily among thorns, she was exempt from original sin and all its consequences. Conceived in sanctifying grace and in a state of the highest innocence, new Eve, purer than the first on coming from the hands of her Creator, she drew to herself the complacency of the Most High. Although in so great a mystery the human mind is forced to confess its weakness and impotence, it is allowable to presume and to believe that her blessed soul, so greatly privileged, enjoyed, from the moment of its union with the body that developed reason with which God adorned the first woman, and that the august prerogative of Mother of God seemed to exact from her Son, then her Creator, before becoming her first born. Is it not indeed just, to think that what the divine Word could do to enhance the glory of his Mother, he effected with as much love as energy? Is it possible to push things too far on this point?

Founded upon this two-fold testimony of reason and of faith, it is therefore true to say that, from the first instant of her immaculate conception, Mary was in a disposition of holiness, superior to that of all the angels and of all men, and from that instant in a condition capable of glorifying God, in a purer and more excellent manner than all creatures united; nothing inclined her to ill, and all things, on the contrary induced her to seek the most sublime supernatural good.

Thence it becomes easy to form a just, although imperfect, idea of the interior of Mary at her birth. An understanding illuminated with the clearest light, an upright will conformed in all things to God's, a more perfect liberty than that of Adam in the state of innocence, no ignorance, no concupiscence, passions always governed, constantly in order, ever conspiring with reason and grace, interior reign of God, a pure and most holy flesh, destined and worthy of being one day the flesh of a Man-God; an eminent degree of sanctifying grace; actual graces of a superior order for all her thoughts, affections, and actions; no evil propensity, an extreme horror of ill, even the most trifling; an attraction, a relish, an inexpressible facility for every virtue; a continual union with God. an inviolable fidelity to grace, a total forgetfulness of self, an ineffable purity of intention, which referred all without exception, and without reserve to the greater glory of God, and that exalted her above all incentive of merit, of personal sanctity and of recompense; such were the first traits of the interior of Mary, which has ever acquired new increase, proportioned to her primitive perfection. Such are the features that we should find reflected, although less purely and perfectly, in the interior of souls whom the Lord predestines to that divine maternity, which consists in fidelity in following courageously the way that he has traced out, and which caused our Lord to exclaim, in the transport of his love: He that doeth the will of my Father in heaven is my brother, and sister, and *mother*.—(St. Mark, 3, 35.) Who does not discover, in the special choice that God makes of certain souls destined to reproduce the more perfect characteristics of virtue, a singular and divine privilege which should awaken gratitude, love and admiration towards his infinite bounty. Thus, the august prerogatives of Mary, which at first sight appear to dispense us from imitating her, become, by reflection, very capable of confounding and condemning all our weaknesses; for in that abundance, and in that plenitude of graces, which place between it and sin an almost infinite space, Mary did not think herself capable of escape and conservation, except by a continual vigilance and fidelity. Her virtue, superior to the greatest dangers, dreads the smallest peril; her heart, that the most powerful attractions could not seduce, believes it is not in safety, but by flight of objects the least seductive. Follow Mary; you will always find her attentive to herself and distrustful. Can we, without confusion, read the details that St. Ambrose gives us of the occupations of her life? He can hardly find expressions capable of explaining the rigor of her abstinence, as though she were subject to the revolts of the flesh; he admires her silence and her circumspection when speaking, as though she needed to distrust the discretion of her tongue; he praises her attachment to labor, as though idleness were dangerous for her; he extols her love for solitude, as if the air of society could have poisoned her virtue; he remarks her precaution in never going out of her house, not even to the temple of God, without attendants, as if she were incapable of watching over herself. In a word, her flight from the world, her austere penance, her uninterrupted toil, fervent prayer, extreme self-distrust, her love of retreat, teach all souls that aspire to perfection, what must be avoided, corrected, and observed for retaining grace. Alas! we dare, after all this, excuse ourselves on the plea of our weakness of heart; but it is not so much the heart we have received, which is the cause of our infidelities, as the heart that each one of us makes by his imprudent facility in following the first impulse of the passions. Were our origin wholly pure and holy, with such conduct we could never be just. Was not the first man created in that state of innocence and grace that we regret? As rash as we, his temerity rendered him a sinner and unfaithful before God.

Mary in her Immaculate Conception, received the most abundant grace; but upon what grace rolled that of her predestination? Upon a grace of flight and separation, upon a grace of vigilance and precaution. For this reason, the pious author of the *Spiritual Combat*, fears not to assure a soul, that did she possess as great self-distrust as did Mary, she would be always preserved, like her, in a state of grace, without ever committing the smallest fault.

SENTIMENTS.

O pure and immaculate Virgin, Mary, my tender Mother; thou whom the Lord hast been pleased to load with his ineffable bounties, deign to lend an attentive ear to the accents of my gratitude. Whilst admiring thy sublime prerogatives, and blessing the Lord who has endowed thee so magnificently, I cannot resist breaking forth into a transport of joy, while considering in my soul its necessity of a more interior piety, and an attraction to more perfect exercises. Augment in my heart, with the esteem of the gift thou hast bestowed on me, the desire and energy requisite for devoting myself wholly to thee. Pre-

serve me from the baneful contagion of worldly
passions and prejudices, so that like thee, entirely
occupied in fulfilling God's holy will, I may please
thy divine Son, and form through thee but one heart
with him.   Amen.

ASPIRATION AND PRACTICE.

O Mary, conceived without sin, pray for us who
have recourse to thee!

Recite the Little Office of the Immaculate Conception.

The Maternity.

The human tongue is incapable of describing what
the heart of Mary experienced during her residence
in Bethlehem.   It will never be given to any created
intelligence, to understand the emotions of the heart
of the Mother of God, after the birth of her divine
Son.   Who can tell or who can appreciate, in effect,
the lively transports of soul of the august Virgin,
when, contemplating in her chaste arms, him whom
the angels tremblingly adore, and pressed him to her
heart?   Who will depict the consolations of her
pure and ardent soul, when the caressing looks of
Jesus were blended with hers, and the love of Mary
was answered not only with gratitude, but also with
effusion of divine favors?   The caresses of Jesus in
regard to Mary were not like those of ordinary
infants, caresses of simple instinct, they were rational
testimonies of charity, emanations of the divinity,
proofs of his predilection; they were caresses which
produced by their own power, (as remarks a master
of a spiritual life,) delicious effects of suavity and

perfection. Hence, what holy delight must they not have dispensed to that pure heart, to that burning charity! How is it possible to express all that the Lord communicated that is divine to his mother, and all the correspondent gratitude of the heart of Mary.

How carefully, says St. Bonaventure, did Mary watch over Jesus! how respectfully did she touch him whom she knew to be her God! with what tenderness and veneration did she not embrace him! with what recollection must she have considered his delicate members! with what holy eagerness must she have nourished him.

All motives and incentives for loving Jesus are found blended, as it were, in Mary in the most eminent degree. She loved Jesus as her God, and her love far surpassed the ardor of the highest seraph; she loved Jesus as her Saviour, and her grateful love, in effacing the inflamed desires of the Patriarchs, became a perpetual model, that succeeding ages have followed, and which will never be equalled; she loved with a love whose vivacity and extent exceed those of all the hearts of the elect, united.

She loved Jesus, as her only son, and we know how deep is a mother's love, that faithful copy of the providential tenderness of the Creator. We know all that God has bestowed of nobility, generosity, devotedness and sublimity, on the maternal heart; but never shall we comprehend how that depth of tenderness, that generous devotedness is inferior and feeble in comparison with the ineffable affections of the heart of Mary; of that heart whose love was as much more sublimely exalted above every species of ordinary maternal affection, as her maternity is elevated above all other maternities. Ah! if the father of Origen went, in the silence of midnight, to kiss

10

with overflowing affection, the breast of his child, as the tabernacle of God who cherishes innocence, how much more must the piety of Mary have conducted her to the cradle of her divine Infant. How pure her love! there, there was no excess to dread. The object of her love is infinitely amiable, and required to be infinitely loved; and had she any reproach to make herself, it was that she did not love him enough. But she loved with all the capacity of her heart, with all the strength of her soul, and exactly in accordance with the measure of grace that had been dispensed to her.

If the love that Mary bore to Jesus was the source of her joy, it was also the source of her trials; and whatever the divine Infant suffered in the manger, pierced the heart of the mother in the most sensible manner. The quickness of her apprehensions and of her alarms, corresponded to that of her affection; and she was in a continual transition from the extreme of delight to the excess of sorrow, without losing her peace of mind; never suffering herself to be inebriated with consolation, nor dejected with grief; desiring not the one nor fearing the other; neither seeking the first nor avoiding the second.

Mary teaches us, by these sentiments of her perfect soul, to love Jesus for himself, to be piously passive in regard to his caresses without being insensible to them, and to endure, as she did, in a spirit of faith, the adversities through which his love may cause us to pass.

God, in allowing the soul that devotes itself to his service, a sort of fore-taste of the pure and intimate pleasures of which he is the source, intends inspiring it with disgust and aversion for the deceitful pleasures attached to creature enjoyments. This experience is more efficacious for disabusing it than any argument that can be presented to the judgment. The Lord, to win a soul, gives it a feeble fore-taste of promised blessedness, but perfect enjoyment is reserved to the other life; this is the time of trial and of merit. God prepares naught but crosses for his friends here below; and it is only to dispose them to accept them from his hand, that he commences by rendering that hand most amiable to them, by inundating them with sweetness. The more delicious and intoxicating the consolations, the ruder and more burdensome will be the crosses that succeed.

MEDITATION

For the Feast of St. Joseph.

(M. Abbe Bletton.)

1. The sublime virtues of St. Joseph, may be attributed to the happiness he enjoyed of being in the society of Mary. If the presence of that Virgin Mother, sanctified the family of Saint Elizabeth, during her short sojourn with them, what graces must not St. Joseph have received from the Queen of heaven, as he dwelt with her continually. The innumerable favors which he received from Mary softened all his trials. It may be said that St. Joseph is *great* in reference to Mary. The Holy Spirit informs us that we may be judged according to the merit of the persons with whom we associate. What may we then infer concerning the merit of St. Joseph? Had God given to us the honorable commission of selecting for the blessed Virgin a guardian of her virginity, would we not have chosen the greatest saint that ever appeared upon earth? Well, can we presume that the Holy Spirit who is the author of this choice had less affection or less wisdom in choosing than we? O blessed Joseph! how happy thou wert in having found so many favors and graces before the eternal Father, who gave thee his Son to guard, and before the ever blessed Spirit, who entrusted thee with his Spouse, by establishing thee like the cherubim in the terrestrial paradise, to guard the tree of life.

We need, in order to accomplish our salvation, to be surrounded by virtuous persons; and we ought to be aware, with even very little experience, of the good that the soul finds in her relations with the neighbor. Consider at what period you began to relish the gifts of God; you will see that this favor dates from the happy meeting with some virtuous companion, of a discreet associate or friend, or of an edifying neighbor. May not the same be said of such as brave a love of piety? was it not after some unbecoming conversation, that assiduity in prayer and love of pious reading were destroyed, and the sacraments neglected?

2. We do not find in the life of this Patriarch such splendid actions as in that of other saints; it is not said that he performed miracles, or practiced great austerities; he followed the ordinary way, because it is less exposed to pride. He passed his life in his little dwelling at Nazareth, occupied as a carpenter, laboring to support the infant Jesus and the blessed Virgin. He did not see the great world, he did not even know it; his delight was to pray and lament in secret over the iniquities that are committed in it. It is indeed admirable, that he was never seen frequenting the streets and public squares of Nazareth; he was a hidden treasure that God reserved to make known hereafter. There were then kings, emperors, men of learning, men of renown, who caused others to speak of them; where are they now? They have disappeared from the earth many a century ago; and now they are never mentioned, except when their evil deeds are narrated; whilst St. Joseph, who led a modest, retired life, who was not ambitious of worldly honors, who served God in silence, sighing only for the happiness of the saints, is exalted above them all. O you therefore, who aspire to the bliss of saints, love retirement; do

not seek the praises and admiration of a fleeting and misjudging world; dread flattery, do all your good works secretly, concealing "from your right hand what your left hand doeth;" or if you are obliged to exhibit your actions to the world, purify your intentions and your motives, so that you may be able to say that they were done solely for the glory of God and the welfare of the neighbor.

3. Persons generally die as they have lived; what then must have been the consolations that attended the departure of St. Joseph, after so many good deeds, touching examples and noble employments. Let us represent to the mind that holy and venerable man, on his bed of poverty, with Jesus holding his right hand, and Mary holding his left, as though to support the last fleeting instants of mortality. What words of encouragement, and of gratitude, and holy hope they offered him, are the secrets of heaven! How comforting to assist at the death scene of the *just*, of *him*, who, like St. Joseph, lived in the practice of good, and suffered his heart to adopt no earthly attachments, who despised the world and its false allurements. He calmly perceives the arrival of his last moments, as a traveler that expects impatiently the term of a stormy voyage; as a prisoner who gladly beholds the walls of his dungeon give way, and chants the song of deliverance; as a stranger who goes forth from the land of exile and returns to his own, his native land; as a suffering patient who arrives at the conclusion of protracted illness. He kisses his crucifix; he offers his life to him from whom he holds it, and who died to expiate our sins; he bedews with tears of contrition that holy cross which is his passport to heaven; despair dares not intrude, for he relies on the mercy of Jesus, who

shed his blood to expiate his sins; he lifts his hands
and eyes to heaven, and expires pronouncing the
dear names of Jesus, of Mary, and of Joseph.

4. In the eternal tabernacles, St. Joseph is glorified
as the worthy head of the Holy family; on earth he
was nearest to Jesus and Mary; he was the most
faithful companion of their toils and sufferings; how
could he fail of enjoying a position near them in
heaven. If king Ahasuerus exalted Mordecai to
such great honor because he delivered him from a
conspiracy; what will not our Lord, the king of
heaven, do for him who delivered him from the
pursuit of Herod? St. Bernardin of Sienna, says,
that it is beyond doubt, that our Saviour refuses not
to St. Joseph that familiarity and tender respect with
which he honored him in the world, as a respectful
child towards a father, and many saints do not hesitate in declaring that St. Joseph does not implore
but requires from our Lord with paternal authority.
St. Teresa, says that we may hope for all that we
implore through the intercession of St. Joseph. Let
us then take him for our special protector; conjuring
him to assume the important affair of our salvation,
promising to walk in his footsteps, to imitate his virtues, to love retirement, and to detach our affections
from earthly goods. And as he is so powerful in
heaven, let us beseech him with earnestness to obtain
for us the gift of virginity and chastity, which is of
inestimable value, and will merit for us the grace of
reigning with him in a blessed eternity.

SENTIMENTS.

We humble ourselves in thy presence, O most
compassionate Joseph, and entreat thee to receive us
in the number of thy devoted servants. Thou wast

humble, pure, meek, and patient; obtain us the grace of becoming so. But chiefly enrich our souls with that faith, hope and charity, which were so plentifully diffused in thy heart. We commend our whole life to thy powerful protection; we recommend to thee also the moment of our death; may we, like thee, expire in the arms of Jesus and Mary. Amen.

ASPIRATION.

Jesus, Mary and Joseph, aid us now, and at the hour of death.

PRACTICE.

Observe the month of St. Joseph—and recite his litany or office on Wednesdays.

Devotion to St. Joseph.

Pope Pius VII., granted to all the faithful, who recite with contrite heart the following seven prayers:

1. A hundred days' indulgence once every day.

2. An indulgence of three hundred days every Wednesday in the year.

3. Three hundred days' indulgence on the nine days preceding the 19th of March, and on the third Sunday after Easter.

4. A plenary indulgence on the 19th of March, and on the third Sunday after Easter on accomplishing the ordinary conditions.

5. A plenary indulgence once a month, to those who will daily recite this exercise during a month, on the day they may select for confessing and praying for the Church. These indulgences are applicable to the souls in purgatory.—(*From the Raccolta.*)

St. Teresa, in the sixth chapter of her life, writes: "I choose the glorious St. Joseph, for my patron, and I commend myself in all things to his intercession. I do not remember ever to have asked God anything by his means, which I did not obtain. I never knew any one, who by invoking him, did not advance exceedingly in virtue, for he assists in a wonderful manner, all who address themselves to him."

ST. JOSEPH.

Prayers containing the Seven Sorrows and Seven Joys of St. Joseph.

FIRST PRAYER.

Chaste spouse of the Immaculate Mother of Jesus, glorious St. Joseph, as intense as was thy grief and interior anguish when believing it thy duty to separate from thy stainless spouse, so ineffable was thy joy when the angel of God revealed to thee the mystery of the Incarnation. We implore thee by this sorrow and this joy, deign to console us now, and in our agony, that after leading a devout life, we may like thee, sweetly die in the arms of Jesus and Mary.

Pater Noster. Ave Maria. Gloria Patri.

SECOND PRAYER.

Illustrious Patriarch, glorious St. Joseph, who enjoyed the eminent dignity of reputed Father of the Word made man, the grief that pierced thy heart, when contemplating the divine Infant lying in a manger and weeping and trembling with cold, was suddenly changed into a celestial joy, on beholding the choirs of angels adoring him, and chanting his praises, the three kings prostrate before him, and all the glorious events of that resplendent night. We entreat thee, by this sorrow and this joy, to obtain for us, that after this earthly pilgrimage, we may enter the mansions of bliss, and there enjoy the immortal chorus of the angels amid the brightness of eternal light.

Pater. Ave. Gloria.

THIRD PRAYER.

Perfect model of submission to the divine precepts, glorious St. Joseph, if the sight of the precious blood shed by the Infant Redeemer in the painful rite of circumcision overwhelmed thy heart with grief—the appointment of the sweet name of Jesus, according to the revelation made thee by the angel, revived thy fainting spirits, and filled thee with unutterable consolation.

Obtain for us that after being washed and purified by the precious blood of thy Son, we may die joyfully, pronouncing, heart and voice, the sacred names of Jesus and Mary.

Pater. Ave. Gloria.

FOURTH PRAYER.

O thou to whom were communicated the divine mysteries of our redemption, glorious St. Joseph, if Simeon's prophecy penetrated thy soul with a mortal sorrow, by fore-telling thee what Jesus and Mary were to suffer, it also filled thee with a holy joy, by announcing to thee, that these sufferings would be followed by the salvation of innumerable souls resuscitated to a blissful immortality.

Ask for us, by this sorrow, and by this joy, that, through the merits of Jesus and the intercession of Mary, we may become partakers of the glorious resurrection.

Pater. Ave. Gloria.

FIFTH PRAYER.

O vigilant guardian of God made man, pious comforter of his holy mother, glorious St. Joseph, by the trouble, weary and anxious sorrow thou didst undergo in the "Flight into Egypt," and by thy unmingled joy on perceiving the idols of the heathen falling from their pedestals before the presence of the true God, pray for us, that, avoiding dangerous occasions, we may merit to see the idols of our terrestial affections overthrown, and our hearts being consecrated wholly to the service of Jesus and Mary, we may live but for them, and calmly offer them our latest sigh.

Pater. Ave. Gloria.

SIXTH PRAYER.

Angel of earth, glorious St. Joseph, who was lost in admiration on beholding the King of heaven submissive to thy orders; the consolation thou didst experience when bringing him back from Egypt was embittered by the dread of Archelaus; however, on being encouraged and fortified by the angel, thou didst joyfully enter Nazareth in company with Jesus and Mary.

Obtain for us that being disengaged from all hurtful fears, we may enjoy tranquility of conscience, living securely in union with Jesus and Mary, and that in the dread hour of death, we may commend our souls to their holy keeping.

Pater. Ave. Gloria.

SEVENTH PRAYER.

Mirror of sanctity, glorious St. Joseph, who can conceive thy excessive grief, at the loss of the Child Jesus, (without thy fault,) or the joy that transported thee, when, after three days of anxious search, thou didst find him in the temple, amid the Doctors of the law.

We humbly entreat thee, by this sorrow and thy succeeding joy, to condescend to intercede for us with God, that we may never lose our amiable Jesus by the commission of mortal sin; or should this misfortune occur, may we seek him anew with sincere contrition, until we enjoy the light of his gracious countenance; and after death, may we be united to him in heaven, and with thee bless his divine mercies world without end.

Pater. Ave. Gloria.

℣. Pray for us, blessed Joseph.

℟. That we may be made worthy of the promises of Christ.

LET US PRAY.

O God, who by thy ineffable providence, vouchsafed to select St. Joseph to become the Spouse of thy holy Mother, grant, we implore thee, that while venerating him on earth as our protector, we may merit his intercession for us in heaven. O thou who livest and reignest world without end.

PRAYER TO ST. JOSEPH.

Great Saint, faithful servant to whom God confided the care of the Holy Family—and established thee protector of the Infancy of Jesus, the comfort and support of his blessed Mother, and co-operator in the great plan of man's redemption—who enjoyed the happiness of living with Jesus and Mary, and expiring in their arms; chaste Spouse of the Mother of God, model and pattern of pure, humble, patient and interior souls, be moved by the confidence we repose in thee, and receive with benevolence the testimonies of our devotion. We bless God for the favors with which he distinguished thee, and entreat him, through thy intercession, to grant us the grace of imitating thy virtues.

Pray for us great Saint; and by thy love for Jesus and Mary, and by the love of Jesus and Mary for thee, procure for us the happiness of living and dying in their love.   Amen.

Jesus Christ, hear us.

Jesus Christ, graciously hear us.

V̇. Pray for us O blessed Joseph.

Ṙ. That we may be made worthy of the promises of Christ.

DEVOTIONS TO ST. ALOYSIUS.

The Six Sundays of St. Aloysius.

CONSIDERATION FOR THE FIRST SUNDAY.

St. Aloysius an example of compunction of heart.

Consider 1st—What was the subject of his sorrow? small faults, which worldlings hardly believed to be faults.

At four or five years of age, he had taken, by stealth, some powder from the pouches of the soldiers, to fire a small field piece, which was allowed him for diversion, and with a view of training him up for the army. He had also been heard occasionally to utter some improper expressions, which he had gathered from the soldiers, though without reflecting on the import and meaning of them. Nevertheless, he bitterly bewailed these two faults during his whole ensuing life.

Consider 2d—That, although the faults of St. Aloysius were small, his grief was most intense and sincere.

So lively was his sorrow, that entering upon a general confession of his whole life, at Florence, he was siezed with such great grief, and overwhelmed with such a torrent of tears, that, unable to support the anguish, he fainted away, and was obliged not only to interrupt, but to postpone his confession, already begun, to a further time; and ever after, a sincere sorrow expressed by sighs and tears, attended the remembrance of his past faults.

Consider 3d—The perseverance of his repentance. He never ceased to repent, till he ceased to live. Often was he heard to say, with tears, Thy judgments, O God! are a deep abyss: Who knows whether the sins I committed before my entrance into religion are yet forgiven!

He feared, lest he should be cast off by Almighty God, and accounted in the number of the reprobate.

REFLECTIONS AND RESOLUTIONS.

What an unhappy reflection will it prove for me when in *eternal misery*; I am here, because I would not do what I could have performed with so much ease—I will daily humble myself before God, whom I have so often offended—I will offer him sincere contrition for my past sins, resolving to make amends as far as I can, by my fervor and devotion. I will say often, in the sincerity of my heart, *permit O Lord, that my love and affection in serving thee, may equal (if possible) my malice in having offended thee.* I will be exact in my examination at night, and resolve never to retire to rest, without begging pardon of Almighty God for those offences of my past life, which I know to be the most displeasing to him. I will endeavor to excite within me, *that compunction of heart*, St. Aloysius experienced, and will beg it through his intercession.

CONSIDERATION FOR THE SECOND SUNDAY.

St. Aloysius an example of Mortification.

Consider what was his mortification: 1st—*In the world.* 2d—*In a religious state.* 3d—*On his death-bed.*

Consider 1st—That every christian is commanded by his Redeemer, to walk *in the narrow way that leads to life;* MATT. vii. 14. Consequently the spirit of christianity is a spirit of mortification. Under the influence of divine grace, Aloysius was early imbued with this heavenly doctrine. · He practiced the most rigid austerities from his childhood, even in the world, and notwithstanding the contrary attractions of a magnificent court, he treated his body, innocent as it was, with the greatest severity. His disciplines were frequent and bloody; his fasts almost continual, his very refection was so sparing, that it never exceeded one ounce at any set meal. When deprived of his usual instruments of mortification, he was ever ingenious in finding means to supyly their want. Instead of hair shirts, he would make use of small iron spikes and rowels of spurs, and would strew his bed with chips of wood, that his very rest might be in uniformity with his other actions, which were ever seasoned with mortification.

Consider 2d—That Aloysius in a religious state, with due subordination to superiors, continued to practise the same rigorous austerities. No action

seemed to please him, unless accompanied with some
mortification. Besides fasting, iron chains and disciplines, he would find some means to afflict his body,
in what position soever it was, and would not allow
any opportunity to escape, of overcoming himself.
To such as appeared surprised at his austerities, he
would frequently answer : *It is practice and custom
that make these things easy and agreeable; neglect
and dis se render them hard and difficult.*

Consider 3d—The mortification of St. Aloysius at
the hour of death. From the knowledge of the
astonishing mortifications of this Saint, many imag-
ined, that at the hour of his death, he would be
troubled, as though by his voluntary chastisements
he had shortened his life. On the contrary, having
received the last sacraments of the Church, he declared, *that, far from being troubled at the mortifications he had inflicted on himself, his only concern
was, that he had omitted many austerities, which his
strength probably would have been able to support.*

REFLECTIONS AND RESOLUTIONS.

Remember that it is the undoubted sign of predestination, according to St. Paul.—(GAL. v. 24)
*that those who are Christ's, have crucified their flesh,
with its vices and lusts;* consequently to avoid sin,
and to be a disciple of Jesus Christ, I must oppose
with vigor my evil inclinations; I must deny my
senses that freedom and liberty, in which I have
often indulged them. Had I done this on such or
such an occasion, in my conversations with others, in
my manner of acting with them and myself, I would
not have so frequently excited the anger of the
Almighty. At my baptism I promised to the Church
of Christ, that I would renounce the *world* with its

pomps, the *devil* with his works, the *flesh* and its pleasures—can I do so without constant mortification? My God, I was made to serve and love thee alone. I will ever resist the first incitement to vice, and *bring my body into subjection.* My *mortification* in so doing will be *short,* my reward *eternal.* Enable me to keep these my resolutions; bless me as thou didst bless St. Aloysius, I beg this favor through his intercession.

CONSIDERATION FOR THE THIRD SUNDAY.

St. Aloysius an example of purity of body.

Consider 1st—That St. Aloysius though possessing every virtue, seems to have excelled in that of purity of body. From his earliest youth, his domestics and all who knew him, could not help admiring the integrity of his morals; they usually styled him, the *little prince exempt from the weakness of the flesh.* The holy Church does not fear to name him "*the angelical youth,*" even in her most solemn and public service. No one dared to utter a word that savored of immodesty, or even had a tendency to it, in his presence; they knew that nothing would displease him more. Cardinal Bellarmine, his director in matters of conscience, a most wise and prudent man, hesitates not to declare, that he looked upon him as confirmed in the favor and grace of his Creator.

Consider 2d—How singular were the prerogatives with which God adorned the purity of his servant. In his tender years, he consecrated himself at Florence, to the mother of purity, who seems to have rewarded him, in a particular manner on that account. The acts of his canonization testify, that no one was ever more privileged—reflect on the words themselves. Aloysius never suffered in his body the stings of the flesh, and never had in his mind an impure thought; which thing we read not in the lives of other saints. Such are the gifts of God, such those in particular that are imparted to us through the hands of the most pure Virgin, in themselves singular and angelical.

Consider 3d—With what care St. Aloysius preserved this precious treasure of purity. No advantage was given to his enemies; he kept a strict guard over all his senses; particularly over his eyes, as the most dangerous inlet. When Page to the Empress, Mary of Austria, upon whom he waited many years, he never once looked her in the face, nor was he less circumspect when he conversed with his own mother. He kept his eyes modestly inclined towards the ground, so that the greater number of his friends could not distinguish of what color they were. In a word, he was ever watchful and modest—he showed a diffidence in himself similar to one walking in a difficult path, holding in his hand a frail vessel filled with precious liquor.

REFLECTIONS AND RESOLUTIONS.

Ought I not to follow this striking example of St. Aloysius? He was *moderate* in conversation, *considerate* in action, *meek* in his exterior, *watchful* over his senses; in every motion of his body, he showed himself an angelical youth.

I will here reflect that to follow my loving Redeemer, and to please him I must love purity. I must offer him a heart which sincerely detests the smallest incitements towards impurity. Thousands are buried in *hell* for this dreadful sin. *O my loving Saviour! take my heart to thyself; thou hast loved me upon the cross.*

O most holy Mary! my dearest mother! defend me from the enemy of my salvation, who wishes to make me trample under foot the precious blood which thy beloved Son shed for my redemption. Take pity on me, O holy Mary! defend me from his rage. I will beg this virtue through the intercession of St. Aloysius.

CONSIDERATION FOR THE FOURTH SUNDAY

St. Aloysius an example of purity of mind.

Consider 1st—That St. Aloysius from his youth seemed to possess a knowledge of the vanities of the world. Of this he showed evident signs, by publicly despising its pomps and honors. What engrosses the attention of other men, power, riches, command, were of no merit in his estimation. The rich, who while they might have gained eternal wealth, remained lost and bewildered in the pursuit of what was vain and transient, were so many objects of his pity and compassion. His delight was to resemble the poor; he chose for himself the meanest dress in the midst of the greatest splendor, to show that he cordially despised worldly grandeur. What could he desire upon earth, whose thoughts were centered in heaven?

Consider 2d—That his disengagement from worldly affairs caused him in a short time totally to renounce the world. Deliberating on the choice of a state of life he addressed his prayers to our blessed Lady. On the feast of the Assumption, he clearly saw that he was called to the Society of Jesus. Great were

the obstacles he had to surmount, in order to obey
that call. His father's consent was obtained, only
by prayer, tears and rigorous mortifications. In fine,
St. Aloysius publicly renounced the principality,
which by birth devolved upon him, and transferred
his right to his younger brother; then from amidst
the tears of a large assembly, he proceeds to the
Society of Jesus; exchanging the ease and splendor
of a court, for the poverty, mortification and humiliation of a religious life.

Consider 3d—That this purity of mind which St.
Aloysius possessed in so perfect a degree, received
its life from the saint's intimate union with God.
While a child, he frequently spent whole hours in
contemplating the divine perfections of Almighty
God, exciting tears of tenderness and love towards
him. His thoughts were continually on God. His
countenance would be inflamed, his soul would melt
with tenderness at the mere memory of his Creator,
who was ever before his eyes and present in his heart.
An uninterrupted conversation with God accompanied his whole life. In prayer especially, he was so
absorbed in the object of his love, that no distraction
could avert his mind; of this we have the authentic
testimony in the acts of his canonization, which
declare *that he was free from distractions and dissipation of mind in prayer;* a favor he had not purchased without much labor.

REFLECTIONS AND RESOLUTIONS.

The example St. Aloysius gives me, of purity of
mind, deserves my most serious reflections. By the
possession of this great virtue, my soul is raised to a
union with God; by the assistance of divine grace,
it contemns the follies of this world, despises its

perishable objects, and seeks its Lord and Creator. It is in vain for me to think I do this, unless all my actions tend purely to the honor and glory of Almighty God.

Do I *seek* his glory and a *greater union* with him in performing them?—I must render a most rigorous account of all my thoughts, words and actions.

I will frequently make acts of faith in this truth, and say within myself, I believe, O my God! that I am to give a strict account of all I do, because thou hast said, *that thou wilt judge all men according to their works.* Short aspirations, repeated frequently during my actions, would draw upon me the choicest blessings of Almighty God.

CONSIDERATION FOR THE FIFTH SUNDAY.

St. Aloysius an example of charity toward his neighbor.

Consider 1st—He who knows not how to bear with the defects of others, does not possess the virtue of charity. The first quality ascribed to christian charity by St. Paul is, that *charity is patient*—1. Cor. xiii. 14. It may be affirmed that St. Aloysius carried this virtue to an *eminent* degree. He suffered not only with patience, every contempt, outrage, and insult, but showed on these occasions an exterior cheerfulness of countenance; a disposition not natural to him (being of a warm, hasty temper) but entirely the effect of frequent meditation, and the use he had made of his particular examen. Hence, he had obtained so absolute a command over himself, that the very first motions of anger, not always voluntary and in our power, either could not be observed in him, or were under perfect control.

Consider 2d—His charity was ever industrious in discovering means to relieve the wants of his neighbor. Aloysius, even when a child, was remarkable for his compassionate tenderness. He would notwithstanding his high birth, associate with the ignorant and more uncouth class of men, instruct them in the principles of the christian doctrine, reprove their vices, settle difficulties, disputes or disagreements, too common among them, drawing all to the love of God, and the frequent and due use of the sacraments.

Consider 3d.—The most heroic deed of christian charity, is to sacrifice our lives in the service of our neighbor. The charity of St. Aloysius extended to this sublime degree of perfection Whilst the plague infested Rome, he obtained permission of his superiors to serve such as were infected; the more abject and abandoned the object, that greater was his care and vigilance. We may truly say that he laid down his life in the discharge of so charitable an employment: for contracting the distemper, it soon proved fatal to him.

REFLECTIONS AND RESOLUTIONS.

What comfort to a pious client of St. Aloysius, to contemplate his patron at the hour of death. This Saint expressed his delight at the approach of the happy moment which was to unite him to his Saviour. This favor he received in the exercise of love towards his neighbor. I will reflect that to secure my salvation, I must religiously observe these three commands of my loving Redeemer. 1st—*I must love my neighbor as myself.*—Matt. 22d. 2d—*I must do as I would be done by.*—Matt. 7. 3d—*I must love my neighbor as Christ has loved me.*—John 13.

If I love my Saviour as I ought, I shall love all those for whom he suffered.

I will make it my duty to humble myself for my many faults against charity—and will endeavor by a mild and sweet disposition joined with a virtuous example, to make atonement and reparation. I will often say, *I cannot love God unless I love my neighbor,* and daily pray for this virtue through the intercession of St. Aloysius.

CONSIDERATION FOR THE SIXTH SUNDAY.

St. Aloysius an example of the love we owe to God.

Consider 1st—St. Aloysius, who excelled in all other virtues, was truly seraphic in the love of God. He was so transported with this holy flame, that when he thought of God or heard others speak of him, his countenance was, as it were, on fire, and his heart beat with violence. His superiors obliged him to moderate this fervor which was consuming his remaining strength, and at intervals, to divert his mind from a continual meditation on his Creator.

Consider 2d—The goodness of God, which appears most remarkable in our crucified Saviour, was the nourishment which maintained and increased the love of God in Aloysius. If our Saint was pleased with the contemplation of the humility, sufferings, and bitter passion of Christ crucified; he was not less delighted at the prospect of following an example given him by so admirable an instructor. The remembrance of what our Saviour underwent, gave a constant stimulus to his sufferings which he deemed inconsiderable, because they fell far below what he contemplated in him, and the desire he had formed in his heart of suffering for him.

Consider 3d—The excessive goodness Christ shows in the holy sacrament of the Eucharist, was another source of his love for God. *He has loved them to the end.*—John 13. So it was with St. Aloysius. From the first time he received this pledge of love in the holy communion, which was from the hands of St. Charles Borromeus, his constant care was to live as one thoroughly sensible of so singular a favor. When in presence of the blessed sacrament, his soul dissolved into the tenderest affections, and inspired all around him with the same sentiments of devotion. Three whole days were employed in preparing for the reception of so great a guest, and as many in returning thanks for so kind a visit, so excessive a bounty. He usually spent two hours in adoration after communion.

REFLECTIONS AND RESOLUTIONS.

Who is not moved to the love of Almighty God, when he considers all that God has done to gain his affections? I am that happy person whose love God demands. Can I refuse Almighty God the affections of my heart! Can I deny my soul that happiness which proceeds from the love and possession of her Creator! No, my God, I will now begin to love thee at all times and in all places. I seriously resolve to make frequent acts of love, to accompany all my actions with aspirations of divine love. I will strive to engage others in this heavenly practice. If I adopt these sentiments, and correspond with them, I am certain of being happy with Almighty God and his saints during an endless eternity.

CONFESSION.

Among all the methods bestowed by the Saviour of the world, for converting sinners, sustaining the just, and conducting them to perfection, the most efficacious and the most indispensable is confession. By it, man learns to know and humble himself, to measure the wounds of his soul and to heal them. In the sacrament of penance he finds light, counsel and fortitude, to combat the perverse maxims of the world, and the irregular propensities of the heart, to discover the wiles of the enemy of salvation and to elude them, to rise from his falls, nay, even how to profit by his faults. In that sacred laver, in which he mingles repentant tears with the blood of the Redeemer, he purifies and sanctifies his soul, and recovers the most precious of all wealth—peace with God and with his own conscience.

If many persons do not derive fruit from confession, it is because they do not bring to the reception of the sacrament of penance, the requisite dispositions; *some*, do not examine their consciences, others feel no contrition for the past, and adopt no firm resolutions relative to the future; others dare even to conceal some sins from their confessors.— Unhappy souls, they find *death* where they ought to find *life!* In order to avoid this misfortune, conform to the following directions for the examination of conscience, contrition, accusation of sins, etc.

EXAMINATION OF CONSCIENCE.

To do this well, retire to some recollected spot, place yourself in God's presence, adore him, and imagine that the confession you are about to make will be the last of your life, and thus invoke the light of the Holy Spirit.

Spirit of light and of truth, sounding the depths of consciences, and penetrating the inmost recesses of the soul, enlighten me with thy divine torch, that I may be able to discern the number and the loathsome hideousness of my sins; show me the evil which I have committed, and the good I have left undone; display to me also in the clearest manner, what I shall see when I shall be summoned before the tribunal of supreme, unerring justice.

O dear Saviour, who didst experience an unspeakable sorrow at the view of my ingratitude, and didst implore my pardon with tears and deep-drawn sighs, allow me to accompany thee to the garden of Olives; fill my soul with the sentiments which rendered thee *"sad even unto death."* Holy Virgin, secure refuge of sinners, my guardian angel, and my holy patron, intercede for me with the Holy Spirit, so that I may know whatever there exists in my soul that is offensive to the heart of my God.

[Examine your conscience according to the light God gives you. Avoid two extremes, almost equally dangerous: 1. Relying so implicitly on the interrogatories of the priest, as to examine your conscience only superficially. 2. Never being convinced that you have sincerely endeavored to know your sins, incessantly recommencing your examination, and giving at most a slight application to the very essential part of the sacrament, viz: Contrition. Banish that fear which destroys a filial confidence, which God delights to find in his children; his spirit is one of love, and not of dread and servitude.]

CONTRITION AND FIRM PURPOSE OF AMENDMENT.

After examining your conscience, you must of necessity excite yourself to contrition for having offended God, and promise not to offend him any more. Without that, the tears that the most

affecting exhortation might draw from you would prove ineffect-
ual; but never forget that contrition being a gift of God, you
must humbly and earnestly ask it from him.

O my God! thine eyes ever opened on me, have
seen all that is criminal and imperfect in my deeds,
and thy light has exhibited to me the depth of my
wounds. Destroy my hard-heartedness by the breath
of thy divine spirit, and command tears of compunction to flow from it, for thou canst change the rocks
of the wilderness into fountains of living water.

May I mingle my tears with the blood that Jesus
Christ, thy son, shed upon the cross. Grant me
grace to *"love thee much"* and then thou wilt remit
my sins; I solicit this grace at thy adorable feet, and
claim it in the name of Jesus, by the intercession of
Mary, of my good angel, and of all my holy protectors.

MOTIVES FOR CONTRITION.

1. Mortal sin deprives my soul of grace.
2. It deprives me of the friendship of God.
3. It takes away my right to glory, and accumu-
lates on my guilty head all the ills of the present life
and all the evils of a miserable eternity.

Form acts of contrition in the heart, and be not contented
with reciting them, but strive to penetrate your heart with true
and deep regret.

ACT OF CONTRITION.

O my God, suffer thy merciful heart to be moved
by my true repentance. Oh! would that the vivacity
of my regret could equal the extent of my faults!
Supply sorrow for me, O agonizing Heart of Jesus;
distil into my sin-sick heart one drop of that bitterness which drenched thy soul in the ga

Pardon, O my God, all the evil th

mitted or caused others to commit. Pardon me all the good that I have omitted or performed badly; pardon for all the sins that I know, or that my self-love hides from me. I detest them, and I desire to repair them at the price of all that I hold most dear.

RESOLUTION.

Now, O my God, I desire to immolate to thee, all that I value most, rather than displease thee. Alas! because thou art good, I have abused thy benefits in order to offend thee; but I now firmly resolve to avoid sin, to shun its occasions, and labor efficaciously in eradicating my faults. (*Here specify the fault of which you are most frequently guilty.*)

Yes, my God, I will endure death rather than infringe my resolution of serving you with inviolable fidelity. My passions will rise, and it will cost me to repress them; but with the help of grace I will faithfully accomplish the promise I deposite at thy sacred feet. Henceforth no more thoughts, words or deeds contrary to charity or modesty; no more impatience or anger, no more irreverence in the holy place, languor in thy service, or omissions in my duties; no more attachment to my own thoughts, or to my own will, I will rather die, O my God, than displease thee.

PRAYER TO OBTAIN GRACE FOR OVERCOMING A FALSE SHAME.

Divine Jesus, who didst deign to pass for a sinner, and suffer as though thou hadst been guilty, deliver me from that shame that sometimes hinders the penitent from confessing all his sins. I am aware, O my God, that it is thyself I address in the person of the priest; how should I dare omit acknowledging what thou knowest, since thou knowest the secrets of hearts, and nothing that passes in mine can be hidden from thee? O my God prevent me from making a sacrilegious confession, grant me simplicity and sincerity so that I may disclose to my confessor all the wounds of my soul, making him acquainted with their number, their quality and their aggravating circumstances, without disguise or diminuition, and by thus bringing to the reception of the sacrament of penance the necessary dispositions, I may merit to receive the pardon of all of my sins.

OF THE GRACE OF ABSOLUTION.

When we receive absolution, Jesus Christ washes us in his blood, we are clothed in the nuptial garment of the Lamb, hell is closed beneath our feet, and a place is destined for us in heaven; let us, therefore, receive this grace with respect, confidence and love; and take care to preserve it, so as not to fall again, and to advance in the service of God.

When leaving the tribunal of confession retire apart, and reflect on the benefits just received, and give to God heartfelt thanks.

PRAYER AFTER HAVING RECEIVED ABSOLUTION.

O my soul, render thanks to God, and confess his wonderful benefits. A moment since, and thou wert criminal, but now thou art absolved through the merits of Christ's precious blood. Instead of fearful torments which thou didst merit, the God of mercy deigns to be content with a trifling satisfaction, to pardon all, and to forget all.

O my God, what thou hast just done in my favor inspires me with a lively horror of sin, and excites me to renew my resolution of never again offending thee. Augment in my soul the desire I experience of changing my life, fortify my good resolutions, especially that of avoiding the occasions of my predominant fault; and grant that I may have such magnanimity in vanquishing myself that I may become thy beloved child on earth, and reign forever with thee in heaven.

Do not delay performing the penance prescribed you by the priest, and in order to testify to God that your return to him is sincere, adopt measures for retrenching the occasions of your faults, foresee the causes that lead you to sin, and prescribe a penance for yourself if you relapse into them anew.

If the confessor did not think proper to give you absolution, lament interiorly, and admit that you are unworthy of receiving it, resolve to increase your efforts to deserve it by a total change of manners.

PRAYER WHEN ONE HAS NOT RECEIVED ABSOLUTION.

O Jesus! I have shown thee the interior of my soul; thou hast fathomed its wounds, and I have retired from thee without being healed; thou knowest my infidelities, and thou didst not pardon them; when shall I be so happy as to obtain this grace? "Save me, or I perish." Thou canst do all things, and without thee I can do nothing, behold me prostrate before thee; "O God, be merciful to me a sinner"—enlighten my mind and strengthen my love.

LITANY OF THE SAINTS.

Ant. Remember not, O Lord, our offences, nor those of our parents, and take not revenge of our sins.

Kyrie eleison.	Lord, have mercy on us.
Christe eleison.	Christ, have mercy on us.
Kyrie eleison.	Lord, have mercy on us.
Christe audi nos.	Christ, hear us.
Christe exaudi nos.	Christ, graciously hear us.
Pater de cœlis Deus, miserere nobis.	God, the Father of heaven, have mercy on us.
Fili Redemptor mundi Deus miserere nobis.	God the Son, Redeemer of the world, have mercy on us.
Spiritus Sancte Deus, miserere nobis.	God the Holy Ghost, have mercy on us.
Sancta Trinitas unus Deus, miserere nobis.	Holy Trinity, one God, have mercy on us.
Sancta Maria, ora pro nobis.	Holy Mary, pray for us.
Sancta Dei genitrix.	Holy Mother of God,
Sancta Virgo virginum.	Holy Virgin of virgins,
Sancte Michael.	St. Michael,
Sancte Gabriel.	St. Gabriel,
Sancte Raphael.	St. Raphael,
Omnes sancti Angeli et Archangeli, orate pro nobis.	All ye holy Angels and Archangels,
Omnes sancti beatorum Spirituum ordines, orate, &c.	All ye holy orders of blessed spirits,
Sancte Joannes Baptista.	St. John the Baptist,
Sancte Joseph,	St. Joseph,
Omnes sancti Patriarchæ et Prophetæ, orate pro nobis,	All ye holy Patriarchs and Prophets,
Sancte Petre,	St. Peter,
Sancte Paule,	St. Paul,
Sancte Andrea,	St. Andrew,
Sancte Jacobe,	St. James,
Sancte Joannes,	St. John,

(Left column responses marked: Ora, etc. — Right column responses marked: Pray, etc.)

Sancte Thoma,		St. Thomas,
Sancte Jacobe,		St. James,
Sancte Philippe,		St. Philip,
Sancte Bartholomæ,		St. Bartholomew,
Sancte Matthæe,		St. Matthew,
Sancte Simon,	*Ora, etc.*	St. Simon,
Sancte Thaddæe,		St. Thaddeus,
Sancte Mathia,		St. Matthias,
Sancte Barnaba,		St. Barnaby,
Sancte Luca,		St. Luke,
Sancte Marce,		St. Mark,

Omnes sancti apostoli et evangelistæ, orate pro nobis.　　All ye holy apostles and evangelists,

Omnes sancti discipuli Domini, orate pro nobis,　　All ye holy disciples of our Lord,

Omnes sancti innocentes, orate pro nobis,　　All ye holy innocents,

Sancte Stephane, ora, etc.	St. Stephen,
Sancte Laurenti, ora, etc.	St. Lawrence,
Sancte Vincenti, ora, etc.	St. Vincent.

Sancti Fabiane et Sebastiane, orate pro nobis.　　SS. Fabian and Sebastian,

Sancti Joannes et Paule, orate pro nobis.　　SS. Paul and John.

Sancti Cosma et Damiane, orate, etc.　　SS. Cosmas and Damian,

Sancti Gervasi et Protasi, orate, etc.　　SS. Gervase and Protase,

Omnes sancti martyres, orate, etc.　　All ye holy martyrs,

Sancte Sylvester,		St. Sylvester,
Sancte Gregori.		St. Gregory,
Sancte Ambrosi,	*Ora pro nobis.*	St. Ambrose,
Sancte Augustine,		St. Augustine,
Sancte Hieronyme,		St. Jerome,
Sancte Martine,		St. Martin,
Sancte Nicolæ,		St. Nicholas,

Omnes sancti pontifices et confessores, orate, etc.　　All ye holy bishops and confessors.

Pray for us.

Omnes sancti doctores, orate, etc.

All ye holy doctors,

Sancte Antoni, orate, etc.

St. Anthony,

Sancte Benedicte, ora, etc.

St. Bennet,

Sancte Bernarde, ora, etc.

St. Bernard,

Sancte Dominice, ora, etc.

St. Dominic,

Sancte Francisce, ora, etc.

St. Francis,

Omnes sancti sacerdotes et levitæ, orate, etc.

All ye holy priests and levites,

Omnes sancti monarchi et eremitæ, orate, etc.

All ye holy monks and hermits,

Sancta Maria Magdalena,

St. Mary Magdalen,

Sancta Agatha,

St. Agatha,

Sancta Lucia,

St. Lucy,

Sancta Agnes,

St. Agnes,

Sancta Cæcilio,

St. Cecily,

Sancta Catharina,

St. Catharine,

Sancta Anastasia, ora, etc.

St. Anastasia, pray, etc.

Ora, etc.

Pray for us.

Omnes sancta virgines et viduæ, orate, etc.

All ye holy virgins and widows, pray, etc.

Omnes sancti et sanctæ Dei, intercedite pro nobis.

All ye men and women, saints of God, make intercession for us.

Propitius parce nobis Domine.

Be merciful unto us, spare us, O Lord.

Propitius esto, exaudi nos, Domine.

Be merciful unto us, graciously hear us, O Lord.

Ab omni malo, libera nos, Domine.

From all evil, O Lord deliver us.

Ab omni peccato,

From all sin,

Ab ira tua,*

From thy wrath,

A subitanea et improvisa morte,

From a sudden and unprovided death,

Ab insidiis diaboli,

From the deceits of the devil,

Ora, etc.

Pray for us.

---

*Here, for the devotion of the Forty Hours, is inserted:

Ab imminentibus periculis,

From all dangers that threaten us,

A peste, fame, et bello.

From plague, famine and war.

Ab ira, et odio, et omni mala voluntate,

A spiritu fornicationis,

A fulgure et tempestate,

A morte perpetua,

Per mysterium sanctæ incarnationis tuæ,

Per adventum tuum,

Per nativitatem tuam,

Per baptismum et sanctum jejunium tuum,

Per crucem et passionem tuam,

Per mortem et sepulturam tuam.

Per sanctam resurrectionem tuam,

Per admirabilem ascensionem tuam,

Per adventum Spiritus sancti Paracliti,

In die judicii,

Peccatores, te rogamus, audi nos.

Ut nobis parcas,

Ut nobis indulgeas,

Ut ad veram pœnitentiam nos perducere digneris,

Ut Ecclesiam tuam sanctam regere et conservare digneris,

Ut domnum Apostolicum et omnes ecclesiasticos ordines in sancta religione conservare digneris.

Libera nos, Domine.

Te rogamus audi nos.

From anger, hatred, and all ill-will,

From the spirit of fornication,

From lightning and tempest,

From everlasting death,

Through the mystery of thy holy incarnation,

Through thy coming,

Through thy nativity,

Through thy baptism, and holy fasting,

Through thy cross and passion,

Through thy death and burial,

Through thy holy resurrection,

Through thy admirable ascension,

Through the coming of the Holy Ghost, the Comforter,

In the day of judgment,

We sinners do beseech thee to hear us.

That thou spare us,

That thou pardon us,

That thou vouchsafe to bring us to true penance,

That thou vouchsafe to govern and preserve thy holy Church,

That thou vouchsafe to preserve our apostolic prelate, and all ecclesiastical orders in holy religion.

O Lord, deliver us,

We beseech thee to hear us.

Ut inimicos sancta Ecclesiæ humiliare digneris,

Ut regibus et principibus Christianis pacem et veram concordiam donare digneris,

Ut cuncto populo Christiano pacem et unitatem largiri digneris,

Ut nosmetipsos in tuo sancto servitio confortare et conservare digneris,

Ut mentes nostras ad cœlestia desideria erigas,

Ut omnibus benefactoribus nostris sempiterna bona retribuas,

Ut animas nostras, fratrum, propinquorum, et benefactorum nostrorum, ab æterna damnatione eripias,

Ut fructus terræ dare et conservare digneris,

Te rogamus, audi nos.

Ut omnibus fidelibus defunctis requiem æternam donare digneris, te, etc.

Ut nos exaudire digneris, te, etc.

Fili Dei, te, etc.

Agnus Dei, qui tollis peccata mundi, parce nobis Domine.

Agnus Dei, qui tollis peccata mundi, exaudi nos Domine.

That thou vouchsafe to humble the enemies of the holy Church,

That thou vouchsafe to give peace and true concord to Christian kings and princes,

That thou vouchsafe to grant peace and unity to all Christian people,

That thou vouchsafe to confirm and preserve us in thy holy service,

That thou lift up our minds to heavenly desires,

That thou render eternal good things to all our benefactors,

That thou deliver our souls, and those of our brethren, kinsfolks, and benefactors, from eternal damnation,

That thou vouchsafe to give and preserve the fruits of the earth.

We beseech thee to hear us.

That thou vouchsafe to give eternal rest to all the faithful departed, we, etc.

That thou vouchsafe graciously to hear us, we, etc.

Son of God, we, etc.

Lamb of God, who takest away the sins of the world, spare us, O Lord.

Lamb of God, who takest away the sins of the world, graciously hear us, O Lord.

Agnus Dei, qui tollis peccata mundi, miserere nobis.

Christe audi nos. Christe, exaudi nos. Kyrie eleison. Christe eleison.— Kyrie eleison. Pater noster, *secreto.*

V. Et ne nos inducas in tentationem.

R. Sed libera nos a malo.

Lamb of God, who takest away the sins of the world, have mercy on us.

Christ hear us. Christ graciously hear us. Lord have mercy on us. Christ have mercy on us. Our Father, *in an under tone.*

V. And lead us not into temptation.

R. But deliver us from evil.

PSALM LXIX.

Deus, in adjutorium meum intende: *Domine ad adjuvandum me festina.

Confundantur et revereantur, *qui quærunt animam meam :

Avertantur retrorsum, et erubescant, *qui volunt mihi mala :

Avertantur statim erubescentes, *qui dicunt mihi : Euge, euge.

Exultent et lætentur in te nmnes qui quærunt te, *et dicant semper: Magnificetur Dominus; qui diligunt salutare tuum.

Ego vero egenus et pauper sum : *Deus, adjuva me.

Adjutor meus et liberator meus es tu : *Domine, ne moreris.

Gloria Patri, etc.

V. Salvos fac servos tuos.

R. Deus meus, sperantes in te.

O God, come to my assistance : *O Lord, make haste to help me.

Let them be confounded and ashamed *that seek my soul :

Let them be turned backward, and blush for shame *that desire evils to me :

Let them be presently turned away blushing for shame *that say to me : 'Tis well, 'tis well.

Let all that seek thee rejoice and be glad in thee, *and let such as love thy salvation say always: The Lord be magnified.

But I am needy and poor, *O God, help me.

Thou art my helper and my deliverer : *O Lord, make no delay.

Glory be to the Father, etc.

V. Save thy servants.

R. Trusting in thee, O my God.

V. Esto nobis, Domine, turris fortitudinis.

R. A facie inimici.

V. Nihil proficiat inimicus in nobis.

R. Et filius iniquitatis non apponat nocere nobis.

V. Domine, non secundum peccata nostra facias nobis.

R. Neque secundum iniquitates nostras retribuas nobis.

V. Oremus pro pontifice nostro *N.*

R. Dominus conservet eum, et vivificet eum, et beatum faciat eum in terra, et non tradat eum in animam inimicorum ejus.

V. Oremus pro benefactoribus nostris.

R. Retribuere dignare, Domine, omnibus nobis bona facienticus, propter nomen tuum, vitam æternam, *Amen.*

V. Oremus pro fidelibus defunctis.

R. Requiem æternam dona eis, Domine : et lux perpetua luceat eis.

V. Requiescant in pace.

R. Amen.

V. Pro fratribus nostris absentibus.

R. Salvos fac servos tuos, Deus meus, sperantes in te.

V. Mitte eis, Domine aux-

V. Be unto us, O Lord, a tower of strength.

R. From the face of the enemy.

V. Let not the enemy prevail against us at all.

R. Nor the son of iniquity have any power to hurt us.

V. O Lord, deal not with us according to our sins.

R. Neither reward us according to our iniquities.

V. Let us pray for our chief bishop, *N.*

R. The Lord preserve him and give him life, and make him blessed upon earth, and deliver him not to the will of his enemies.

V. Let us pray for our benefactors.

R. Vouchsafe, O Lord, for thy name's sake, to reward with eternal life all those who have done us good, *Amen.*

V. Let us pray for the faithful departed.

R. Eternal rest give them O Lord : and let perpetual light shine upon them.

V. May they rest in peace.

R. Amen.

V. For our absent brethren.

R. O my God, save thy servants trusting in thee.

V. Send them help, O

11

ilium de sancto.

R. Et de Sion tuere eos.

V. Domine, exaudi orationem meam.

R. Et clamor meus ad te veniat.

OREMUS.*

Deus, cui proprium est misereri semper, et parcere; suscipe deprecationem nostram; ut nos et omnes famulos tuos, quos delictorum catena constringit, miseratio tuæ pietatis clementer absolvat.

Exaudi, quæsumus, Domine, supplicum preces, et

Lord, from thy holy place.

R. And from Sion protect them.

V. O Lord, hear my prayer.

R. And let my cry come unto thee.

LET US PRAY.*

O God, whose property is always to have mercy and to spare; receive our humble petition; that we with all thy servants, who are bound by the chains of sin, may, by the compassion of thy goodness, mercifully be absolved.

Graciously hear, we beseech thee, O Lord, the

---

* For the Devotion of the Forty Hours the following Collects are used:

Deus, qui nobis sub sacramento mirabili Passionis tuæ memoriam reliquisti; tribue, quæsumus, ita nos Corporis et Sanguinis tui sacra mysteria venerari, ut redemptionis tui fructrum in nobis jugiter sentiamus. Qui vivis et regnas in sæcula sæculorum. Amen.

O God, who under this wonderful sacrament has left us a memorial of thy Passion; grant us, we beseech thee, so to venerate the sacred mysteries of thy Body and Blood, that we continually feel in our souls, the fruit of thy redemption. Who livest and reignest forever and ever. Amen.

From Advent to Christmas.

Deus, qui de beatæ Mariæ Virginis utero Verbum tuum. angelo nuntiante, carnem suscipere voluisti; præsta supplicibus tuis, ut qui vere eam Genitricem Dei credimus, ejus apud, te intercessionibus adjuvemur. Per eundem Christum Dominum nostrum.

R. Amen.

O God, who wast pleased that thy Word, at the message of an angel, should take flesh in the womb of the blessed Virgin Mary; grant to us, thy suppliants, that we, who believe her to be truly the Mother of God, may be assisted by her intercessions with thee. Through &c.

R. Amen.

confitentium tibi parce peccatis; ut pariter nobis indulgentiam tribuas benignus et pacem.

prayers of thy suppliants, and forgive the sins of them that confess to thee: that, in thy bounty, thou mayest grant us both pardon and peace.

Ineffabilem nobis, Domine, misericordiam tuam clementer ostende: ut simul nos et a peccatis omnibus exuas, et a pœnis, quas pro his meremur, eripias.

Shew forth upon us, O Lord, in thy mercy, thy unspeakable loving kindness: that thou mayest both loose us from all our sins, and deliver us from the punishments which we deserve for them.

Deus, qui culpa offenderis pœnitentia placaris; preces populi tui supplicantis propitius respice; et flagella

O God, who by sin art offended, and by penance pacified; mercifully regard the prayers of thy people mak-

---

From Christmas to the Purification

Deus, qui salutis æternæ, beatæ Mariæ virginitate fœcunda, humano generi præmia prætitisti; tribue, quæsumus, ut ipsam pro nobis intercedere sentiamus, per quam meruimus auctorum vitæ suscipere Dominum nostrum Jesum Christum Filium tuum. Qui tecum vivit et regnat in unitate Spiritus Sancti, Deus, per omnia sæcula sæculorem.
R. Amen.

O God, who by the fruitful virginity of blessed Mary, hast given to mankind the rewards of eternal salvation; grant, we beseech thee, that we may experience her intercession for us, through whom we have merited to receive the author of life, our Lord Jesus Christ thy Son. Who liveth and reigneth with thee in the unity of the Holy Ghost, God, world without end.
R. Amen.

From the Purification to Advent.

Concede nos famulos tuos, quæsumus, Domine Deus, perpetua mentis et corporis sanitate gaudere; et gloriosa beatæ Mariæ semper Virginis intersessione, a præsenti liberari tristitia, et æterna perfrui lætitia.

Grant, we beseech thee, O Lord God, that we, thy servants, may enjoy perpetual health of mind and body; and by the intercession of the blessed Mary, ever Virgin, may be delivered from present sorrow, and attain eternal gladness.

tua iracundiæ, quæ pro peccatis nostris meremur, averte.

Omnipotens, sempiterne Deus, miserere famulo tuo Pontifici nostro N., et dirige eum secundum tuam clementiam in viam salutis æternæ: ut te nonante tibi placita cupiat, et tota virtute perficiat.

Deus, a quo sancta desideria, recta consilia, et justa sunt opera; da servis tuis illam, quam mundus dare

ing supplication to thee, and turn away the scourges of thine anger, which we deserve for our sins.

Almighty, everlasting God, have mercy upon thy servant N., our Sovereign Pontiff, and direct him according to thy clemency, into the way of everlasting salvation; that by thy grace he may both desire those things that are pleasing to thee, and perform them with all his strength.

O God, from whom all holy desires, all right counsels, and all just works do come; give to thy servants

Then follows the Collect for the Pope, after which is said:

Deus, refugium nostrum et virtus: adesto piis Ecclesiæ tuæ precibus, auctor ipse pietatis, et præsta ut quod fideliter pecimus, efficaciter consequamur.

Omnipotens, sempiterne Deus in cujus manu sunt omnes potestates, et omnia jura regnorum; respice in auxilium Christianorum, ut gentes paganorum et hæreticorum, quæ in sua feritate et fraude confidunt, dexteræ tuæ potentia conterantur.

O God, our refuge and strength, who art the author of all piety; hearken unto the devout prayers of thy Church, and grant that what we ask faithfully, we may obtain effectually.

Almighty, everlasting God, in whose hand are all the powers and all the rights of kingdoms; come to the assistance of thy Christian people, that all pagan and heretical nations who trust in their own violence and fraud, may be broken by the might of thy right hand.

Then follows the last Collect, Omnipotens, sempiterne Deus, &c., Almighty, everlasting God, &c., with the Versicles; except that, in the last response but one, &c., instead of the simple Amen, is said:

R. Et custodiat nos semper. Amen.

R. And ever preserve us. Amen.

non potest, pacem; ut et corda nostra mandatis tuis dedita, et hostium sublata formidine, tempora sint tua protectione tranquilla.

Ure igne Sancti Spiritus renes nostros et cor nostrum, Domine: ut tibi casto corpore serviamus, et mundo, corde placeamus.

Fidelium Deus omnium Conditor et Redemptor, animabus famulorum famularumque tuarum remissionem cunctorum tribue peccatorum: ut indulgentiam, quam semper optaverunt, piis supplicationibus consequantur.

Actiones nostras, quæsumus, Domine, aspirando præveni, et adjuvando prosequere: ut cuncta nostra oratio et operatio a te semper incipiat, et per te cœpta finiatur.

Omnipotens, sempiterne Deus, qui vivorum dominaris simul et mortuorum, omniumque misereris, quos tuos fide et opere futuros esse prænoscis: te supplices exoramus, ut pro quibus effundere preces decrivimus, quosque vel præsens sæculum adhuc in carne retinet, vel

that peace which the world cannot give; that our hearts being given up to obey thy commandment, and the fear of enemies being taken away our days, by thy protection, may be peaceful.

Inflame, O Lord, our reins and heart with the fire of the Holy Ghost; that we may serve thee with a chaste body, and please thee with a clean heart.

O God, the Creator and Redeemer of all the faithful, give to the souls of thy servants departed, the remission of all their sins; that through pious supplications they may obtain the pardon which they have always desired.

Prevent, we beseech thee, O Lord, our actions by thy inspirations, and further them with thy continual help; that every prayer and work of ours may always begin from thee, and through thee be likewise ended.

Almighty, everlasting God, who hast dominion over the living and the dead, and art merciful to all, who thou foreknowest will be thine by faith and works; we humbly beseech thee, that they for whom we intend to pour forth our prayers, whether this present world still de-futurum jam exutos corpore suscepit, intercedentibus omnibus Sanctis tuis, pietatis tuæ clementia omnium delictorum suorum veniam consequantur. Per Dominum nostrum.

R. Amen.

tain them in the flesh, or the world to come hath already received them, stripped of their mortal bodies, may, by the grace of thy loving kindness, and by the intercession of all the Saints, obtain the remission of all their sins. Through thy Son, Jesus Christ, our Lord, who liveth and reigneth with thee in the unity of the Holy Spirit, God, for ever and ever.

R. Amen.

V. Domine, exaudi orationem.

R. Et clamor meus ad te veniat.

V. Exaudiat nos omnipotens et misericors Dominus.*

R. Amen.

V. Et fidelium animæ, per misericordiam Dei, requiescant in pace.

R. Amen.

V. O Lord, hear my prayer.

R. And let my cry come unto thee.

V. May the almighty and merciful Lord graciously hear us.

R. Amen.

V. And may the souls of the faithful, through the mercy of God, rest in peace.

R. Amen.

* *For the Forty Hours:* R. Et custodiat nos semper. Amen.

THE SEVEN PENITENTIAL PSALMS.

Remember not, O Lord! our offences, nor those of our parents, and take not revenge on our sins.

PSALM VI.

Domine ne in Furore.

O Lord, rebuke me not in thy indignation, nor chastise me in thy wrath.

Have mercy on me, O Lord, for I am weak; heal me, O Lord, for my bones are troubled.

And my soul is troubled exceedingly; but thou O Lord, how long?

Turn to me, O Lord, and deliver my soul: O save me for thy mercy's sake.

For there is no one in death that is mindful of thee: and who shall confess to thee in hell?

I have labored in my groanings: every night I will wash my bed, I will water my couch with my tears.

My eye is troubled through indignation: I have grown old amongst all my enemies.

Depart from me all ye workers of iniquity, for the Lord hath heard the voice of my weeping.

The Lord hath heard my supplication: the Lord hath received my prayer.

Let all my enemies be ashamed, and be very much troubled: let them be turned back, and be ashamed very speedily.

Glory be, etc.

PSALM XXXI.

Beati quorum.

Blessed are they whose iniquities are forgiven, and whose sins are covered.

Blessed is the man to whom the lord hath not imputed sin, and in whose spirit there is no guile.

Because I was silent, my bones grew old; whilst I cried out all the day long.

For day and night thy hand was heavy upon me: I am turned in my anguish, whilst the thorn is fastened.

I have acknowledged my sin to thee, and my injustice I have not concealed.

I said I will confess against myself my injustice to the Lord; and thou hast forgiven the wickedness of my sin.

For this shall every one that is holy pray to thee, in a seasonable time.

And yet in a flood of many waters, they shall not come nigh unto him.

Thou art my refuge from the trouble that hath encompassed me: my joy, deliver me from them that surround me.

I will give thee understanding, and I will instruct in this way in which thou shalt walk: I will fix my eyes upon thee.

Do not become like the horse and the mule, who have no understanding.

With bit and bridle bind fast their jaws, who come not near unto thee.

Many are the scourges of the sinner, but mercy shall encompass him that hopeth in the Lord.

Be glad in the Lord, and rejoice ye just: and glory all ye right of heart.

Glory be, etc.

PSALM XXXVII.

Domine, ne in furore.

Rebuke me not, O Lord, in thy indignation, nor chastise me in thy wrath.

For thy arrows are fastened in me: and thy hand hath been strong upon me.

There is no health in my flesh, because of thy wrath; there is no peace for my bones, because of my sins.

For my iniquities are gone over my head; and as a heavy burden have become heavy upon me.

My sores are putrified and corrupted, because of my foolishness,

I am become miserable, and am bowed down even to the end: I walked sorrowful all the day long.

For my loins are filled with illusions; and there is no health in my flesh.

I am afflicted and humbled exceedingly; I roared with the groaning of my heart.

Lord, all my desire is before thee: and my groaning is not hidden from thee.

My heart is troubled, my strength hath left me, and the light of mine eyes itself is not with me.

My friends and my neighbors have drawn near and stood against me.

And they that were near me stood afar off; and they that sought my soul used violence.

And they that sought evils to me spoke vain things, and studied deceits all the day long.

But I, as a deaf man heard not; and as a dumb man not opening his mouth.

And I became as a man that heareth not, and that hath no reproofs in his mouth.

For in thee, O Lord, have I hoped; thou wilt hear me, O Lord, my God.

For I said: lest at any time my enemies rejoice over me; and whilst my feet are moved, they speak great things against me.

For I am ready for scourges; and my sorrow is continually before me.

For I will declare my iniquity; and I will think for my sin.

But my enemies live and are stronger than I; and they that hate me wrongfully are multiplied.

They that rendered evil for good have detracted me, because I followed goodness.

Forsake me not, O Lord my God; do not thou depart from me.

Attend unto my help, O Lord, the God of my salvation.

Glory be, etc.

PSALM CXXIX.
De profundis.

Out of the depths I have cried to thee, O Lord, Lord, hear my voice.

Let thy ears be attentive to the voice of my supplication.

If thou, O Lord, wilt mark iniquities, Lord, who shall stand it!

For with thee there is merciful forgiveness, and by reason of thy law I have waited for thee, O Lord.

My soul hath relied on his word; my soul hath hoped in the Lord.

From the morning watch even until night, let Israel hope in the Lord.

Because with the Lord there is mercy, and with him plentiful redemption.

And he shall redeem Israel from all his iniquities.

Glory be to the Father, etc.

PSALM CXLII.
Domine exaudi.

Hear, O Lord, my prayer; give ear to my supplication in thy truth; hear me in thy justice.

And enter not into judgment with thy servant; for in thy sight no man living shall be justified.

For I did eat ashes like bread, and mingled my drink with weeping.

Because of thy anger and indignation; for having lifted me up thou hast thrown me down.

My days have declined like a shadow, and I am withered like grass.

But thou, O Lord, endurest forever; and thy memorial to all generations.

Thou shalt arise and have mercy on Sion; for it is time to have mercy on it; for the time is come.

For the stones thereof have pleased thy servants, and they shall have pity on the earth thereof.

And the Gentiles shall fear thy name, O Lord, and all the kings of the earth thy glory.

For the Lord hath built up Sion; and he shall be seen in his glory.

He hath had regard to the prayer of the humble and he hath not despised their petition.

Let these things be written unto another generation: and the people that shall be created shall praise the Lord:

Because he hath looked forth from his high sanctuary: from heaven the Lord hath looked upon the earth.

That he might hear the groans of them that are in fetters: that he might release the children of the slain.

That they may declare the name of the Lord in Sion, and his praise in Jerusalem.

When the people assembled together, and kings, to serve the Lord.

He answered him in the way of his strength: Declare unto me the fewness of my days.

Call me not away in the midst of my days: thy years are unto generation and generation.

In the beginning, O Lord, thou foundest the earth, and the heavens are the work of thy hands.

They shall perish, but thou remainest: and all of them shall grow old like a garment.

And as a vesture thou shalt change them, and they shall be changed. But thou art always the self-same, and thy years shall not fail.

The children of thy servants shall continue: and their seed shall be directed forever.

Glory be to the Father, etc.

PSALM L.

Miserere.

Have mercy on me, O God, according to thy great mercy.

And according to the multitude of thy tender mercies, blot out my iniquity.

Wash me yet more from my iniquity, and cleanse me from my sin.

For I know my iniquity and my sin is always before me.

To thee only have I sinned, and have done evil before thee: that thou mayest be justified in thy words, and mayest overcome when thou art judged.

For behold I was conceived in iniquities; and in sins did my mother conceive me.

For behold thou hast loved truth; the uncertain and hidden things of thy wisdom thou hast made manifest to me.

Thou shalt sprinkle me with hyssop and I shall be cleansed; thou shalt wash me, and I shall be made whiter than snow.

To my hearing thou shalt give joy and gladness; and the bones that have been humbled shall rejoice.

Turn away thy face from my sins, and blot out all my iniquities.

Create a clean heart in me, O God; and renew a right spirit within my bowels.

Cast me not away from thy face; and take not thy Holy Spirit from me.

Restore unto me the joy of thy salvation; and strengthen me with a perfect spirit.

I will teach the unjust thy ways; and the wicked shall be converted to thee.

Deliver me from blood, O God, thou God of my salvation: and my tongue shall declare thy praise.

For if thou hadst desired sacrifice, I would indeed have given it; with burnt offerings thou wilt not be delighted. A sacrifice to God is an afflicted spirit; a contrite and humble heart, O God, thou wilt not despise.

Deal favorably, O Lord, in thy good will, with Sion; that the walls of Jerusalem may be built up.

Then shalt thou accept the sacrifice of justice, oblations and whole burnt offerings: then shall they lay calves upon thy altar.

Glory be, etc.

PSALM CL.

Domine Exaudi.

Hear, O Lord, my prayer; and let my cry come unto thee.

Turn not away thy face from me: in the day when I am in trouble, incline thy ear to me.

In what day soever I shall call upon thee, hear me speedily.

For my days are vanished like smoke, and my bones are grown dry like fuel for the fire.

I am smitten as grass, and my heart is withered; because I forgot to eat my bread.

Through the voice of my groaning, my bone hath cleaved to my flesh.

I am become like to a pelican of the wilderness: I am like a night raven in the house.

I have watched, and have become as a sparrow all alone on the house top.

All the day long my enemies reproach me; and they that praised me did swear against me.

For the enemy hath persecuted my soul: he hath brought down my life to the earth.

He hath made me to dwell in darkness, as those that have been dead of old; and my spirit is in anguish within me: my heart within me is troubled.

I remember the days of old; I meditate on all thy works: I meditated on the works of thy hands.

I stretched forth my hands to thee: my soul is as earth without water unto thee.

Hear me speedily, O Lord, my spirit hath fainted away.

Turn not away thy face from me, lest I be like unto them that go down into the pit.

Cause me to hear thy mercy in the morning; for in thee have I hoped.

Make the way known to me wherein I should walk; for I have lifted up my soul to thee.

Deliver me from my enemies, O Lord, to thee have I fled: teach me to do thy will, for thou art my God.

Thy good spirit shall lead me into the right land: for thy name's sake, O Lord, thou wilt quicken me in thy justice.

Thou wilt bring my soul out of trouble: and in thy mercy thou wilt destroy my enemies.

And thou wilt cut off all them that afflict my soul: for I am thy servant. Glory be to the Father, etc.

Remember not, O Lord! our offences, nor those of our parents, and take not revenge of our sins.

PRAYER BEFORE A CRUCIFIX.

PLENARY INDULGENCE.

Pope Pius VII., by a decree of the S. Congr. of Indulgences, dated April 10, 1821, granted a Plenary Indulgence to all who recite devoutly the following prayer before a crucifix, with contrite hearts, and praying for the wants of the church, after having confessed and communicated.

O gentle and compassionate Jesus, humbly prostrate before thee, I conjure thee with all the ardor of my soul to deign to imprint in my heart deep and fervent sentiments of FAITH, HOPE, and CHARITY, a true repentance for my transgressions with a firmly determined will to correct myself—while with sincere affection and heartfelt sorrow I interiorly contemplate thy five sacred wounds and call to mind the prediction of thy royal Prophet. *They pierced my hands and my feet; they numbered all my bones.* (Ps. xii. 17. 18.)

(From the Raccolta.)

PRAYER FOR THE CONVERSION OF SINNERS.

(By St. Francis of Sales.)

Pardon, O my God, pardoning grace for so many souls that daily sink into eternal perdition? Behold Satan darts from the abyss marching forward to horrible conquest—he excites his infernal legions, crying souls! souls!—fly to the destruction of souls! and souls like autumn leaves fall into the eternal gulf! *We* also, O my God, cry to thee—souls! souls!—we would win souls *to thee* to prove our love, and to cancel our debt of gratitude. Canst thou refuse us O my God? we supplicate thee by the wounds of Jesus our Saviour and spouse—those adorable wounds press thee as so many eloquent mouths—" Pardon, O Father, pardon those guilty ones, for they are the price of thy blood, give me the souls that have cost me so dear." O merciful God wilt thou refuse them to thy Son, we ask them of thee with him and in his name, for thy greater glory, and through the intercession of the heart of Mary. *Say three times.* Heart of Jesus, refuge of sinners, have mercy on us.

Heart of Mary, refuge of sinners, pray for us.

STABAT MATER.

Stabat Mater dolorosa,
Juxta crucem lacrymosa,
Dum pendebat filius.

At the cross her station keeping,
Stood the mournful Mother weeping,
Close to Jesus to the last.

Cujus animam gementem,
Contristatam et dolentem,
Pertransivit gladius.

Through her heart his sorrow sharing,
All his bitter anguish bearing,
Now at length the sword had passed.

O quam tristis et afflicta,
Fuit illa benedicta,
Mater unigeniti!

Oh, how sad and sore distressed,
Was that Mother highly blest,
Of that sole-begotten One!

Quæ mœrebat, et dolebat,
Pia Mater dum videbat,
Nati pœnas inclyti.

Christ above in torment hangs;
She beneath beholds the pangs
Of her dying glorious Son.

Quis et homo qui non fleret,
Matrem Christi si videret,
In tanto supplicis!

Is there one who would not weep,
Whelm'd in miseries so deep
Christ's dear Mother to behold?

Quis non posset contristari,
Christi Matrem contemplari
Dolentum cum Filio?

Can the human heart refrain
From partaking in her pain,
In that Mother's pain untold?

Pro peccatis suæ gentis,
Vidit Jesum in tormentis,
Et flagellis subditum.

Bruised, derided, cursed, defiled,
She beheld her tender child
All with bloody scourges rent.

Vidit suum dulcem natum,
Moriendo desolatum,
Dum emisit spiritum.

Eia Mater, fous amoris,
Me sentire vim doloris,
Fac, ut tecum lugeam.

Fac ut ardeat cor meum,
In amando Christum Deum,
Ut sibi complaceam.

Sancta Mater istud agas,
Crucifixi fige plagas,
Cordi meo valide.

Tui nati villnerati,
Tam dignati pro me pati,
Pænas mecum divide.

Fac me vere tecum flere,
Crucifixo condolere,
Donec ego vixero.

Juxta crucem tecum stare,
Te libenter sociare,
In planctu desidero.

Virgo virginum præclara,
Mihi jam non sis amara,
Fac me tecum plangere.

For the sins of his own nation,
Saw him hang in desolation,
Till his spirit forth he sent.

O thou Mother! fount of love!
Touch my spirit from above,
Make my heart with thine accord.

Make me feel as thou hast felt;
Make my soul to grow and melt,
With the love of Christ my Lord.

Holy Mother! pierce me through;
In my heart each wound renew,
Of my Saviour crucified.

Let me share with thee his pain,
Who for all my sins was slain,
Who for me in torments died.

Let me mingle tears with thee,
Mourning him who mourn'd for me,
All the days that I may live.

By the cross with thee to stay;
There with thee to weep and pray;
Is all I ask of thee to give.

Virgin of all virgins best!
Listen to my fond request:
Let me share thy grief divine.

Fac ut portem Christi mortem,
Passionis ejus sortem,
Et plagas recolere.
Fac me plagis vulnerari,
Cruci hac inebriari,
Ob amorem Filii.

Inflammatus et accensis,
Per te, virgo, sim defensus.
In die judicii.

Fac me cruce custodiri,
Morte Christi præmuniri,
Confoveri gratia.

Quando corpus morietur,
Fac ut animæ donetur,
Paradisi gloria.

Let me, to my latest breath,
In my body bear the death,
Of that dying Son of thine.

Wounded with his every wound,
Steep my soul till it has swoon'd
In his very blood away.
Be to me, O Virgin, nigh,
Lest in flames I burn and die,
In his awful judgment-day.
Christ, when thou shalt call me hence,
Be thy Mother my defence,
Be thy cross my victory.
While my body here decays,
May my soul thy goodness praise,
Safe in Paradise with Thee.

--

VIVAT JESUS.

Vivat Jesus, vivat Jesus, vivat Jesus,
Vivat Jesus, homo Deus,
Vivat Salvator Dominus,
Rex nostri cordis unicus.
        Vivat, etc.
Ubi, mors, ubi stimulus?
Vixit et surrexit Jesus:
Ut caput, membra surgemus.   Vivat, etc.

Sub cruce gemit infernus,
Tremit caro, fremit mundus,
Victor, subactis hostibus.
        Vivat, etc.

Live Jesus! live Jesus! God made man. Our Saviour and sole monarch of our hearts—live!

O Death, where is thy victory, where is thy sting?— Jesus has risen, and as he is the head, we who are his members shall also rise.
Hell groaned beneath the empire of the cross, humanity trembled, the vanquished world quaked with consternation.

Agnos, vocat Pastor bonus,
Agnos amat Dei agnus:
Ite, agni, præit Jesus.
    Vivat, etc.

The Shepherd invites his sheep, the Lamb of God cherishes the little ones of the flock: go little lambs, Jesus leads onward in triumph.

Jesus spes pœnitentibus,
Jesus pax morientibus,
Jesus, esto nobis Jesus.

O Jesus, hope of repenting souls, peace and consolation of the dying, be to us a Saviour.

O! meæ sint voces Jesus,
Mores, amores sint Jesus;
In me non ego, sed Jesus.

May my voice utter no accent that does not give praise to the name of Jesus; may Jesus be my delight, my life; may I no longer live, but Jesus live alone.

Vivat per quem nos vivimus;
Vincat per quem nos vincimus;
Regnet per quem regnabimus.

Live Jesus, by whom we have life; let him triumph who conquered for us, let him reign by whom we shall forever reign.

Vivat per quam vivit Jesus,
Vivat Mater, vivat Natus,
Vivat Maria et Jesus.

O live Mary, who gave life to our amiable Saviour! live, the Mother, the Son, live Mary—live Jesus!

OFFERING OF THE BEADS.

(A favorite way of reciting them.)

My God we offer to thee the beads (or Chaplet) that we are going to recite, to thy greater honor and glory, for the salvation of our souls, to thank thee for all the graces thou hast bestowed on the blessed Virgin Mary, and to implore through her intercession those of which we have need, for the deliverance of the souls in purgatory, the conversion of sinners, the perseverance of the just, for all persons who are recommended to our prayers, in particular for the children of Mary, for the conversion of England and Poland and for (N. N.) lately deceased.

St. Stanislas. O God, who among the wonders of thy divine wisdom, accorded to the most tender age the grace of an accomplished sanctity, grant we entreat thee that imitating the example of St. Stanislas, we may hasten to redeem the time by continual good works, and thus attain eternal rest through Jesus Christ our Lord.

St Joseph. Great saint, faithful servant to whom God confided the care of the holy family, and whom he established the protector of the infancy of Jesus, the comfort and support of his blessed Mother, and co-operator in the great plan of man's redemption— who enjoyed the happiness of living with Jesus and Mary and expiring in their arms; chaste spouse of the Mother of God, model of pure, humble, patient and interior souls, be moved by the confidence we repose in thee, and receive with benevolence the testimonies of our devotion. We bless God for the favors which he bestowed on thee, and entreat him through thy intercession, to grant us the grace of imitating thy virtues.

Pray for us great saint; and by thy love for Jesus and Mary, and by the love of Jesus and Mary for thee, procure us the happiness of living and dying in their love.

℣. I believe in God the Father, etc.

℟. I believe in the Holy Ghost, etc.

℣. Glory be to the Father and to the Son, etc.

℟. As it was in the beginning, etc.

℣. Glory be to the Sacred Hearts of Jesus and Mary.

℟. Throughout the whole world, and forever.

℣. Our Father, etc.

℟. Give us this day, etc.

Asp. Daughter of God the Father. Hail Mary.

Asp. Spouse of the Holy Ghost. Hail Mary.

Asp. Mother of God the Son. Hail Mary.

℣. Glory be to the Father, etc.

℣. Glory be to the Sacred Hearts, etc.

Our Father, etc.

1. With the Angels. Hail Mary, etc.
2. With the Archangels. Hail Mary, etc.
3. With the Principalities. Hail Mary, etc.
4. With the Powers. Hail Mary, etc.
5. With the Virtues. Hail Mary, etc.
6. With the Dominations. Hail Mary, etc.
7. With the Thrones. Hail Mary, etc.
8. With the Cherubim. Hail Mary, etc.
9. With the Seraphim. Hail Mary, etc.
10. With all the heavenly court and all the just on earth. Hail Mary, etc.

Glory be to the Father, etc.

Glory be to the SS. CC. etc.

At the close add:

We fly to thy patronage, O holy Mother of God, despise not our petitions in our necessities but deliver us from all dangers, O ever glorious and blessed Virgin.

O divine Heart of Jesus, centre of a Society consecrated to thy greater honor and glory, unite the hearts of its members, inflame them with thy divine charity, and bestow on them the virtues of meekness and humility, so that they may gain souls to thy service.

Hail Mary, etc. (*For any particular intention.*)

De profundis clamavi ad te Domine, Domine exaudi vocem meam.

Fiant aures tuæ intendentes in vocem deprecationis meæ.

Si iniquitates observaveris Domine, Domine quis
sustinebit.

Quia apud te propitiatio est et propter legem tuam
sustinui te Domine.

Sustinuit anima mea in verbo ejus speravit anima
mea in Domino.

A custodia matutina usque ad noctem speret Israel
in Domino.

Quid apud Dominum misericordia et copiosa apud
eum redemptio.

Et ipse redinet Israel ex omnibus iniquitatibus ejus.

Requiem æternam dona eis Domine, et lux perpetua luceat eis.

Requiescat in pace.   Amen.

(For one person deceased.)

Oremus.   Quæsumus, Domine pro tua pietate miserere animæ famulæ tuæ (the name) et a contagiis
mortalitatis exutam in æternæ salvationis partem
restituæ.

Fideluim, Deus omnium conditor et redemptor,
animabus famulorum famularumque tuarum remissionem cunctorem tribue peccatorum ut indulgentiam
quam semper optaverunt piis supplicationibus consequantur, qui vivis et regnas in sæcula sæculorum.
Amen.

Requiem æternam, etc.

Monday and Tuesday.

JOYOUS MYSTERIES.

1. The Incarnation,   Fruit,   Humility.
2. The Visitation,   "   Charity.
3. The Birth of Jesus,   "   Poverty of spirit.

4. The Presentation,   Fruit,   Purity.
5. The finding of Jesus
    in the Temple,   "   Obedience.

Wednesday and Saturday.
SORROWFUL MYSTERIES.

1. The agony in the Garden,   Fruit,   Contrition.
2. The scourging at the Pillar,   "   Love of suffering.
3. The crowning with Thorns,   "   Love of humiliation.
4. The carrying of the Cross,   "   Love of crosses.
5. The Crucifixion,   "   Perseverance.

Thursday and Sunday.
GLORIOUS MYSTERIES.

1. The Resurrection,   Fruit,   Hope and Charity.
2. The Ascension,   "   Detachment.
3. The descent of the   "   Seven gifts of the
    Holy Ghost,   Holy Ghost.
4. The Assumption,   "   A happy Death.
5. The coronation of   "   Union with Jesus
    Mary in Heaven,   "   and Mary.

Beads of the Seven Dolors.

On Fridays, it is recommended to say the beads of the Seven Dolors. These must be blessed by a Priest having special faculties for so doing. Benedict XIII., granted 100 days for every Our Father and Hail Mary, recited with sincere contrition after having confessed; and twice as much on Fridays in Lent, and on the Feast of the Seven Dolors.

Begin as shown for the Rosary above mentioned.

1. St. Simon's Prophecy,   Ask for Resignation to
    God's will.

2. The Flight into Egypt,   Ask for Prompt obedience
                                 to the voice of God.
3. The three days Loss,   Ask for a Contrite heart.
4. Meeting Jesus bearing
    the Cross,   "   Patience.
5. The Crucifixion,   "   Mortification.
6. Descent from the Cross,   "   Preparation for
                                   Communion.
7. Burial of Jesus,   "   Act for God alone.

Let us recite three times *Ave Maria*, in honor of the tears that the blessed Virgin shed in her sufferings, so as to obtain through her mediation, the grace of shedding tears of true contrition for our faults.

Hail Mary, etc.   (*For some private intention.*)

ACT OF CONTRITION.

O my God, I am extremely sorry for having offended thee, because thou art infinitely good, amiable and deserving of my love, and because sin offends thee, and I firmly resolve by the assistance of thy grace, no more to offend thee, and to do penance for my sins.

Then conclude as on the ordinary beads.

The Little Crown of the Immaculate Conception.

METHOD OF SAYING THE ROSARY.

In the name of the ✠ Father, and the Son, and the Holy Ghost.   Amen.

℣. Incline unto my aid, O God.

℟. O Lord, make haste to help us.

℣. Glory be to the ✠ Father, and to Son, and to the Holy Ghost.

℞. As it was in the beginning, is now, and ever shall be, world without end.   Amen.

We thank thee, O eternal Father, because by thy power thou didst preserve Mary, thy most blessed daughter, from the stain of original sin.

Then, on the large bead, say: Our Father, and on the four small: Hail Mary, adding each time: Blessed be the pure, holy, and Immaculate Conception of the Blessed Virgin Mary.

We thank thee, O eternal Son, because by thy wisdom, thou didst preserve Mary, thy most blessed mother, from the stain of original sin.

Our Father, four Hail Mary's, with the rest as before.

We thank thee, O Holy Ghost eternal, because by thy love thou didst preserve Mary, thy most blessed spouse, from the stain of original sin.

Our Father, four Hail Mary's, with the rest as before.

At the end, one *Glory be to the Father, &c.*, in honor of the purity of St. Joseph, spouse of Mary, most holy.

INDULGENCES.

One hundred days for each recitation.
A plenary indulgence once a month on the usual conditions.

Renovation of the Baptismal Vows.

FOR THE DAY OF THE FIRST COMMUNION.

Adorable Trinity, Omnipotent and Eternal God, who in thy mercy regenerated us in the sacred waters of baptism, what thanks can we render to thee for this inestimable favor? We were born children of wrath, but by receiving the sacrament of baptism, we became thy adopted children. By our nature we were captives of Satan, and forever excluded from thy kingdom: now, in virtue of thy divine adoption, Jesus Christ is our brother, and heaven our eternal inheritance. O God of infinite goodness, what was there in us, that could invite thy prediliction. Alas! at the very moment thou wert bestowing these precious titles, thou didst foresee that we would basely profane them, and yet the view of our future perfidy could not arrest the course of thy infinite beneficence. Humbly prostrate in thy presence, in all the bitterness of repentant sorrow, we deplore our enormous and culpable ingratitude.

What, O my God, would have been our destiny, hadst thou obeyed the dictates of holy justice? but attentive only to the voice of thy mercy, thou didst meekly bear with us in our guilty wanderings: *even* offering us pardon and reconciliation before we implored it! Like the Father of the prodigal, thine arms embraced us as soon as we returned to thee, and now as the crowning blessing, we have been admitted to partake of the bread of angels. This then, O sweetest Saviour is thy revenge! but if *thou* dost so easily forget our transgressions, *we* shall not lose their remembrance. The more *thou* hast shown thyself patient and prompt in forgiving, the more firmly *we* resolve to be faithful and constant in return.

Lamb of God, whose blood washed us, and whose flesh became our food, prostrate at thy feet, we freely and with the whole heart, renounce Satan and his works.

We pledge ourselves never to blush for thy Gospel, nor be ashamed of the title of Christian—but remaining inviolably attached to thy service, to prefer death a thousand times before the commission of mortal sin.

Divine Jesus, engrave these holy engagements in our hearts, and confirm us in our resolution to be faithful to them until death. Amen.

Act of Consecration to the Blessed Virgin.
FOR THE DAY OF THE FIRST COMMUNION.

Queen of angels and of men, august Mary, on this, the most beautiful day of our lives, the day in which Jesus deigned to admit us to his holy table; we humbly present thee the homage of our youthful hearts, and claim thy powerful protection. Condescend, O holy Virgin, to become our queen, our advocate and mother, and deign to number us among thy happy and privileged children. Banish from our souls whatever breathes the contagion of vice; and never allow us to sully the robe of innocence, in which, purified by the blood of thy divine Son, we have for the first time approached his heavenly banquet. O most excellent of mothers, imprint in our filial hearts *thy* horror of sin, *thy* contempt of earthly vanities, and thy ardent and generous love for Jesus.

In mercy, bestow thy choicest benedictions on all those who have contributed to our present happiness by their prayers or toil: but above all, we conjure thee, bless most abundantly, our beloved Parents, whose salvation interests us so deeply: could we be happy if they shared not in our joy? And couldst thou, O tender mother, who art never invoked in vain, refuse to obtain their sanctification and ours— so that united before thy throne in heaven, both parents and children may bless thee evermore. Amen.

Consecration to the Blessed Virgin.
FOR THE FEAST OF THE IMMACULATE CONCEPTION.

Immaculate Mary, Mother of God and perpetual

Virgin, special patroness of a house consecrated to thy honor, cast a benign look on us, the children of the Heart of Jesus. We choose thee unanimously for our Queen and our Mother, and here promise never to forsake thy devotion nor the interests of thy glory: we resolve, and pledge ourselves never to say anything nor do anything, which might attack ever so lightly, the respect and homage due to thee by so many titles. We unite our intentions with those of all our companions who are consecrated to the Heart of thy Son, and to thy sacred Heart, O Immaculate Mary, confessing thy glorious and exalted privileges, in atonement for the blasphemies that the powers of darkness pronounce against thee. Deign, august Queen of Heaven and earth, to accept us in the number of thy fervent and persevering children, shield us from the vain spirit and maxims of the world, watch over our innocence, and above all, O powerful Mother, protect us in the dread hour of death. Amen.

Consecration to the Blessed Virgin.
FOR THE FIRST OF MAY.

August Mary, immaculate and ever virgin, mother of God and our mother, prostrate before thy altar, we humbly offer thee the first-fruits of *this month* consecrated to thy honor. From thy immortal throne, gently regard the children of the Heart of Jesus, kindly accept their infantine homage, and deign to hear the petitions they strew before thy maternal Heart. We present thee the days of our childhood and youth, with the mature years of our future existence.

Permit not sin, the spirit of the world, nor Satan, to ravish from thee, the hearts we this day commit to thy powerful protection. Ah! shield us from every lurking danger, for we invoke thee with filial confidence, actuated by the remembrance of thy bounty, and we consecrate ourselves anew to thy devotion and thy love. Reject us not, O Mary! but pray for us now and at the hour of death, that after having imitated thy virtues, we may continue to praise thee in eternity, forever blessing the Omnipotent hand that formed thee, so noble, so holy, so surpassingly lovely. Amen.

Consecration to the Infant Jesus.
FOR LITTLE CHILDREN.

Blessed Infant Jesus, kindly take us "little children," under thy especial protection. We promise to try to avoid sin, and humbly ask thee to bless us and teach us how to practice Obedience, Patience, and Humility, virtues which thou camest down from heaven to teach. Grant us grace to love thee daily more and more, and to reign with thee forever in heaven. Amen.

Act of Consecration to St. Aloysius.

O glorious and seraphic Aloysius, I ....
.... humbly prostrate before thy throne, in presence of the whole heavenly court, choose thee for my special patron and protector. Graciously deign to receive me among thy faithful imitators, and consider me as belonging entirely to thee. Watch over me, and present my heart to Jesus and Mary, so that they may come and dwell therein, and preserve my tender innocence. As I increase in years may I like thee advance in piety and true wisdom,

and merit by my fidelity, to praise God with thee in a blessed eternity.   Amen.

Act of Atonement to the Guardian Angel.

Angel from Heaven, my faithful and charitable guardian, I present myself before thee to ask forgiveness for my past years of waywardness, inattention and ingratitude.   Deeply sensible of my coldness, I resolve in future to love and honor thee and implore thy powerful aid: and to prove my sincerity, I hope with thy assistance to merit a reception into the Sodality consecrated to the Holy Angels.   By the interest thou dost condescend to manifest towards my soul, mercifully receive my act of atonement, shield me from all my enemies, and conduct my docile steps in the path that leads to Heaven.   Amen.

Act of Consecration to the Holy Angels.

Blessed spirits of the heavenly court! Zealous defenders of God's greater glory—I .... in presence of the Immaculate Queen of Angels, humbly adopt you as my patrons and advocates.   I consecrate to your friendly and tender guardianship, my soul and body, and all that I have or am, and resolve by your gracious assistance to be more faithful in the observance of my baptismal engagements.   Teach me how to imitate your humility, obedience, purity and zeal.   Shield me, when (having quitted this asylum,) I may be exposed to the snares of a corrupt world, and in the awful hour of death and judgment, protect me from the powers of darkness, and bear my victorious soul to heaven, that in union with the celestial choirs, it may chant forever the praises of our King and Redeemer.   Amen.

Act of Consecration to the Blessed Virgin Mary.

Holy Mary, Immaculate Virgin, Mother of God, I .... choose thee this day for my mother, queen, patroness, and advocate, and I firmly resolve never to depart, either in word or action, from the duty I owe thee, or suffer those committed to my charge to say or do anything against the honor and respect to which thou art entitled.— Receive me then, to be forever thy servant and child. Assist me in all my necessities, and forsake me not at the hour of my death.   Amen.

Little Office of the Immaculate Conception.

℣. Let my lips open.

℟. To celebrate the praises and dignity of the ever blessed Mary.

℣. Incline unto mine aid, O powerful Queen.

℟. From the hand of my enemies deliver me.

℣. Glory be to the Father, and to the Son, and to the Holy Ghost.

℟. As it was in the beginning, is now, and ever shall be, world without end. Amen.

HYMN.

Hail, sovereign lady, Queen of the heavenly hosts, Virgin of virgins, Star of the morning!

Hail Mary, full of grace and of the spirit of wisdom, hasten to aid this unfortunate world, of which thou art the guardian and queen.

God predestined thee from all eternity to become the mother of his only Son, the incarnate Word, by whom all things were created, the heavens, earth and sea.

To render thee worthy of becoming his spouse, he adorned thy soul with incomparable beauty, which the sin of Adam never stained.

℣. God chose and predestined her.

℟. He prepared himself an abode and tabernacle.

℣. Hear my prayer, O most excellent Queen.

℟. And be propitious to my desires.

PRAYER.

Holy Mary, Queen of Heaven, Mother of our Lord Jesus Christ, who never forsakest or despisest any one, cast on me a look of pity, and obtain for me of thy dear Son the pardon of all my sins, that

393

I, who with devout affection do now celebrate thy Immaculate Conception, may hereafter enjoy the reward of eternal bliss, through the merits of thy Son, Jesus Christ our Lord, who with the Father and the Holy Ghost, lives and reigns world without end. Amen.

℣. Hear my prayer, O most excellent Queen.

℟. And be propitious to my desires.

℣. Bless the Lord.

℟. To him give immortal thanks.

℣. May the souls of the faithful departed through the mercy of our God, rest in peace.   Amen.

PRIME.

℣. Incline unto my aid, O powerful Queen.

℟. Deliver me from the hands of my enemies.

Glory be, etc.

HYMN.

Hail! immaculate Virgin, replete with heavenly wisdom, enriched with adornments, of which those of the temple of Solomon were but feeble types.

Thou wert holy from thy conception, and preserved from the corruption common to our race.

Hail, mother of the living, gate of heaven, queen of angels, the new star of Jacob, that announced salvation to a ruined world!

Hail, terror of the demons! defence in our spiritual combats—sure haven of refuge for thy faithful servants.

℣. God created her, and filled her with his own spirit.

℟. He lavished upon her all his gifts.

The rest as at Matins.

TIERCE.

℣. Incline unto my aid, O powerful Queen.

℞. Deliver me from the hands of all my enemies.
Glory be to the Father, etc.

Hail, holy Mary! Ark of the new covenant,
throne of the true Solomon, token of peace between
God and man.

Prefigured by the rainbow, the burning bush, the
blossoming rod of Aaron, Gideon's fleece, the closed
gate of Ezekiel, and the honey-comb of Samson.

It was becoming the glory of the eternal Word, to
preserve from the stain of original sin the Mother
he had chosen, and to forbid that so excellent a
mother be ever subject to the infamy of sin.

℣. Thy dwelling is in the highest heavens.

℞. And thy throne on a pillar of clouds.

As at Matins.

SEXT.

℣. Incline unto my aid, O powerful Queen.

℞. From the hands of my enemies deliver me.

Glory be to the Father, etc.

HYMN.

Hail, august temple of the adorable Trinity, at
once virgin and mother, joy of the angels, fountain
of purity, consolation of the afflicted, "garden of
delights," model of patience and chastity, prefigured
by the palm-tree and cedar.

Thou wert always, from the first instant of thy
being, a land of benediction, exempt from the curse
of original sin.

Thou art the dwelling of the Most High, the mystical "Eastern Gate" through which entered the
Redeemer of mankind.

O incomparable Virgin, in thee are united all the
graces and gifts of heaven.

℣. As the lily among thorns.

℟. So is my beloved among the daughters of Adam.

As at Matins.

NONE.

℣. Incline unto my aid, O powerful Queen.
℟. Deliver me from the hands of my enemies.
Glory be to the Father, etc.

HYMN.

Hail, most excellent Queen! our refuge and asylum, prefigured by David's tower, in which were stored all weapons of defence. From the first moment of thy conception, inflamed with the fire of charity, thou hast triumphed over the infernal dragon, destroyed him and trampled him in the dust.

O valiant woman! O invincible Judith! wiser and more beautiful than Abigail, thou hast merited the love and tenderness of the true David. Rachel was the mother of the Saviour of Egypt; Mary brought forth the Redeemer of the world.

℣. Thou art all beautiful, O my beloved!
℟. The stain of original sin was never in thee.

As at Matins.

VESPERS.

℣. Incline unto my aid, O powerful Queen.
℟. Deliver me from the power of my enemies.
Glory be to the Father, etc.

HYMN.

Hail, most excellent virgin, in whose womb the Son of Justice became man.

The eternal Word became flesh; the Immense lowered himself beneath the angels, to draw man from hell, and to exalt him to heaven.

Mary shines with the delight of this divine sun. At the moment of the conception she was radiant as the dawn of the morning.

She is as the lily among thorns. From the moment of her life, she crushed the head of the old serpent. She is fair as the moon, and her light shines for those who are in the darkness of error.

℣. I kindle a fire in the heavens, which shall never be extinguished.

℞. And I have covered the whole earth as with a beneficent cloud.

As at Matins.

COMPLIN.

℣. Convert us by thy prayers, O holy Mary!

℞. Appease the anger of thy Son, and cause him to be propitious to us.

℣. Incline unto my aid, O powerful Queen!

℞. Deliver me from the hands of my enemies.

HYMN.

Hail, incomparable virgin, adorned with all virtues, and with all the gifts of grace. Mother, ever virgin, crowned with the stars, purer than the angelic host, thou art enthroned in heaven at the right hand of the king of glory, clothed with all that is most precious in his royal treasures.

O mother of grace, sweet hope of sinners, star of the sea, secure haven of the shipwrecked, and ever-opened gate of heaven, health of the sick, obtain that by thy intercession we may one day enjoy the vision of the King of glory, in the heavenly Jerusalem.

℣. Thy name, O Mary, is a perfume shed abroad.

℞. Thy servants find their delight in the tender love they bear thee.

As at Matins.

PRAYER.

Prostrate at thy feet, august virgin, we offer thee these songs of praise. Deign, O mother of bounty

12

and mercy, to be our guide during the course of this perishable life, and to aid us in the hour of death.

Ant. Behold that admirable virgin, who hath no blemish of original sin nor actual sin.

℣. Thou wast conceived without sin, O most excellent virgin!

℞. Pray for us to God the Father, whose Son thou didst bring forth.

PRAYER.

Great God, who in preserving the most holy Virgin from original sin, prepared for thy Son a worthy abode in the immaculate womb, we entreat thee, that as thou hast preserved her from sin by the precious merits of the death of her Son, thou wilt also deign, by his intercession, to grant us the grace of coming to thee, cleansed from every stain, through our Lord Jesus Christ. Amen.

METHODS.

Extracted from the Spiritual Exercises of St. Ignatius. Approved by the Holy See.

PARTICULAR EXAMINATION.

This examination is directed towards one sin or defect, exterior or interior, which the fervent soul desires to correct. It is made daily, and in the following manner:

1. On rising in the morning, resolve to watch over yourself during the day, in order to avoid the commission of that sin or imperfection.

2. At noon, ask God's grace to remember how many times you have fallen, and implore a particular grace to be able to resist in future; then examine by running over the hours that have elapsed from the time of rising to the present moment, the number of faults committed against the point proposed, which should be marked by some sign on a formula or little book prepared for that purpose. This done, take a fresh resolution for the remainder of the day.

3. In the evening, before retiring to rest, make a second examination, similar in all respects to the first, but dwelling only on the time that has elapsed since noon.

OBSERVATIONS.

1. At each fault committed against the good resolution, instantly lay your hand on your heart, (in a manner not to attract the notice of others,) and at the same time humble yourself interiorly.

2. In the evening, compare the results of the two examinations, to discern whether there is any amendment.

3. Similar comparison should be made between the day and the week that are closing, with the day or the week that preceded.

399

4. It is to be presumed that the faults will diminish each day, *if not*, try to discover the cause.

GENERAL EXAMINATION

Is made at the close of the day, and in the following manner:

1. Thank God for all his benefits.

2. Entreat him to give you the light to discover your sins or transgressions, and a special grace to detest them.

3. Examine your thoughts, words and actions of the day just elapsed, repassing its hours one after the other.

4. Ask pardon for your faults.

5. Resolve to correct them with the help of divine grace, and conclude with reciting the *Pater Noster.*

Meditation.

Meditation consists in recalling to mind some truth and reflecting or reasoning upon it, (according to one's mental capacity or strength of intellect,) but in such a way as to excite the *will* to resolve to become better.

Let us suppose that you are going to meditate on the sin of the angels. Recall to your mind that having refused *obedience* to the Creator, these spirits lost grace and were directly precipitated into hell. Next, reason or reflect upon this with fixed attention —comparing your *numerous* sins with this *one* sin, then blush interiorly and be overwhelmed with confusion—consider that if the angels merited hell by only *one* transgression, how *many times* you have deserved the same degree of punishment.

In order to meditate well, and obtain such results as this exercise should produce, it will be extremely useful to attend to the following practices, or additions.

1. Divide the subject into a certain number of points. Recall the points just before falling to sleep. From the first instant of awaking, think on the meditation exclusively, and try to excite in your heart sentiments that correspond with it. The preparation of meditations that are to be performed during the day, is made a little before commencing them.

2. The hour for meditation having arrived, stand a step or two from the spot in which the meditation is to be made, and there, after interiorly adoring our Lord Jesus Christ, as though he were actually present to you and observing you, take an humble and respectful posture. Ask of him to grant that all operations of your mind, heart and soul, may contribute purely to his greater honor and glory.

3. Imagine a place, which shall be as it were actually present to you, but in strict accordance with the theme selected for meditation; thus, if the subject is sin, consider the body as a prison of clay in which the soul is enchained—or, think of a valley of exile and tears, etc.

Ask of God the grace you desire to obtain, conformably to the subject in question; then, while kneeling, sitting or standing, in fine, in that posture which you find most conducive to facility in obtaining good thoughts and affections, begin your meditation.

1. You should apply less to thinking much, than to endeavoring to understand, appreciate and relish interiorly, the point that occupies you.

2. If you find facility in awakening pious affections, and a train of holy sentiments which fill you with consoling devotion, beware of indulging in self-complacency, but humble yourself. If some consideration impresses you forcibly, dwell upon it as long as its influence lasts, without reference to the other points.

3. If your soul is arid, tempted, etc.; excite yourself to a holy courage and patience, continue the exercise, and prolong it—this would be conquering nature and the demon. Hope for a quick return of sensible favors. Even in such a state, God and his grace are assisting us and remain with us.

4. During the course of the meditation you may sometimes converse with God, or with our divine Saviour, or with the blessed Virgin, or with the Saints and Angels: in such colloquies use confidence and liberty, but also profound respect.

5. Meditations should terminate with one colloquy or with several colloquies, in which you may accuse yourself of your defects, and implore that grace which is the fruit of the truth that has just been meditated. These colloquies may be held with the blessed Virgin, with our Lord, or with the Eternal Father, and occasionally with the three successively, and they conclude with a prayer in accordance with the person to whom they have been addressed, viz: by *Ave Maria, Anima Christi,* or by a *Pater Noster.*

6. Examine whether your meditation has been performed well; if so, thank God; if not, seek the cause, excite yourself to sorrow and resolve to amend.

Three Methods of Praying.

According to the method of St. Ignatius.

First Method.—This consists in reflecting on the

commandments of God, the capital sins, the three powers of the soul, and the five corporal senses—it is less a prayer than a spiritual exercise.

1st. Before commencing, dwell a few moments on what you are going to do? 2d. Then ask of God the grace to know what sins you have committed against his commandments, with grace to correct yourself in future. 3d. Consider each commandment separately, and ask yourself how you have accomplished it, or how you have violated it. Implore forgiveness for the sins which recur to your memory, and recite the *Pater Noster*. It is sufficient to dwell upon each precept the time necessary for reciting three *Pater*—and even this may be diminished or prolonged, in proportion as the soul finds more or less materials for self-reproach on any one of the commandments. 4th. After having thus run over all of the precepts, humble and accuse yourself, ask for grace to observe them better in future, and terminate with a colloquy addressed to God, in conformity with the state and dispositions in which you may find yourself.

In regard to the capital sins, the three powers of the soul, the five senses, etc., the examination merely passes to different subjects; the rest is accomplished as was directed for the commandments.

If you desire to imitate our Lord Jesus Christ in the use of the senses, implore that grace from God the Father; then dwell some time on each particular sense, examining how your soul approaches or is remote from that divine model; before passing from one sense to the other, recite the Lord's prayer. If you propose to imitate the blessed Virgin, recommend your soul to her, asking her to procure you this favor from her divine Son, and after the examination of each sense, recite the angelical salutation.

Second Method.—This consists in the recitation of some vocal prayer, and stopping at each consecutive word or phrase, as long as the soul experiences a relish or devotion. 1st. Recollect yourself interiorly. 2d. Address yourself to the person to whom you are going to pray. 3d. For example, commence "Our Father"—meditate on these two words as long as they will furnish you with thoughts, affections, etc., then pass on to the following phrase and consider it in the same manner. 4. The time to conclude arriving, recite currently the remainder of the prayer, and hold a short colloquy with the person to whom you have just been praying, petitioning that grace or virtue that your soul most needs.

Observe that if only one word or phrase of the prayer, had offered matter for occupying the mind or heart, during the whole time that was destined to the prayer, the meditation of the rest can be deferred until the following day; then on the morrow, begin by reciting the portion of the prayer that you meditated on the previous day, and continue to reflect on the other parts of the prayer.

The Credo—the Salve Regina and the *Anima Christi*, and indeed, any vocal prayer may be recited in this way.

Third Method.—It consists in pronouncing the words of some vocal prayer, and dwelling a little, either on the meaning of the word, or on the dignity of the person to whom the prayer is addressed—or on your personal unworthiness, or at the great distance there is between you. Take for example, the "*Ave Maria.*" 1st. Think on the action you are about to perform. 2d. Think a moment on the word Hail, or on the exalted dignity of the blessed Virgin, whom you thus address, or on your miseries which create such a wide distance between you and the mother of God. 3d. Pronounce the remaining words, dwelling on each one the period requisite for respiration.

Confraternity of the Sacred Heart.

Form of admission into the Confraternity of the Sacred Heart of Jesus.

I........................for the greater glory of Jesus Christ crucified, and of his divine Heart, burning with love in the blessed Eucharist, and also to atone for the insults he receives in this august sacrament, associate myself freely and cordially to the faithful, received into this pious Confraternity; I desire to participate in the indulgences with which it is enriched, and in the good works therein performed; both for the expiation of my own sins and for the relief of the suffering souls in Purgatory.

O sweet Jesus! enclose in thy sacred Heart all the members of this association; grant, that faithfully observing the precepts of thy law, and fulfilling the duties of their state, they may continually increase in thy love. Amen

N. B.—To gain the eight plenary indulgences, it is requisite, 1. To be inscribed on the register of the Confraternity, to pray for the Pope's intentions, and recite habitually, each day, the Pater, Ave, and Credo, with the following aspiration:

O sweetest Heart of Jesus, I implore
That I may ever love thee more and more.

PLENARY INDULGENCES.

1. The day of entrance into the Confraternity.
2. On the Feast of the Sacred Heart, or on the Sunday following it.
3. On the first Friday or Sunday of every month.
4. One day in every month, at the will of the members.
5. At the hour of death, on condition of invoking interiorly, the holy name of Jesus, if it cannot be pronounced.
6. On Christmas day, holy Thursday, Easter and the Ascension.

7. On the festivals of the Conception, of the Nativity, Annunciation, Purification and Assumption of the Blessed Virgin, All Saints, All Souls, Sts. Peter and Paul, St. Joseph and St. John the Evangelist.

8. The six Fridays or the six Sundays that immediately precede the feast of the Sacred Heart.

These, besides many partial indulgences are applicable to the souls in purgatory. To gain all the above, confession and communion are required, and for Nos. 6 and 7, visit the chapel of the Confraternity, or if that is not practicable, perform some pious work enjoined by the confessor, not as a sacramental penance, but as a condition of the indulgence. The confessor can give a general permission for this change. To obtain No. 8, it is necessary to visit a church or chapel in which the Feast of the Sacred Heart is celebrated, and if that cannot be done, do some pious work prescribed by one's confessor.

The partial indulgences are :

1. Thirty years and as many times forty days on the three days after Christmas, the Festivals of the Circumcision and the Epiphany, the Sundays of Septuagesima, Sexagesima, and Quinquagesima, Good Friday and Holy Saturday, every day in the Octave of Easter, Quasimodo Sunday, the four days of St. Mark and Rogation days, the day of Pentecost and during its Octave.

2. Twenty-five years and twenty times forty days on Palm Sunday.

3. Fifteen years and fifteen times forty days on Ash Wednesday, the fourth Sunday of Lent, the third Sunday of Advent, the vigil of Christmas, at midnight and sunrise Mass.

4. Ten years and ten times forty days on the second and fourth Sunday of Advent, every day during Lent, not including those already named, the eve of Pentecost and the three Ember days at the four seasons of the year.

5. Seven years and seven times forty days on the Feasts of the Presentation and Visitation, on the Feasts of the Apostles not mentioned above.

6. Same indulgences every day of the Novena, preceding the Feast of the Sacred Heart.

7. Seven years and seven times forty days on the four Sundays directly preceding the Feast of the Sacred Heart.

8. Sixty days indulgence for every work of piety performed by the associates.

For the partial indulgences Nos. 1, 2, 3, 4, 5, visit the chapel of the Confraternity, or perform a good work named by the confessor, such as to visit the blessed Sacrament in a certain church, but this should not be given as a sacramental penance, but in the view of obtaining the indulgence.

VESPERS,

Pater noster, etc.

Ave Maria, etc.

P. Deus, in adjutorium meum intende.

R. Domine, ad adjuvandum me festina.

V. Gloria Patri, et Filio, * et Spiritui Sancto.

R. Sicut erat in principio, et nunc, et semper,, * et in sæcula sæculorum. Amen. Alleluia.

In Lent. Laus tibi, Domine, Rex æternæ gloriæ. .

PSALM CIX.

Dixit Dominus Domino meo: * sede a dextris meis;

Donec ponam inimicos tuos: * scabbellum pedum tuorum.

Virgam virtutis tuæ emittet Dominus ex Sion: *dominare in medio inimicorum tuorum.

Tecum principium in die virtutis tuæ in splendoribus sanctorum : * ex utero ante luciferum genui te.

Juravit Dominus, et non pœnitebit eum : * tu es sacerdos in æternam, secundum ordinem Melchisedec.

Our Father, etc.

Hail Mary, etc.

P. Incline unto my aid, O God.

R. O Lord, make haste to help me.

V. Glory be to the Father and to the Son, and to the Holy Ghost.

R. As it was in the beginning, is now, and ever shall be, world without end. Amen. Alleluia.

In Lent. Praise be to thee O King of eternal glory.

PSALM 109.

The Lord said to my Lord sit thou at my right hand.

Until I make thy enemies thy footstool,

The Lord will send forth the sceptre of thy power out of Sion : rule thou in the midst of thy enemies.

With thee is the principality, in the day of thy strength, in the brightness of the saints : from the womb before the day-star, I begot thee.

The Lord hath sworn, and he will not repent : thou art a priest for ever, according to the order of Melchisedec.

407

Dominus a dextris tuis: * confregit in die iræ suæ reges.

Judicabit in nationibus, implebit ruinas ; * conquassabit capita in terra multorum.

De torrente in via bibet: * propterea exaltabit caput.

Gloria Patri, etc.

PSALM CX.

Confitebor tibi Domine in toto corde meo: * in concilio justorum, et congregatione.

Magna opera Domini: * exquisita in omnes voluntates ejus.

Confessio et magnificentia opus ejus; * et justitia ejus manet in sæculum sæculi.

Memoriam fecit mirabilium suorum misericors et miserator Dominus: *escam dedit timentibus se.

Memor erit in sæculum testamenti sui : * virtutem operum suorum annunciabit populo suo.

Ut det illis hæreditatem Gentium ; * opera manuum ejus veritas et judicium.

Fidelio omnia mandata ejus; confirmata in sæculum sæculi ; * facta in veritate et æquitate.

The Lord, at thy right hand, hath broken kings, in the day of his wrath.

He shall judge among nations : he shall fill ruins ; he shall crush the heads in the land of many.

He shall drink of the torrent in the way : therefore shall he lift up the head.

Glory be to the Father, etc

PSALM 110.

I will praise thee, O Lord, with my whole heart ; in the council of the just, and in the congregation.

Great are the works of the Lord, sought out according to all his wills.

His work is praise and magnificence, and his justice continueth for ever and ever.

He hath a remembrance of his wonderful works, being a merciful and gracious Lord ; he hath given food to them that fear him.

He will be mindful forever of his covenant : he will show forth to his people the power of his works.

That he may give them the inheritance of the Gentiles: the works of his hands are truth and judgment.

All his commandments are faithful, confirmed for ever and ever, made in truth and equity.

Redemptionem misit populo suo; * mandavit in æternum testamentum suum.

Sanctum et terribile nomen ejus: * initium sapientiæ timor Domini

Intellectus bonus omnibus facientibus eum: * laudatio ejus manet in sæculum sæculi.

Gloria Patri, etc.

PSALM CXI.

Beatus vir, qui timet Dominum: * in mandatis ejus volet nimis.

Potens in terra, erit semen ejus: * generatio rectorum benedicetur.

Gloria et divitiæ in domo ejus: et justitia ejus manet in sæculum sæculi.

Exortem est in tenebris lumen rectis: * misericors, et miserator, et justus.

Jucundus homo qui miseretur et commodat; disponet sermones suos in judicio: * quia in æternum non commovebitur.

In memoria æterna erit justus: * ab auditione mala non timebit.

Paratum cor ejus sperare in Domino, confirmatum est

He hath sent redemption to his people : he hath commanded his covenant for ever.

Holy and terrible is his name : the fear of the Lord is the beginning of wisdom.

A good understanding to all that do it: his praise continueth for ever and ever.

Glory, etc.

PSALM 111.

Blessed is the man that feareth the Lord; he shall delight exceedingly in his commandments.

His seed shall be mighty upon earth : the generation of the righteous shall be blessed.

Glory and wealth shall be in his house : and his justice remaineth for ever and ever.

To the righteous a light has sprung up in darkness : he is merciful, compassionate and just.

Acceptable is the man that showeth mercy, and lendeth : he shall order his words with judgment; because he shall not be moved for ever.

The just shall be in everlasting remembrance : he shall not fear the evil hearing.

His heart is ready to hope in the Lord : his heart is

cor ejus: * non commove-
bitur, donec despiciat inimicos suos.

Dispersit, dedit pauperi-
bus: justitir ejus menet in
sæculum sæculi, * cornu
ejus exaltabitur in gloria.

Peccator videbit, et iras-
cetur; dentibus suis fremet
et tabescet: * desiderium
peccatorum peribit.

Gloria Patri, etc.

PSALM CXII.

Laudate pueri Dominum :
* laudate nomen Domini.

Sit nomen Domini bene-
dictum, * ex hoc nunc, et
usque in sæculum.

A solis ortu usque ad oc-
casum, * laudabile nomen
Domini.

Excelsus super omnes gen-
tes Dominus, * et super cœlos gloria ejus.

Puis sicut Dominus Deus
noster, qui in altis habitat,
* et humilia respicit in cœlo
et in terra?

Suscitans a terra inopem :
* et de stercore erigens pau-
perem ;

Ut collocet eum cum prin-
cipibus populi sui.

strengthened: he shall not
be moved until he look over
his enemies.

He hath distributed: he
hath given to the poor: his
justice remaineth for ever
and ever: his horn shall be
exalted in glory.

The wicked shall see, and
shall be angry: he shall
gnash with his teeth, and
pine away: the desire of the
wicked shall perish.

Glory, etc.

PSALM 112.

Praise the Lord, ye chil-
dren: praise ye the name of
the Lord.

Blessed be the name of
the Lord, from henceforth,
now and forever.

From the rising of the
sun unto the going down of
the same, the name of the
Lord is worthy of praise.

The Lord is high above
all nations; and his glory
above the heavens.

Who is as the Lord our
God, who dwelleth on high,
and looketh down on the low
things in heaven and in
earth?

Raising up the needy from
the earth, and lifting up the
poor out of the dung-hill.

That he may place him
with princes, with the princes of his people.

Qui habitare facit sterilem in domo, * matrem filiorum lætantem.

Who maketh a barren woman to dwell in a house, the joyful mother of children.

Gloria Patri, etc.

Glory, etc.

PSALM CXIII.†

PSALM 113.

In exitu Israel de Ægypto * Dominus Jacob de populo barbaro.

Facta est Judæa sanctificatio ejus, * Israel potestas ejus.

Mare vidit, et fugit; * Jordanis conversus est retrorsum.

Montes exultaverunt ut arietes; * et colles sicut agni ovium.

Quid est tibi mare, quod fugisti? * et tu Jordanis, quia conversus es retrorsum?

Montes exultastis sicut arietes? * et colles sicut agni ovium?

A facie Domini mota est terra, * a facie Dei Jacob.

Qui convertit petram in stagna aquarum, * et rupem in fontes aquarum.

Non nobis, Domini, non nobis; * sed nomini tuo da gloriam.

When Israel went out of Egypt, the house of Jacob from a barbarous people?

Judea was made his sanctuary, Israel his dominion.

The sea saw and fled; Jordan was turned back.

The mountains skipped like rams, and the hills like the lambs of a flock.

What aileth thee, O thou sea, that thou didst flee? and thou, O Jordan, that thou wast turned back?

Ye mountains, that ye skipped like rams; and ye hills like the lambs of the flock?

At the presence of the Lord, the earth was moved: at the presence of the God of Jacob.

Who turned the rock into pools of water, and the stony hills into fountains of waters.

Not unto us, O Lord, not unto us, but to thy name give glory.

† Instead of 113, the Psalm 116, is often sung.

Super misericordia tua, et veritate tua; * ne quando dicant gentes; ubi est Deus eorum?

Deus autem noster in cœlo: * omnia quæcumque voluit, fecit.

Simulacra gentium argentum et aurum, * opera manuum hominum.

Os habent, et non loquentur; * oculos habent, et non videbunt.

Aures habent, et non audient; * nares habent, et non odorabunt.

Manus habent, et non palpabunt; pedes habent, et non ambulent; * non clamabunt in guttere suo.

Similes illis fiant qui faciunt ea; * et omnes qui confidunt in eis.

Domus Israel speravit in Domino; * adjutor eorum et protector eorum est.

Domus Aaron speravit in Domino; * adjutor eorum et protector eorum est.

Qui timent Dominum, speraverunt in Domino; * adjutor eorum et protector eorum est.

Dominus memor fuit nostri; * et benedixit nobis:

Benedixit domui Israel; * benedixit domui Aaron.

For thy mercy and for thy truth's sake; lest the Gentiles should say, where is their God?

But our God is in heaven; he hath done all things whatsoever he would.

The idols of the Gentiles are silver and gold; the work of the hands of men.

They have mouths and speak not; they have eyes and see not.

They have ears and hear not; they have noses and smell not.

They have hands and feel not; they have feet and walk not; neither shall they cry out through their throats.

Let them that make them become like unto them; and such as trust in them.

The house of Israel hath hoped in the Lord; he is their helper and their protector.

The house of Aaron hath hoped in the Lord; he is their helper and their protector.

They that fear the Lord have hoped in the Lord; he is their helper and their protector.

The Lord hath been mindful of us, and hath blessed us.

He hath blessed the house of Israel; he hath blessed the house of Aaron.

Benedixit omnibus qui timent Dominum, * pusillis cum majoribus.

Adjiciat Dominus super vos; super vos, et super filios vestros.

Benedicti vos a Domino; * qui fecit cœlum et terram.

Cœlum cœle Domino; * terram autem dedit filiis hominum.

Non mortui laudabunt te, Domine; * neque omnes qui descendunt in infernum.

Sed nos qui vivimus, benedicimus Domino; * ex hoc nunc et usque in sæculum.

Gloria Patri, etc.

He hath blessed all that fear the Lord, both little and great.

May the Lord add blessings upon you and upon your children.

Blessed be you of the Lord, who made heaven and earth.

The heaven of heavens is the Lord's: but the earth he hath given to the children of men.

The dead shall not praise thee, O Lord, nor any of them that go down to hell.

But we that live bless the Lord, from this time now and forever.

Glory, etc.

PSALM CXVI.

Laudate Dominum omnes Gentes; * laudate eum omnes populi.

Quoniam confirmata est super nos misericordia ejus; * et veritas Domini manet in æternum.

Gloria Patri, etc.

PSALM 116.

Praise the Lord, all ye nations: praise him all ye people.

Because his mercy is confirmed upon us, and the truth of the Lord remaineth for ever.

Glory, etc.

Capitulum, 2 Cor., 1, 3.

Benedictus Deus et Pater Domini nostri Jesu Christi, Pater misericordiarum, et Deus totius consolationis, qui consolatur nos in omni tribulatione nostra.

R. Deo Gratias.

Little Chapter, 2 Cor., 1, 3.

Blessed be the God and Father of our Lord Jesus Christ, the Father of mercies, and the God of all comfort, who comforteth us in all our tribulations.

R. Thanks be to God.

[Here is usually sung a Hymn, appropriate to the season of the year.]

HYMN FOR SUNDAY.

FOR SUNDAY.

Lucis Creator optime,
Lucem dierum proferens,
Primordiis lucis novæ,
Mundi parans originem.

O, great Creator of the light,
Who from the darksome
womb of night,
Brought'st forth new light
at nature's birth,
To shine upon the face of
earth.

Qui mane junctum vesperi,
Diem vocari præcipis;
Illabitur tetrum chaos:
Audi preces cum fletibus.

Who by the morn and even-
ing ray,
Hast measured time and
called it day,
Whilst sable night involves
the spheres,
Vouchsafe to hear our prayers and tears.

Ne mens gravata crimine,
Vitæ sit exul munere;
Dum nil perenne cogitat,
Seseque culpis illigat.

Lest our frail mind with sin
defiled,
From gifts of life should be
exiled,
Whilst on no heavenly thing
she thinks,
But twines herself in Satan's
links.

Coeleste pulsit ostium:
Vitale tollat præmium.
Vitemus omne noxium:
Pergemus omne pessimum.

O, may she soar to heaven
above,
The happy seat of light and
love;
Meantime all sinful actions
shun,
And purge the foul ones she
hath done.

Præsta, Pater, piissime,
Patrique compar unice,

This prayer, most gracious
Father, hear;

Cum Spiritu Paraclito,
Regnans per omne sæculum.
Amen.

Thy equal Son, incline his ear,
Who, with the Holy Ghost and thee,
Doth live and reign eternally.

The Magnificat: or the Canticle of the Blessed Virgin Mary. Luke 1.

Magnificat * anima mea Dominum.

My soul doth magnify the Lord;

Et exultavit Spiritus meus * in Deo salutari meo.

And my spirit hath rejoiced in God my Saviour.

Quia respexit humilitatem ancillæ suæ; * ecce enim ex hoc beatem me dicent omnes generationes.

Because he hath regarded the humility of his handmaid, for behold from henceforth all generations shall call me blessed.

Quia fecit mihi magna qui potens est; * et sanctum nomen ejus.

For he that is mighty hath done great things to me; and holy is his name.

Et misericordia ejus a progenie in progenies, * timentibus eum.

And his mercy is from generation to generation, to them that fear him.

Fecit potentiam in brachio sue; * dispersit superbos mente cordis sui

He hath showed might in his arm; he hath scattered the proud in the conceit of their heart.

Deposuit potentes de sede, * et exaltavit humiles.

He hath put down the mighty from their seat, and hath exalted the humble.

Esurientes implevit bonis: * et divites dimisit inanes.

He hath filled the hungry with good things; and the rich he hath sent away empty.

Suscepit Israel puerum suum, * recordatus misericordiæ suæ.

He hath received Israel his servant; being mindful of his mercy.

Sicut locutus est ad patres nostros, * Abraham, et semini ejus in sæcula.

As he spoke to our fathers, to Abraham, and to his seed forever.

Gloria Patri, etc.

Glory, etc.

Then follows the Prayer, which is different every day.

P. Dominus vobiscum.

R. Et cum spiritu tuo.

P. Benedicamus Domino.

R. Deo gratias.

P. Fidelium animæ, per misericordiam Dei, requiescant in pace.

R. Amen.

P. The Lord be with you.

R. And with thy spirit.

P. Let us bless the Lord.

R. Thanks be to God.

P. May the souls of the faithful, through the mercy of God, rest in peace.

R. Amen.

Then is sung one of the following Anthems, according to the time.

FROM ADVENT TO THE PURIFICATION.

Alma Redemptoris mater, quæ pervia cœli,

Porta manes, et stella maris, succurre cadenti,

Surgere qui curat populo, tu quæ genuisti,

Natura mirante, tuum sanctum genitorem,

Virgo prius ac posterius: Gabrielis ab ore,

Sumens illud ave, peccatorum miserere.

Mother of Jesus, heaven's open gate,

Star of the sea, support the fallen state

Of mortals; thou whose womb thy maker bore,

And yet, strange thing, a virgin as before;

Who didst from Gabriel's hail, this news receive;

Repenting sinners by thy prayers relieve.

IN ADVENT.

P. Angelus Domini nuntiavit Mariæ;

R. Et concepit de Spiritu Sancto.

P. Oremus.

Gratiam tuam qæsumus, Domine, mentibus nostris infunde; ut qui, angelo nuntiante, Christi Filii tui incarnationem cognovimus, per passionem ejus et crucem, ad resurrectionis gloriam perducamur; per eumdem Christum, Dominum nostrum.

R. Amen.

P. The angel of the Lord declared unto Mary,

R. And she conceived of the Holy Ghost.

P. Let us pray.

Pour forth, we beseech thee, O Lord, thy grace into our hearts, that we, to whom the incarnation of Christ thy Son has been made known by the message of an angel, may by his passion and cross be brought to the glory of his resurrection; through the same Christ, our Lord.

R. Amen.

AFTER ADVENT.

P. Post partum virgo inviolata per mansisti.

R. Dei genitrix, intercede pro nobis.

P. Oremus.

Deus, qui salutis æternæ beatæ Mariæ Virginitate fœcunda humano generi præmia prætitisti; tribue, quæsumus, ut ipsam pro nobis intercedere sentiamus, per quam meruimus Auctorum vitæ suscipere Dominum nostrum, Jesum Christum, Filium tuum.

R. Amen.

P. After childbirth thou didst remain a pure virgin.

R. Mother of God intercede for us.

P. Let us pray.

O God, who by the fruitful virginity of the blessed Virgin Mary, hast given to mankind the rewards of eternal salvation; grant, we beseech thee, that we may be sensible of the benefits of her intercession, by whom we have received the Author of life, our Lord Jesus Christ thy Son.

R. Amen.

FROM THE PURIFICATION TILL EASTER.

Ave, Regina Cœlorum,
Ave, Domina Angelorum,
Salve, radix, salve, porta,
Ex qua mundo lux est orta;
Gaude, Virgo gloriosa,
Super omnes speciosa;
Vale, O valde decora,
Et pro nobis Christum exora.

Hail, Mary, queen of heavenly spheres!
Hail, whom the angelic host reveres!
Hail, fruitful root, hail sacred gate!
Whence the world's light derives its date.
O glorious maid, with beauty blessed!
May joys eternal fill thy breast,
Thus crowned with beauty and with joy,
Thy prayers with Christ for us employ.

P. Dignare me laudare te, Virgo sacrata.

R. Da mihi virtutem contra hostes tuos.

P. Vouchsafe, O sacred Virgin, to accept my praises.

R. Give me power against thy enemies.

P. Oremus.

Concede misericors Deus, fragilitati nostræ præsidium; ut qui sanctæ Dei genitricis memoriam agimus, intercessionis ejus auxilio a nostris iniquitatibus resurgamus; per eumdem Christum, Dominum nostrum.

R. Amen.

P. Let us pray.

Grant us, O merciful God, strength against all our weakness; that we, who celebrate the memory of the holy Mother of God, may by the help of her intercession, rise again from our iniquities; through the same Christ our Lord.

R. Amen.

FROM EASTER UNTIL TRINITY.

Regina cœli, lætare, Alleluia.
Quia quem meruisti portare, Alleluia.
Resurrexit, sicut dixit, Alleluia.
Ora pro nobis Deum, Alleluia.
P. Guade et lætare, Virgo Maria, Alleluia.
R. Quia surrexit Dominus vere, Alleluia.
P. Oremus.

Deus qui, per resurrectionem Filii tui, Domini nostri, Jesu Christi, mundum lætificare dignatus es, præsta, quæsumus, ut per ejus genitricem Virginem Mariam perpetuæ capiamus gaudia vitæ: per eumdem Christum, Dominum nostrum.
R. Amen.

O Queen of Heaven, rejoice, Alleluia.
For he whom thou didst deserve to bear, Alleluia.
Is risen again as he said, Alleluia.
Pray for us to God, Alleluia.
P. Rejoice and be glad, O Virgin Mary; Alleluia.
R. Because our Lord is truly risen, Alleluia.
P. Let us pray.

O God, who by the resurrection of thy Son, our Lord Jesus Christ, hath been pleased to fill the world with joy; grant, we beseech thee, that by the Virgin Mary, his mother, we may receive the joys of eternal life: through the same Christ our Lord.
R. Amen.

FROM TRINITY SUNDAY UNTIL ADVENT.

Salve, Regina, mater misericordiæ, vita, dulcedo, et

Hail, O queen, O mother of mercy, hail our life, our

spes nostra salve. Ad te clamamus, exules filii Evæ. Ad te suspiramus gementes et flentes, in hac lacrymarum valle. Eia ergo, advocata nostra, illos tuos misericordes oculos ad nos converte. Et Jesum benedictum fructum ventris tui nobis post hoc exilium ostende; O clemens, O pia, O dulcis Virgo Maria!

P. Ora pro nobis sancta Dei Genitrix!

R. Ut digni efficiamur promissionibus Christi.

P. Oremus.

Omnipotens, sempiterne Deus, qui gloriosæ Virginis Matris Mariæ corpus et animam, ut dignum Filii tui habitaculum effici mereretur, Spiritu Sancto co-operante, præparasti; da, ut cujus commemoratione lætamur ejus pia intercessione ab instantibus malis, et a morte perpetua liberemur; per eumdem Christum, Dominum nostrum.

R. Amen.

P. Divinum auxilium maneat semper nobiscum.

R. Amen.

comfort, and our hope. We the banished children of Eve, cry out unto thee. To thee we send up our sighs, groaning and weeping in this vale of tears. Come, then, our advocate, and look upon us with those thy pitying eyes. And after this our banishment, show us Jesus, the blessed fruit of thy womb; O merciful, O pious, O sweet Virgin Mary!

P. Pray for us, O holy mother of God!

R. That we may be made worthy of the promises of Christ.

P. Let us pray.

Almighty and eternal God who, by the co-operation of the Holy Ghost, didst prepare the body and the soul of the glorious Virgin Mother Mary, that she might become a worthy habitation for thy Son, grant, that as with joy we celebrate her memory, so by her pious intercession we may be delivered from present evils and eternal death: through the same Christ our Lord.

R. Amen.

P. May the divine assistance always remain with us.

R. Amen.

Benediction of the Blessed Sacrament.

Tantum ergo sacramentum
Veneremur cernui,
Et antiquum documentum
Novo cedat ritui :
Præstet fides supplementum
Sensuum defectui.

To this mysterious table now
Our knees, our hearts and
sense we bow,
Let ancient rites resign their
place,
To nobler elements of grace,
And faith for all defects sup-
ply,
While sense is lost in mys-
tery.

Genitori, Genitoque
Laus et jubilatio,
Salus, honor, virtus, quo-
que
Sit et benedictio ;
Procedenti ab utroque
Compar sit laudatio. Amen.

To God the Father born of
none,
To Christ, his co-eternal Son,
And Holy Ghost, whose
equal rays,
From both proceed one
equal praise;
One honor, jubilee and fame
Forever bless his glorious
name. Amen.

P. Panem de cœlo præ-
stitisti eis.

R. Omne delectamentum
in se habentem.

P. Ora pro nobis, sancta
Dei genitrix.

R. Ut digni efficiamur
promissionibus Christi.

P. Oremus.

Deus qui sub sacramento
mirabili passionis tuæ memoriam reliquisti, tribue,
quæsumus, ita nos corporis
et sanguinis tui sacra mysteria venerari, ut redemptionis tui fructum in nobis

P. Thou hast given them
bread from heaven.

R. Replenished with all
sweetness and delight.

P. Pray for us, O holy
mother of God!

R. That we may be made
worthy of the promises of
Christ.

P. Let us pray.

O God, who hast left us,
in this wonderful sacrament
a perpetual memorial of thy
passion : grant, we beseech
thee, so to reverence the sacred mysteries of thy body
and blood, that we may con-

jugiter sentiamus. Qui vivis et regnas Deus in sæcula sæculorum. Amen.

tinually find in our souls the fruit of thy redemption, who livest and reignest, etc.

When the Priest gives the benediction with the Blessed Sacrament, bow down, and profoundly adore your Saviour there present. Give him thanks for all his mercies; offer your whole self to him, to be his forever; and earnestly beg his blessing upon you and yours, and upon his whole Church.

After Benediction, the Choir generally sing "Laudate Dominum," etc., see page 413.

Vespers of the Blessed Virgin.

Ave Maria, etc.
V. Deus, etc.

Hail Mary, etc.
V. Incline, etc.

[Page 407.

PSALM CIX.

Dixit dominus, etc.

The Lord, etc.

[Page 407.

PSALM CXII.

Laudate, etc.

Praise ye, etc.

[Page 410.

PSALM CXXI.

Lætatus sum in his, quæ dicta sunt mihi : * in domum Domini ibimus.

I rejoiced at those things which were said to me ; we shall go into the house of our Lord.

Stantes erant pedes nostri, * in atriis tuis Jerusalem.

Our feet were standing in thy courts, O Jerusalem.

Jerusalem quæ ædificatur ut civitas : * cujus participatio ejus in idipsum.

Jerusalem, which is built as a city, whose inhabitants are united together.

Illuc enim ascenderunt tribus, tribus Domini, * testimonium Israel ad confitendum nomini Domini.

For thither did the tribes ascend, the tribes of the Lord, the testimony of Israel ; to praise the name of the Lord.

Quia illic sederunt sedes in judicio, * sedes super domum David.

Because seats sat there in judgment ; seats upon the house of David.

Rogate quæ ad pacem sunt Jerusalem: et abundantia diligentibus te.

Ask the things that are for the peace of Jerusalem, and abundance to them that love thee.

Fiat pax in virtute tua: * et abundantia in turribus tuis.

Let peace be made in thy strength, and abundance in thy towers.

Propter fratres meos, et proximos meos, * loquebar pacem de te.

For my brethren and my neighbors; I spoke peace of thee.

Propter domum Domini Dei nostri, * quæsivi bona tibi.

For the house of the Lord our God: I have sought good things for thee.

Gloria Patri, etc.

Glory, etc.

PSALM CXXVI.

Nisi Dominus ædificaverit domum, * in vanum laboraverunt qui ædificant eam.

If the Lord build not the house, they have laboured in vain that build it.

Nisi Dominus custodierit civitatem, * frustra vigilat qui custodit eam.

If the Lord keep not the city, he watches in vain that keeps it.

Vanum est vobis ante lucem surgere: * surgite postquam sederitis, qui manducatis panem doloris.

It is in vain for you to rise before light: rise after ye have sat, you that eat the bread of sorrow.

Cum dederit dilectis suis somnum: * ecce hereditas Domini filii: merces, fructus ventris:

When he shall give sleep to his beloved: behold children are an inheritance from the Lord, and the fruit of thy womb is a reward.

Sicut sagittæ in manu potentis: * ita filii excusorum.

As arrows in the hand of the mighty, so are the children of them that are rejected.

Beatus vir qui implevit desiderium suum ex ipsis: * non confundetur cum loquetur inimicis suis in porta.

Blessed is the man that has filled his desire of them: he shall not be confounded, when he shall speak to his enemies in the gate.

Gloria Patri, etc.

Glory, etc.

PSALM CXLVII.

Lauda Jerusalem Dominum : * lauda Deum tuum Sion.

O Jerusalem, praise the Lord : praise thy God, O Sion.

Quoniam confortavit seras portarum tuarum : * benedixit filiis tuis in te.

Because he has strengthened the locks of thy gates, he has blessed thy children in thee.

Qui posuit fines tuos pacem : * et adipe frumenti satiat te.

Who has set thy borders in peace : and fills thee with the fat of corn.

Qui emittit eloquium suum terræ : * velociter currit sermo ejus:

Who sends forth his speech to the earth : his words run swiftly.

Qui dat nivem sicut lanam : * nebulum sicut cinerem spargit.

Who gives snow as wool : scatters mist as ashes.

Mittit crystallum suam sicut buccellas : * ante faciem frigoris ejus quis sustinebit.

He casts his crystal as morsels : before the face of his cold who shall abide ?

Emittet verbum suum, et liquefaciet ea : * flabit spiritus ejus, et fluent aquæ.

He shall send forth his word, and shall melt them : his spirit shall breathe, and the waters shall flow.

Qui annuntiat verbum suum Jacob : * justitias, et judicia sua Israel.

Who declares his word to Jacob, his justice and judgments to Israel.

Non fecit taliter omni nationi : * et judicia sua non manifestavit eis.

He has not done so to every nation : and his judgments he has not made manifest to them.

Gloria Patri, etc.

Glory, etc.

THE LITTLE CANTICLE. Ec. 24.

Ab initio, et ante sæcula et creata sum, et usque ad futurum sæculum non desinam, et in habitatione sancta coram ipso ministravi.

From the beginning, and before the world, was I created, and unto the world to come I shall not cease : and in the holy habitation have I ministered before him.

R. Deo gratias.

R. Thanks be to God.

HYMN.

Ave maris stella.
Dei mater alma,
Atque sempe virgo,
Felix cæli porta.

Bright Mother of our Maker,
  hail,
Thou virgin ever blest,
The ocean's star by which we
  sail,
And gain the port of rest.

Sumens illud Ave,
Gabrielis ore,
Funda nos in pace,
Mutans Hevæ nomen.

Whilst we this *Ave* thus to thee,
From Gabriel's mouth rehearse:
Prevail that peace our lot may
  be,
And Eva's name reverse.

Solve vincla reis,
Profer lumen cæcis,
Mala nostra pelle,
Bona cuncta posce.

Release our long entangled
  mind,
From all the snares of ill;
With heavenly light instruct
  the blind,
And all our vows fulfil.

Monstra te esse matrem,
Sumat per te preces,
Qui pro nobis natus,
Tulit esse tuus.

Exert for us a mother's care,
And us thy children own,
Prevail with him to hear our
  prayer,
Who chose to be thy son.

Virgo singularis,
Inter omnes mitis,
Nos culpis solutos,
Mites fac et castos.

O spotless maid! whose vir-
  tues shine,
With brightest purity:
Each action of our lives refine,
And make us pure like thee.

Vitam præsta puram,
Iter para tuum,
Ut videntes Jesum,
Semper collætemur.

Preserve our lives unstained
  with ill,
In this infectious way;
That heaven alone our souls
  may fill,
With joys that ne'er decay.

Sit laus Deo Patri,
Summo Christo decus,
Spiritui sancto,
Tribus honor unus. **Amen.**

To God the Father, endless
  praise;
To God the Son, the same;
And Holy Ghost, whose equal
  rays,
One equal glory claim. Amen.

V. Diffusa est gratia in labiis tuis.

R. Propterea benedixit te Deus in æternum.

V. Grace is poured forth on thy lips.

R. Therefore God has blessed thee forever.

THE MAGNIFICAT.

[Page 415.

OREMUS.

Concede nos famulos tuos, quæsumus Domine Deus, perpetua mentis et corporis sanitate gaudere; et gloriosa beatæ Mariæ semper virginis intercessione, a præsenti liberari tristitia, et æterna perfui lætitia. Per Christum dominum nostrum.

R. Amen.

LET US PRAY.

Lord God, we beseech thee, grant that we thy servants, may enjoy perpetual health of mind and body; and that by the glorious intercession of the ever blessed Virgin Mary, we may pass from this present sorrow to the enjoyment of everlasting gladness, through our Lord, etc. Amen.

COMMEMORATION OF THE SAINTS.

Antiphona. Sancta Dei omnes intercedere dignemini pro nostra omniumque salute.

V. Lætamini in Domino, et exultate justi.

R. Et gloriamini omnes recti corde.

The Anthem. All ye saints of God, vouchsafe to make intercession for our salvation, and that of all.

V. Ye just rejoice in our Lord, and be exceeding glad.

R. And glory all ye right in heart.

OREMUS.

Protege, Domine, populum tuum, et Apostolorum tuorum Petri et Pauli, et aliorum Apostolorum patrocinio confidentum, perpetua defensione conserva.

Omnes Sancti tui quæsumus Domine, nos ubique adjuvent; ut dum eorum merita recolimus, patrocinia sentiamus; et pacem tuam nostris concede temporibus,

LET US PRAY.

Protect, O Lord, thy people, and let the confidence we have in the intercession of thy blessed apostles Peter and Paul, and of thy other apostles, prevail with thee, to preserve and defend us forever.

May all thy saints, O Lord, we beseech thee, everywhere assist us, that whilst we celebrate their merits, we may be sensible of their protection: grant us thy peace in

et ab Ecclesia tua cunctam repelle nequitiam; iter, actus et voluntates nostras, et omnium famulorum tuorum, in salutis tuæ prosperitate dispone; benefactoribus nostris sempiterna bona retribue; et omnibus fidelibus defunctis requiem æternam concede. Per Dominum nostrum Jesum Christum Filium tuum.

V. Domine exaudi orationem meam.

R. Et clamor meus ad te veniat.

V. Benedicamus Domino.

R. Deo gratias.

V. Fidelium animæ per misericordiam Dei requiescant in pace.

R. Amen.

our times, and repel all wickedness from thy church; prosperously guide the steps, actions and desires of us, and all thy servants, in the way of salvation; give eternal blessings to those who have done good to us, and everlasting peace to the faithful departed. Through the Lord Jesus Christ, thy Son. Amen.

V. Lord hear my prayer.

R. And let my cry come to thee.

V. Let us bless the Lord.

R. Thanks be to God.

V. May the souls of the faithful departed, through the mercy of God, rest in peace. R. Amen.

Complin.

Ave Maria, etc.

V. Converte nos Deus salutaris noster.

R. Et averte iram tuam a nobis.

V. Deus in adjutorium meum intende.

R. Domine ad adjuvandum me festina.

Gloria Patri, etc. Alleluia—*aut* Laus, etc.

Hail Mary, etc.

V. Convert us, O God our Saviour.

R. And turn away thy anger from us.

V. Incline unto my aid, O God.

R. Lord, make haste to help me.

Glory be to the Father, etc. Alleluia—*or*, Praise, etc.

PSALM CXXVIII.

Sæpe expugnaverunt me a juventute mea: * dicat nunc Israel.

Often have they assaulted me from my youth; let Israel now say.

Sæpe expugnaverunt me a juventute mea, * etenim non potuerunt mihi.

Often have they assaulted me from my youth; but they have not prevailed against me.

Supra dorsum meum fabricaverunt peccatores; * prolongaverunt iniquitatem suam.

Sinners have beaten on my back, as on an anvil: they have prolonged their iniquity.

Dominus justus concidit cervices peccatorum : * confundantur et convertantur retrorsum omnes qui oderunt Sion.

The just Lord will cut the necks of sinners: let all be confounded and turned back ward that hate Sion.

Fiant sicut fœnum tectorum, * quod priusquam evelatur, exaruit.

Let them be made as hay on the tops of houses, which is withered before it be plucked up.

De quo non implevit manum suam qui metit, * et sinum suum qui manipulos colligit.

Whereof the reaper shall not fill his hand, nor he that gathers the sheaves his bosom.

Et non dixerunt qui præteribant: Benedictio Domini super vos; * benediximus vobis in nomine Domini.

And they who passed by, said not, the blessing of the Lord be upon you; we have blessed you in the name of the Lord.

Gloria Patri, etc.

Glory, etc.

PSALM CXXIX.

De profundis clamavi ad te Domini: * Domine exaudi vocem meam.

From the depths I have cried to thee, O Lord; Lord, hear my voice.

Fiant aures tuæ intendentes, * in vocem deprecationis meæ.

Let thy ears be attentive to the voice of my petition.

Si iniquitates observaveris, Domine: * Domine, quis sustinebit?

If thou regardest iniquities, O Lord; Lord, who shall bear it.

Quia apud te propitiatio est; et proper legem tuam sustinui te, Domine.

Because with thee there is mercy; and because of thy law, I have waited for thee, O Lord.

Sustinuit anima mea in verbo ejus : * speravit anima mea in Domino.

A custodia matutina usque ad noctem : * speret Israel in Domino.

Qui apud Dominum misericordia : * et copiosa apud eum redemptio.

Et ipse redimet Israel, * ex omnibus iniquitatibus ejus.

Gloria Patri, etc.

My soul has trusted in his word, my soul had hoped in the Lord.

From the morning watch even until night, let Israel hope in the Lord.

Because with the Lord there is mercy, and with him plentiful redemption.

And he shall redeem Israel from all his iniquities.

Glory, etc.

PSALM CXXX.

Domine, non est exaltatum cor meum : * neque elati sunt oculi mei.

Neque ambulavi in magnis : * neque in marabilibus super me.

Si non humiliter sentiebam : * sed exaltavi animam meam.

Sicut ablactatus est super matre sua, * ita retributio in anima mea.

Speret Israel in Domino, * ex hoc nunc et usque in sæculum.

Gloria Patri etc.

Lord, my heart is not exalted ; nor are my eyes lofty.

Nor have I walked in great matters, nor in marvellous things above me.

If I was not humble minded, but exalted my soul ;

As the weaned child is towards his mother, so let it be with my soul.

Let Israel hope in the Lord, from henceforth, now and forever.

Glory, etc.

THE HYMN.

Memento. rerum Conditor,
Nostri quod olim corporis,
Sacra ab alvo Virginis,
Nascendo, forman sumpseris;

Remember thou, O gracious Lord,
The eternal God's co-equal Word,
In virgin's womb a creature made,
Our nature wore for Nature's aid.

Maria mater gratiæ,
Dulcis Parens clementiæ,
Tu nos ab hoste protege,
Et mortis hora suscipe,

O happy Mary chose to be
Mother of grace and clemency!
Protect us at the hour of death,
And bear to heaven our part-
ing breath.

Jesu, tibi sit gloria,
Qui natus es de Virgine,
Cum Patre, et almo Spiritu,
In sempiterna sæcula. Amen.

May age to age forever sing,
The Virgin's son and angel's
king,
And praise with the celestial
host,
The Father, Son, and Holy
Ghost. Amen.

THE CHAPTER. Eccles. 24,

Ego mater pulchræ dilec-
tionis, et timoris, et agni-
tionis, et sancta spei.

I am the mother of beau-
tiful love, and of fear, and
of knowledge, and of holy
hope.

R. Deo gratias.
V. Ora pro nobis sancta
Dei genitrix.
R. Ut digni efficiamur
promissionibus Christi.

R. Thanks be to God.
V. Pray for us Mother of
God.
R. That we may be made
worthy the promises of
Christ.

Antiphona. Sub tuum
præsidium.

The Anthem. Under thy
protection.

CANTICLE OF HOLY SIMEON.

Nunc dimittis servum tu-
um Domine, * secundum
verbum tuum in pace :
Quia viderunt oculi mei, *
salutare tuum,
Quod parasti, * ante fa-
ciem omnium populorum.
Lumen ad revelationem
Gentium, * et gloriam ple-
bis tuæ Israel.
Gloria Patri, etc.
Ant. Sub tuum præsidi-
um confugimus, sancti Dei
genitrix; nostras depreca-

Now, Lord, let thy ser-
vant depart in peace, ac-
cording to thy word.
Because my eyes have
seen thy salvation,
Which thou hast prepared
before the face of all people.
A light to enlighten the
Gentiles : and for the glory
of thy people Israel.
Glory, etc.
Ant. Under thy protec-
tion we take our refuge, O
holy Mother of God : des-

tiones ne despicias in necessitatibus, sed a periculis cunctis libera nos semper, Virgo gloriosa et benedicta.

Kyrie eleison.   Christe eleison.   Kyrie eleison.

V. Domine exaudi orationem meam.

R. Et clamor meus ad te veniat.

OREMUS.

Beatæ et gloriosæ semper virginis Mariæ, quæsumus Domine, intercessio gloriosa nos protegat, et ad vitam perducat æternam.   Per Dominum nostrum Jesum Christum Filium tuum Qui, etc.

R. Amen.

V. Domine exaudi orationem meam.

R. Et clamor meus ad te veniat.

V. Benedicamus Domino.

R. Deo gratias.

Benedictio. Benedicat, et custodiat nos omnipotens et misericors Dominus, Pater, et Filius, et Spiritus Sanctus.

R. Amen.

pise not our petitions in our necessities, but ever deliver us from all dangers, O glorious and blessed virgin.

Lord have mercy on us. Christ have mercy on us. Lord have mercy on us.

V. Lord hear my prayer.

R. And let my cry come to thee.

LET US PRAY.

We beseech thee, O Lord, that the glorious intercession of the ever blessed and glorious Virgin Mary, may protect us, and bring us to life everlasting; through the Lord Jesus Christ, thy Son, who, etc.

R. Amen.

V. Lord, hear my prayer.

R. And let my cry come to thee.

V. Let us bless the Lord.

R. Thanks be to God.

The Blessing. May the Almighty and merciful Lord Father, and Son, and Holy Ghost, bless and keep us.

R. Amen.

One of the Anthems according to the season, is now said, pages 416, etc.

THE END.

CONTENTS.

gt;

432

www.ingramcontent.com/pod-product-compliance
Lightning Source LLC
Chambersburg PA
CBHW032303280326
41932CB00009B/680